Islands of Maine

Islands
of Maine

*Where America
Really Began*

Bill Caldwell

Down East Books
Camden, ME

Copyright © 1981 by Bill Caldwell
Reprinted by arrangement with the author.
All rights reserved.

Cover illustration copyright © 2001 by Kitty Smith

Printed and bound at Versa Press, East Peoria, IL.
5   4   3   2   1

Down East Books
Camden, ME
BOOK ORDERS: 800-685-7962

ISBN: 0-89272-537-0

Library of Congress Control Number: 2001087712

Originally published by Guy Gannett Publishing Co., Portland, ME

*In celebration of the Maine islands
and Maine island people who have given
safe anchorage to* Steer Clear *and much
happiness to all those who have sailed
in her.*

For their expert assistance and patient courtesy in helping me gather historical material for this book, I'd like to express thanks to: The Maine State Archives; Maine State Library Research staff; the Maine State Museum; the Maine Historical Society; town historical societies along the coast of Maine; the Skidompha Library, Damariscotta; the Maine State Island Registry; the Maine Coast Heritage Trust; the Maine Maritime Museum, Bath; the Pierpont Morgan Library of New York.

I am particularly grateful to Spencer Apollonio, Commissioner of Marine Resources, for his expert guidance on the chapters concerning the early fisheries and the men and boats of those days; to Mr. J. W. P. Frost of Elliot for checking the facts in the Isles of Shoals chapter; to Dr. Alta Ashley of Monhegan for her advice and help on the Monhegan chapter; to Mr. Robert Drake of Vinalhaven for his advice on the Fox Islands chapter; to Maine State Archaeologist Bruce J. Bourke for his expert comment on the Early Indians and archaeological history in Chapter One; to Mr. Robert Snowman for copy-editing the manuscript and proofs; to Mrs. Wroth Orrick for typing and indexing; and most important of all to Barbara Caldwell for her help, advice, and patience from start to finish.

Bill Caldwell
Damariscotta, Maine
1980–1981

The Province of Mayne

This beautiful map and chart (circa late 16th century) is from among
those collected by the father of Governor Percival Baxter of Maine.

Courtesy of the Maine State Archives

Contents

1

Island Beginnings
Ice Age to Indians

Here among the islands of Maine is where America really began.

Long before there was a colony at Jamestown, long before the Pilgrims set foot on Plymouth, white men from England and Europe were sailing among the islands of Maine, exploring for a new route to Cathay, drawing charts of unmapped worlds, catching fish in quantities that astounded them, going ashore to cut timber for ships' stoves, filling water barrels from cold island streams, building work places and rough shelters on these island shores. These islands of Maine are the roots from which America grew.

For a full hundred years before the *Mayflower* raised a landfall in the New World, explorers and then fishermen from England, France, Spain, and Portugal were familiar with Maine's islands. By the early 1600s, as many as three hundred foreign fishing vessels were working the waters off the Province of Maine. Maine seafood had a bigger share of the market in Europe in the early 1600s than it has today.

That brave and celebrated band of Pilgrims that steered its way toward religious freedom in 1620 was not sailing through uncharted waters, however often the history books say it. The way to North America, fraught with all the sea's perils though it was, had already been well charted.

Those charts, made by Cabot in 1497, by Verrazano in 1524, by Gomez in 1525, by Walker in 1580, by Gosnold in 1602, by Pring in 1603, by Champlain in 1604, by Weymouth in 1605, and by Smith in 1614, all led to Maine. Maine had been their landfall and their discovery.

The constant traffic between Maine, England, and Europe in

small boats without instruments four hundred years ago is almost incredible today. After the explorers came the treasure hunters and, after them, the commercial fishing boats. It was that everlastingly powerful magnet of money—fish—that made these waters the target of so much action, long before the dream of colonies or religious freedom spurred the famed founding fathers to Jamestown or Pilgrims to Plymouth Rock. Small wonder, therefore, that the first white settlements of the roughest kind were begun in Maine by fishermen, drying and salting their catch on Maine islands; that the first European attempt at a colony was made Down East at St. Croix (or Douchet) Island in 1604; that Weymouth celebrated the first Protestant church service in George's Harbor in Muscongus Bay in 1605; that the first full-fledged attempt at establishing an English colony in North America was in Maine, the Popham colony of 1607.*

From the Isles of Shoals to beyond Mount Desert, the coast of Maine had been a busy, much frequented focus of exploration, fishing and fur trade, long before the *Mayflower* came to Plymouth. So well established were the outposts on Maine islands that when the Plymouth colony was on the brink of starvation in 1621, settlers came to Maine for food, and were freely given it by established settlers in fishing centers on Damariscove and Monhegan islands.

But the islands of Maine are far more than the historic roots where our nation really began, far more than unique and lovely jewels of the North American coast. These islands are special havens where man's spirit is renewed; where a human is dwarfed by nature and timelessness, and yet finds happy unison, instead of rivalry, with the universe.

Stand on a Maine island alone and feel the awesome glory of rock, soil, sky, sea. On a peacock day in summer, these islands, more than most places on earth, can give world-stained mankind the healing balm of natural peace. But the power of the restless sea around you is immense: Two hundred billion tons of water move in and out of the Down East bays every day. In a storm, the force of gales and power of seas that beat upon the islands are terrifying. The only solace is the knowledge that millions of storms have done their worst and the rugged islands have survived.

Stand on a Maine island, surrounded by ocean, and you are actually standing atop a mountain, which many millions of years ago was part of the mainland continent.

---

* In 1585, the Lost Colony at Roanoke began. But within a year, it failed. Most of the 108 colonists, sponsored by Sir Walter Raleigh and led by Ralph Lane, were evacuated by Sir Francis Drake. The fifteen men who stayed soon vanished, leaving no trail and no roots upon which America would grow.

On a Maine island, you are halfway between the equator and the North Pole. You are 300 miles closer to Europe than any other part of the United States. You are south of London, south of Paris, on the same latitude as Madrid, Spain. When each new day dawns over America, here is where the sun's rays first strike. Dawn comes to the islands of Maine while darkness still hangs over most of the United States.

Beneath the ocean around your island there were once forests and open country where giant mastodons roamed. The great bays of Maine—Casco, Muscongus, Penobscot, Blue Hill, Frenchman, and Machias—were once sweeping valleys.

Then came the Ice Ages. Beginning about one million years ago, at four different times, all of Maine was covered with ice thousands of feet thick, weighing many tons per acre. Four times these massive ice sheets advanced and retreated. Maine then looked much like the coast of Antarctica does today.

Only the final Ice Age has left a record still decipherable on our land. That last Ice Age began about 40,000 years ago. The ice rose thousands of feet higher than Cadillac Mountain and towered above the Camden Hills. The final great but gradual meltdown began about 13,000 years ago. As the ice melted, the ocean rose and the land was drowned. The one-time valleys filled with ocean waters and became the great bays of Maine. The waters flooded as far up as Bingham on the Kennebec and Millinocket on the Penobscot. As the land drowned, only the highest hills and mountains still reached above the level of the flooding sea. These are the islands of Maine. Stand on an island and you are standing on a mountain top.

As those massive glaciers moved, they tore the land asunder, ripped the ancient granite mountains, gashed the valleys. The result is the ragged coast, the deep bays, and the heavenly islands of Maine today. The glaciers scoured away all remnants of previous human habitation. We know nothing, because we can find no traces at all of the people who lived here before the meltdown of the last Ice Age.

After that last Ice Age, the first known people, the Paleo Indians, came to the coast of Maine. They were a wandering, Stone Age people, a race that moved vast distances, from northern Mexico, up through the United States, and into Canada, hunting the now extinct giant bisons, giant beavers, giant sloths, mammoths, and mastodons. A few traces of their presence here have been found and carbon-dated as being about 11,000 years old. Those traces are mostly the large, sharp stone tips of spears, hollowed out so that long shafts could be inserted into them for hunting the huge Stone Age animals.

"The uniformity of their spear tips is almost unnerving," said state archaeologist Bruce J. Bourque. "There is little discernible difference between a spear tip made by the Paleo Indians in Mexico and those found in Maine, except in the kind of stone used."

The Paleos lived, roamed, and hunted in Maine for 2,000 years, or about five times longer than white men have been here.

As the climate warmed during those first 2,000 years after the last Ice Age, the giant animals they hunted gradually moved away and the Paleo people vanished 9,500 years ago. There is a mystery about what people, if any, came to Maine after the Paleos left. Archaeologists have found no traces of human presence for the 2,000-year period after the Paleos vanished.

The next archaeological finds are traces of the Early Archaic Indians, who were here about 8,000 years ago. Their spear tips were smaller, indicating perhaps that the animals they hunted were smaller, and that the giant beavers, bison, and mammoths once hunted by the Paleos had become extinct due to the warming climate.

After the Early Archaic Indians came the most fascinating of all Maine's early people, the Red Paint people, who flourished here some 4,000 years ago. Archaeologists have given them the name Red Paint people because of the ochre, stained red and sometimes yellow, which they put into their graves. Close to fifty large grave sites of the Red Paint people have been found in Maine, often with scores of small, individual graves in each burying ground. In every grave there was red "paint," actually clay stained red with iron oxide. Scientists think the Red Paint people traveled regularly to Mount Katahdin to mine the red clay they revered so much, which abounds there. They surmise the red clay was put into each grave either to preserve the bodies or because it had a religious meaning. Maybe it was simply the decorative tradition of a skilled and artistic people.

Among those hunting stones and skinning knives found in the grave sites, archaeologists have also found many strangely large gouging chisels. These outsize chisels, say archaeologists, were probably used to make large dug-out canoes from tree trunks; canoes strong enough to use in the choppy ocean. Further indication that the Red Paint people were the first sea-going fishermen in Maine has been found near a Red Paint village on North Haven island. Diggers there uncovered skeletons of many cod and swordfish. The swordfish skeletons indicate that the big fish could not have been caught in water less than 1,000 feet deep. To get out into water that deep would have required massive canoes gouged from large tree trunks. These Red Paint people, say archaeologists who have examined their well-made tools, were technically the most advanced race to inhabit Maine until the white men came 4,000 years later.

Few bones, skulls, or skeletons of the Red Paint people have ever been found. The acidity of Maine soil apparently dissolved and disintegrated their skeletons as well as the bones of all earlier inhabitants. The earliest human skeletons found in Maine date back about 3,500 years, to the Susquehannas, successors to the Red Paint people. Almost complete skeletons of the Susquehannas were found in 1973 during a routine dig in sites of much later Indian villages. The name Susquehanna comes only from the fact that traces of this tribe were first found in the Susquehanna Valley, Pennsylvania. There is no known link between the Susquehannas and present-day Indian tribes in Maine.

After the Susquehannas disappeared, there is another 1,000-year gap in the archaeological history of Maine's early inhabitants. About 2,500 years ago, shortly before the time of Christ, the Ceramic Group of Indians arrived here. The odd name derives from the fact that these were apparently the first people in Maine to make ceramics, or at least leave behind traces of their work in clay.

These Ceramic people were the first Maine inhabitants to form year-round communities. They lived mostly inland and were farmers and planters of corn. But they also made birch-bark canoes, in which most of the settlement would come down rivers in the summertime and camp on the islands. There they used canoes to fish and hunt seals. They would skin the seals and dry the hides for later use. They'd dry the fish, too, for winter food. They were apparently a social people. For, on various islands and along riverbanks, they left behind huge heaps of various shells. Near where I lived by the Damariscotta River, there is a mammoth pile of ancient oyster shells that measures 45 million cubic feet, the greatest assembly of its kind on the entire earth. The supposition is that, on their annual migrations up and down river according to the seasons, the Indians from scattered settlements would enjoy a huge reunion. Families from scattered settlements would meet for days of feasting at the same spot for thousands of years. Perhaps because oysters always grew in massive quantities in the same places, different races of Indians came to the same place to feast on them. The oyster-shell heaps at Damariscotta are 31 feet deep in places. There are three distinct layers of shells, each separated by a thick layer of mold, indicating that 300 years or more passed between the ending of one layer of shells and the beginning of the next layer. Scientists say it takes about 100 years for 1 inch of vegetable mold to accumulate. The most recent or top layer of mold over these oyster heaps is $3\frac{1}{2}$ inches thick, which may indicate that this top layer began to form about the time the Wawenock Indians began to leave the Damariscotta region in the 1600s. In the second stratum of oyster shells, traces of "red paint" (iron oxide) have been found, indicating the Red Paint people may have feasted on this same riverbank 4,000 years ago. Below is another layer of mold and then still a third layer of ancient oyster shells.

By the time white men set foot on the Maine islands, two principal Indian nations lived in Maine. Down East were the Micmacs, fierce and aggressive. In the rest of Maine were the Abnakis, a more peaceful nation, made up of many tribes, each of which kept mostly to its own territory. The tribes that lived closest to the coast were the Passamaquoddy, Penobscot, and Wawenock. These were the tribes the first white explorers and settlers met.

The records written by those early voyagers refer to the tribes as aborigines, savages, natives, as well as Indians. The words had different and nobler connotations than they do now.

To get a better perspective on the kind of people these Indians were, I quote from detailed descriptions by the first white man who wrote about them.

Captain George Weymouth, in his voyage of 1605, met very often with Indians on the islands. James Rosier, the journalist aboard Weymouth's vessel, reported:

> Their canoes are made without any iron, of the bark of a birch tree, strengthened within with ribs and hoops of oak, in so good fashion and with such ingenuous arts, that they are able to bear seven or eight persons, far exceeding any in the Indies.

The famed Old Town canoe, made in Maine today and considered one of the best-designed canoes in the world, is patterned precisely after the Indian canoes about which Rosier wrote 375 years ago.

These Indians also made far larger, stronger canoes capable of holding many more people at sea on a whale hunt. Rosier described the amazing feat of killing a whale from these canoes:

> One skill in special is their manner of killing the Whale, which they call Powdawe; they say how he bloweth up water and that he is twelve fathoms (72 feet) long and that they go in company with their King with a multitude of boats and strike him with a bone made in

the shape of a harpoon iron fastened to a rope, which they make great and strong from the bark of trees; with such rope and bone, they wear out the Whale; and when he is worn, then all their boats come about him, and as he riseth above the water, with their arrows they shoot him to death; when they have killed him and dragged him to shore, they call all their chief lordes together and sing a song of joy; divide the spoil and give to every man a share, which pieces they hang about their houses in profusion; and when they boil them, blow off the fat, put in their peaze and maize and eat.

The Indians must have been alarmed by the sight of strange vessels disembarking strange white-skinned and bearded men on their islands. A natural reaction might have been to immediately fight them off.

But most of the first contacts were friendly. Rosier describes one:

They gave us of their tobacco, which was excellent, as good as any we ever took, strong and of sweet taste ... They filled their pipes, which were made of the short claw of a lobster, which will hold ten of our pipes full ... They signed to us that the leaf would grow a yard high with a leaf as broad as both their hands. ... They likewise showed me a great piece of fish, whereof I tasted, and it was fat like porpoise; and another kind much like salmon.

The Indians who greeted the early explorers and later the English fishermen made fishing lines that greatly impressed the civilized professionals from across the Atlantic.

Their fishing lines are so even, soft and smooth, they look more like silk than hemp, and are more cunningly wrought and of stronger material than the English lines.

These Indians left the islands before the storms of November came and returned to their permanent settlements upriver, taking back seal hides and dried fish. One precious item they carried on all travels was fire. They placed a piece of smoldering punk between two halves of a large clamshell and further protected its glow by enclosing it all in wet clay, leaving one hole for the air to get through and keep the punk burning. They also had fire strikers of flint and iron pyrites.

At their upriver settlements, the Indians planted corn and worked their gardens with hoes made from clamshells and stone-tipped sticks. They had a written language made up of symbolic drawings. They recorded all important records with these symbols on the inside of birch bark, which served them well as a strong, durable paper.

The early Indian settlements were no slap-dash, haphazard collection of wigwams. Captain John Smith, in his voyages along the Maine coast in 1614, refers with admiration to the orderly plan of the

Indian settlement at Norridgewock, near the Kennebec River close to where Skowhegan stands today.

A Jesuit priest described Norridgewock: "The cottages were distributed with an order very much like the houses in cities ... although built of poles and bark, they were elegant and convenient." Each Indian settlement contained a council house thirty or forty feet long. The wigwams were shaped like large beaver houses rather than in the tent shape of the prairie Indians. Each had a stove of stones, floors covered with colored and woven rushes, and the sides of the wigwams were decorated with ornaments and furs. A protective well-built wall of thick brush, twelve or fifteen feet high, enclosed each Indian settlement. Each settlement was locally governed by a head man and an advisory council. They were, in turn, governed by the Bashaba or Great Chief.

Weymouth describes the dress and appearance of Headmen and Chiefs he met in 1605:

> They had newly painted their faces very deep, some all black, some red, with stripes of excellent blue over their upper lips, nose and chin. One of them wore a kind of coronet about his head, made very cunningly of a substance like stiff hair colored red. Others wore white feathered skins around their heads, jewels in their ears, and bracelets of little white round bone, fastened together with a leather string. They possess very good dyes, which they carry with them in bladders.

Another early explorer wrote that the Indian mothers "fashioned from corn husks queer little dolls for their children. These dolls were about six inches in length with long hair made from cornsilk."

The arts of the Indians swiftly declined after a generation of exposure to white traders. They soon lost the skill and the need to make graceful pottery, when, for a few animal skins, which the Indians could get in a morning, they could obtain an indestructible brass kettle or iron axe from a white man. Knives and hatchets from Europe became their weapons, and later they got firearms. The only arts that lasted were those which English and European craftsmen could not match: the snowshoe, the moccasin, the birch-bark canoe, the woven baskets.

In fewer than a hundred years, the first friendliness between whites and Indians had largely disappeared, replaced by warfare, scalpings, burnings. But these were never large-scale Indian attacks. In all of Maine in the seventeenth century there were probably fewer than three thousand Indians, perhaps a third of whom were scattered along the entire coast. The biggest attacks on white settlements were probably made by fewer than one or two hundred Indians, often by far fewer. But the Indians took back most of Maine in the 1670s, except for a few holdouts in York County.

Sickness, brought over from England and Europe, killed more Indians than did warfare. The tribes weakened. Diminished in numbers and abilities, many sided with the French and moved away to Canada. Today the Indians in Maine have dwindled to a thousand or so, concentrated on two reservations at Penobscot and Pleasant Point. These Indians in the 1970s sued for their lost lands and after eight years won a settlement. Their lawsuit had asked for the return of almost two-thirds of the state of Maine. They finally received $81.5 million and some 350,000 acres, the most land ever involved in settlement of an Indian land claim. The five hundred Indians of the Penobscot nation who live on the reservation at Penobscot invested their $40.3 million. In the first quarter of 1981, they received $700,000 in interest. By June 1981, the landless tribe of Penobscot assumed title to some 150,000 acres of land.

Census figures for 1980 indicated that as many as four thousand Indians were living in Maine. This is almost four times as many as reported in the previous census. The increase may be due to several facts: a better effort by census takers to count minorities; a greater pride in Indian blood, which leads to more people with some Indian blood to claim Indian nationality; and the advent of the new wealth to Maine's Indian tribes. The Census Bureau projects that by 2025, there will be nearly seven thousand Indians in Maine.

2

Treasure Hunters
The First Explorers of Maine

There is a sweet hour in the days of summer, around four o'clock in the afternoon, when a cruising boat drops anchor in an island cove and prepares to spend the night. Behind are the adventures and the chores of a day's cruise; and now a peace comes with the tranquillity and stillness of evening.

Your anchor is down. The children, their mother, and the dog have rowed ashore and are racing along the empty island beach, exploring, shouting, swimming, gathering driftwood for a picnic fire at the tidemark.

Now is the time to sit alone on the forward deck and let the visions creep in; to feel a mystic brotherhood across a thousand years of history with the early voyagers to these islands of Maine.

The Vikings were probably the first white men to land on the islands of North America. They came in 1000 A.D., before William the Conqueror set invading foot on the shore of England. They came not from their homeland in distant Scandinavia, but from closer by, their outpost in Greenland, barely 400 miles from North America. They came not for territory, but for timber. Few trees grew in Greenland. They needed wood to build boats and houses. They came not in the romantic Viking ships of picture-story books, with high prows in the shape of dragons and sea monsters, with twenty men manning longsweep oars and a helmeted Viking in breastplate on the bow, brandishing a sword as he leaped ashore.

Instead, the simpler truth is the first Vikings came in 54-foot sailing boats, 15 feet in the beam, clinker built of stout oak fastened with iron rivets. These boats had space for thirty people plus cargo

21

holds for timber and a pen for several head of cattle. We know this because several such vessels carbon dated to 1000 A.D. were unearthed in 1969 in a Danish fjord. These Viking ships left us the name "starboard." On the right-hand side of their stern was a steering board; and one thousand years later we still call the right-hand side of our vessels "starboard."

The first Viking leader to explore North American shores was Leif Ericson, son of Eric the Red. They were tough men, both. Eric the Red had been banished from his homeland for killing a girl in a drunken brawl. With a band of followers, he sailed west, in exile, and discovered "Greenland." He gave it that enticing but misleading name to attract settlers. About fifteen years after Eric the Red settled in Greenland, his teen-age son Leif sailed back to Norway. There he met King Olaf Tryggvason, was converted to Christianity, and sailed back to Greenland.

One night at dinner, a fellow Norseman, Biarni Herilfson, captain of a trading ship, told young Leif Ericson that, when he had been blown off course on his way to Greenland, he had sighted another country. It was level and heavily wooded, far to the west of Greenland. But he had not landed there. The mention of woods excited Leif Ericson. Timber for boats and houses was lacking in Greenland. He assembled a crew, chartered Biarni's boat, and sailed west. Leif Ericson and his thirty-five men found Newfoundland and took delight in the climate, warmer than Greenland. He marveled at the salmon-filled waters and his men harvested the wild berries from which they made wine. Remembering that his father, Eric the Red, had chosen the name Greenland to attract more settlers, Leif Ericson called his discovery "Vinland the Good," believing that mention of vines might entice thirsty wine drinkers to settle there.

In 1960, two Norwegian archaeologists located a spot in Newfoundland, L'Anse aux Meadows, which some believe is where Leif Ericson and his crew briefly settled. Sites of two great houses, similar to the Norse houses in Greenland, were excavated. The bigger one measured 70 feet long by 55 feet wide, had floors of clay, walls of turf, and roofs of timber covered with sod, in true Nordic style.

One incident in the saga is too colorful to omit. When native Indians attacked the Viking settlement, a woman saved the day. Freydis, half sister to Leif, bared her breasts, slapped them with a sword, and screamed like a fiend. She so alarmed the Indian attackers that they fled. So says the saga.

A different version of Leif Ericson's voyage also exists in legend. It says that he was repelled by the incessant fogs and raiding Indians of Newfoundland and sailed on to the south. Here he found what he was looking for bigger stands of trees on Maine islands, together with rich fishing grounds. In this version, the Vikings encamped at Monhegan and Manana islands and chiseled early Norse inscriptions on the rocks by the water springs. The same or later groups of Vikings supposedly sailed on to Pemaquid, the nearest mainland to the west. Some archaeologists claim that a recently uncovered, deeply buried piece of roadway at Pemaquid was built by these Vikings. Three more runic stones, at first claimed to be of Viking origin, were found at Phippsburg, a little west of Pemaquid. Later tests proved that these, like the Nordic inscriptions at Manana Island, were probably not authentic.

One sure bit of evidence that the Vikings were here 400 years before Christopher Columbus "discovered" North America, is a Viking coin of the eleventh century, made of 25 percent silver and 75 percent copper, found in Blue Hill on Penobscot Bay in 1968. This has been authenticated through tests by Dr. Kolbjorn Skaare, coin expert at the University of Oslo. This Norse penny, dating to the reign of King Olaf Kyrre, 1067–1093, is the oldest European artifact ever found in the United States. How it got to Blue Hill Bay in Maine remains a mystery. No one knows whether the Vikings brought it there; or whether they had given it in trading with Indians in Newfoundland and the Indians had carried it home to their ancient village near Blue Hill.

Some historians say that Viking boats continued making trips among the Maine islands for two hundred years after Leif Ericson. If they did, these white-skinned, bearded strangers made strangely little impression. They are not mentioned in the legends and the myths of the Abnaki Indians, who were on these islands and this coast long before the Vikings came and long after they left. Maybe the Vikings voyaged among the Maine islands. Maybe they didn't.

There is no question that Italians were the first sailors to chart the islands of Maine. These ship captains were mercenaries who hired out to the kings and queens of England, France, and Spain; the rulers who were hungry to seize the rich spice lands and gold and silver mines of the Orient. After the Ottoman Turks seized Constantinople, they slammed shut the gateway east to the East Indies and legendary Cathay. European rulers were determined to find a new way to reach those treasures of the orient through the "back door," by crossing the Atlantic and discovering a North American passage to the Pacific.

That is how an Italian from Venice, Giovanni Caboto, became the first man to claim Maine for England. John Cabot (he changed his name after moving to Bristol, England) hired out to Henry VII of England in 1497. Financed by the king, he sailed west in the track of the Vikings. His ship was only 50 tons and was manned by a crew of only seventeen men. Cabot made his landfall in Nova Scotia, then coasted down to Maine. His written reports to the king vividly describe the dark forests and the treacherous reefs and ledges that guarded the new country. King Henry, his mind filled with dreams of riches from China, was not excited by this mundane news. He abandoned the Cabot voyage of exploration in disappointment. But Cabot's written reports to the King of England became of vast future importance. The Cabot reports became the basis of England's claims to New England.

Twenty-five years later, in May 1524, another Italian master mariner from Tuscany, Giovanni da Verrazano, (whose name now graces the spectacular bridge near Manhattan, the island he discovered) explored the Maine islands.

Verrazano was a well-seasoned expert when he hired out to the King of France. He had previously sailed to Carthage, Damascus, the Levant; was a friend of Magellan and a thoroughly experienced voyager. At age thirty-eight, he sailed to America from France in *La Dauphine*, a ship built for the French navy in 1519 and named in honor of Francois, heir to the throne of France. This ship was 100 tons, twice the size of John Cabot's. It carried a crew of fifty, three times the number of Cabot's crew, and was loaded with provisions for eight months.

Verrazano made his destination clear in the will he wrote just before departure. His intent was to reach the east coast of Asia and to find a new route to Cathay.

La Dauphine sailed January 17, 1524. Heavy storms during late February forced Verrazano to alter course to the westward. On March 1, he made a landfall at Cape Fear in North Carolina. Along the Outer Banks of North Carolina, Verrazano found an isthmus and thought that from his lookout he could see the Pacific Ocean, the sea that flows around the shores of India and China. He turned north, hoping to discover a passage through to the Pacific, so he could steer for the shores of Cathay. His mapmaker brother, Girolamo, drew his charts of North America that way. Consequently, for the next 100 years, maps of North America were circulated showing a narrow strait, something like the Panama Canal, through a pinched waist of North Carolina, with the Pacific Ocean on the other side.

All that March, blessed with fantastic luck and good weather, Verrazano sailed north, somehow missing the reefs and ledges around Hatteras, which have sunk more than six hundred ships. On April 17, he sailed into New York Bay. He and his men were the first Europeans to sight what is now Manhattan, Staten Island, and Brooklyn Heights.

From there, he sailed on again, heading east to Block Island. It reminded him of the Island of Rhodes, "filled with trees, full of hills, well peopled." With foul weather approaching, he took shelter and anchored in Narragansett Bay. That night Verrazano named a future state of the Union. He called Block Island, "Rhode Island." Piloted by friendly Wampanoag Indians in their canoes, *La Dauphine* sailed to deep shelter and its crew spent two weeks in friendly visits with the tribe. This may account in part for the Indians' friendliness to the Pilgrims a hundred years later.

By May 6, 1524, *La Dauphine* was under sail across Massachusetts Bay, heading for the coast of Maine at Casco Bay. But here the Abnaki, though they looked like the Wampanoag Indians, were hostile. Verrazano described them as "being of such crudity and evil manners ... that we could not converse with them even with signs." When the French crew came ashore on Casco Bay to trade, they were shot at with arrows and driven away. *La Dauphine* continued east. Finally, at an island described by Verrazano as at latitude 43 degrees, 40 minutes north, unfriendly Indians let down a basket from a high cliff and grudgingly traded a few items. The only places that tally with Verrazano's log are Seguin Island or Bald Head, at the tip of Cape Small, at the eastern entrance to Casco Bay. The behavior that most enraged the Frenchmen was the way the Indians liked to show their disdain: "by exhibiting bare buttocks and laughing immoderately at us." On their map, the Verrazano brothers called this part of Maine "The Land of Bad People" and sailed on, heading east among the islands.

"In the space of 50 leagues, we counted some thirty-two islands, lying all near the land, being small and pleasant to the view, high, and having many turnings and windings among them, making many fair harbors and channels as they do in the gulf of Venice and Dalmatia," wrote Verrazano.

As we cruise today among these same islands, I like to think of this Italian-born captain, with a French crew, writing in his log for King Francois I of France, about his first sightings of the islands of Maine. That May of 1524, some 457 springtimes ago, were shadbushes in bright white bloom? Were porpoises playing? Were the wildflowers of May and the first green buds of summer bursting?

When *La Dauphine* dropped anchor, did the crew row ashore and find mussels among the seaweed clinging to the island ledges? Did they dig fat clams at the low-tide mark or find lobsters under rocks close to shore? Were the small white clouds of spring scudding in a blue sky? And where they walked on the land behind the shore, did those sailors revel, too, in the smell of spruce and sweet fern? Did they watch the gulls soar and laugh at the quick-legged shore birds racing ahead of the wavelets as they hurriedly dug their sandy meals?

The three biggest, most beautiful Maine islands Verrazano saw, he named after the most beautiful princesses in the court of the king of France—the teen-age daughters of Catherine, Queen of Navarre. The islands were Monhegan, Isle au Haut, and Mount Desert, still the greatest island landmarks on the coast.

On the Verrazano map another name appears, a name that would soon send a generation of treasure hunters to search the Maine coast. The name was "Oranbega," which in the Abnaki Indian language means a stretch of quiet water between two rapids. It describes the Penobscot River. It is the only Indian name on the Verrazano map. Soon after, the map was in circulation in Europe, the name became altered to Norumbega, and was used to describe a larger region; a region supposedly filled with gold, silver, precious gems, and containing a fabled city of enormous wealth.

Down East fogs may have plagued Verrazano before he completed his island cruise, for he missed recording the Bay of Fundy and Nova Scotia and put into land that he plotted at 50 degrees latitude, presumably Funk Island, Newfoundland.

"Having spent all our naval stores and victuals, and having discovered 700 leagues (a league, is equivalent to 3 miles) of new country, we topped off with water and wood, and decided to return to France," wrote Verrazano.

La Dauphine made a fast passage on her return and anchored in Dieppe two weeks later, on July 8, 1524. Verrazano reported personally to King Francis and was promised four more ships for a second voyage, which he never got. The bankers refused to invest more money in explorations of North America. However, Verrazano made two more transatlantic voyages. In 1526, he sailed to Brazil. And in 1528, he sailed to Florida, thence to the Bahamas and on to Guadeloupe. There, at age forty-two, he rowed ashore with his brother to meet the natives gathered on the beach, waving to them. Giovanni da Verrazano waded ashore. That proved to be a fateful decision. The Carib natives were cannibals. They killed the great sailor right on the beach, cut up and then ate his still quivering body. "To so miserable an end came this valiant gentleman," wrote Ramusio, chronicler and mapmaker of such voyages.

The next explorer-navigator was a Spaniard, Estaban Gomez, who was driven by dreams of finding gold and silver in Maine to match the treasures found earlier by Spain in Mexico and Peru. Empty-handed and disappointed by Maine, he sailed hastily away. But this sailor left his mark, which lasts until today. For Gomez and his crew chose to give names to Maine's bays and islands. When his boat put ashore at a lovely island far Down East he christened it Campo Bello. When he sailed through the bay with the highest tides in the world, he christened it Bahia Profundo, "deep bay," the Bay of Fundy. And when sailing further west he came upon another vast bay shaped like a helmet; he named it Bahia de Casco, Casco Bay.

Almost 50 years passed before the next treasure hunter sailed to the Maine islands from Europe. This time, in 1597, it was a Por-tuguese, Simon Ferdinando, who hired out to England. He, too, found nothing here to line his pockets, and left. The magnet that brought these and other treasure hunters to Maine was the fabled land of Norumbega, which supposedly was up the Penobscot River. Norumbega was the Wildcat oil or Klondike of its day. Norumbega was the dream of riches in profusion; the city where little children played with diamonds and pearls for toys; where cooking pots were made from silver and the temples were of filigree gold; where the roofs of homes were gold leafed; where every woman and every man wore rubies and brilliant emeralds; where great palaces shone with silver walls and sparkled with "pyllars of cristol," and the gardens bloomed with everlasting artificial flowers with stems made from pre-cious metals and blooms of priceless jewels.

It is easy to smile today at such wild and foolish dreams. But those were the days when the royal courts of Europe glowed with dreams of riches on distant continents. It was the age of exploration, discovery, and wealth to be taken for the asking by men of courage who would dare to sail to far Cathay, the rich Indies, the Levant.

To minds and imaginations already ripe for such an adventure, the tales of Norumbega were believable. The powerful and the greedy were ready to listen, spellbound, to the greatest liar of his time, David Ingram.

Ingram was a member of an expedition to Mexico in 1568, led by the freebooting pirate Sir John Hawkins. Cast ashore in Mexico, David Ingram and two others started on one of the longest, most unlikely walks in American history. Ingram claimed he walked from Mexico to Maine. Finally he met a French vessel trading on the St. John River and took passage home to Europe. Once home, David Ingram wrote a highly spiced adventure story of his journey. In his lively book he gave a lavish account of the incredible wealth of the city he had found: Norumbega. That glittering city became the pot of gold at the end of the rainbow in the new, undiscovered world of Maine.

Ingram was by no means the first traveler to bring home romantic tales of the New World. The Norumbega legend had been born earlier, with the inclusion of Oranbega on the map drawn in 1529 by Girolamo Verrazano. Then, in 1539, the fabled wealth of Norumbega was played up in Ramusio's *Voyages*, a widely read book. When, in 1580, Sir Humphrey Gilbert, a highly respected figure in England, financed the voyage of John Walker, Gilbert hoped they'd find the fabled city and make him rich. Walker sailed into Penobscot Bay, where Norumbega was said to be. He planted the flag of Queen Elizabeth on shores near Camden and claimed this region to be Norumbega. In his reports to Sir Humphrey,* seeking to please his sponsor, Walker sang not only the praises of Penobscot islands, but also claimed to have seen mountains of silver. Indeed, Walker, and many after him, probably mistook the mica and quartz glinting from the island ledges, shining from Mt. Battie, to be silver.

Then, as today, men are apt to see what they dream of seeing.

The dream had substance enough to send brave and foolhardy men in small boats across the Atlantic. Even when dozens returned empty handed, the dream persisted. More men, hungry for easy fortunes, came to strike it rich in Maine. Such quests continued, as men after them have crossed mountains to hunt for California gold, and others have braved harsh lands, the Arctic, the North Sea, to hunt for oil.

But as the dream of easy fortune finally faded, more level-headed voyagers found in the Maine islands a more reliable although much more mundane source of wealth: Fish.

Fish proved to be the real silver mines of Maine.

---

* Sir Humphrey Gilbert himself led four vessels in June 1583 to Newfoundland. He found thirty fishing vessels there and claimed possession in the name of Queen Elizabeth. On his return trip to England in September, aboard the tiny pinnace *Squirrel*, Sir Humphrey was lost at sea.

3

Fish

The Silver Mines of Maine

The first roots of the United States are not in the soil of the mainland, but in the fishing grounds off the coast of Maine. Fishermen began this nation in rough, temporary settlements on the Maine islands, spreading down the coast from Newfoundland to the Isles of Shoals, off Kittery. Fish, in size and numbers not found in European waters, provided not only a reliable, steady food supply, but also the first "cash crop" to the men who began this nation. America's earliest trading centers were fishing ports; and those were on the islands, stretching from St. Croix and Mt. Desert on through Monhegan, Damariscove, Richmond, to the Isles of Shoals.

It was the pursuit of money more than the search for religious freedom that built the first rough trading posts and settlements. Yet the church had a finger in it. In Catholic Europe, the church calendar decreed more than 160 meatless—or fish eating—days a year. Even in Protestant England, an Act of Parliament declared Wednesdays and Saturdays were meatless or fish-eating days. That was the law of the land. It was this demand for fish in Europe and in England that caused the seafaring rush to exploit the real silver mines of Maine—fish.

For the early fishermen, Europe was a long sail home.

Fish caught by the English vessels had to be dried and preserved on shore for that trip to market. This led to the first rough settlements on the Maine islands.

Settlements also required boat building and repairing. The first boat made by white men in North America was built on the bank of the Kennebec, near Popham, in 1607, the pinnace named *Virginia*.

29

The need for timber led to the beginnings of lumbering in Maine. The English navy also urgently needed tall, strong trees for the masts of its new vessels. Cutting trees for these masts created the first big market for what has long been one of Maine's biggest industries—the lumber business.

For almost four hundred years, the growth of fishing, boat building, and lumbering went hand in hand. Boat building and lumbering became the hallmark skills of Maine. Maine has led the world in building many different kinds of boats for many different uses: boats to carry massive masts, for the lumbering trade; boats for the ice trade, the lime trade, the granite trade, each of which played great roles in Maine's development. Maine's shipyards built the fastest clipper ships for the wheat trade to England, Europe, Australia; which, in turn, brought expansion into world markets and prosperity to American agriculture. Then Maine boatyards again adapted their skills to a changing market and created huge four-, five-, and six-masted schooners, the money-making ships that hauled larger cargoes with less sail and fewer in their crews than the fast, beautiful, pointed clipper ships.

These skills, born in the building of fish boats, were applied 170 years later in defending our fledgling young nation. Boatyards at Kittery built the first warships for the U.S. Navy at the time of the Revolution. From these yards on Badger's Island at Kittery came *Kearsage* and *Ranger*, skippered by John Paul Jones. Developing on from there, Maine contributed the first "ironsides" man o' war, the fastest and best of the World War II destroyers, submarines, and sub chasers, on through to today's guided-missile destroyers at Bath Iron Works, the only yard in the nation regularly able to deliver warships ahead of schedule and under budget.

But fish and fishermen, almost five hundred years ago, began it all on these Maine islands.

It was the abundance of fish, and the money that fishing earned, that lured hundreds of fishing boats across 3,000 miles of ocean to the uncharted but rich fishing grounds off the Maine islands.

Ship captains since Cabot and Gilbert wrote glowingly about the plentiful fishing here. Captain John Smith, a man who had voyaged to most of the known world, wrote that he had never seen such good fishing anywhere as he did in Maine.

In his book *Description of New England*, published in 1616, he wrote:

In March, April, May, and halfe June, heere is Cod in abundance; in May, June, July, and August, Mullet and Sturgion, whoes Roes do make Caviare and Puttargo. Herring, if any desire them; I have taken many out of the bellies of Cod; but the Savages compare their store in the sea to the haires of their heads, so surely there are an incredible Abundance on this Coast. In the end of August, September, October and November, you have Cod againe; Hake you may have when the Cod fails in summer, if you will fish the night, which is better than Cod. Now each hundred fish you take here (in Maine) is as good as two or three hundred in Newfoundland.

Another who shouted the praises of fishing here was Thomas Morton, who wrote in 1632 in his book *New England Canaan*:

This Coast aboundeth with such multitudes of Codd that the inhabitants of New England doe dung their ground with Codd; and it is a commodity better than the golden mines of the Spanish Indies; for without dried Codd the Spaniard, Portugal, and Italian would not be able to vittel a ship for the Sea.

And so by the hundreds, the early fishing boats came to the "silver mines of Maine." Money—the demand of the marketplace in the early 1600s—was what caused men to risk their lives and ships in the rough, cold, foggy waters of fishing grounds 3,000 miles from home. The market was assured in fish-eating Catholic Europe.

Fish eating was so ingrained a habit that consumption was higher even than the law demanded. For example, according to the ship's stores stocked by Frobisher for his North American voyage of 1578, the crew ate fish fourteen days a month. By comparison today, the average American eats only 12 pounds of fish in an entire year.

Europe's demand for fish from New England has not changed through the centuries. In 1975, just as in 1475, five hundred years before, foreign fishing fleets were reaping the sea harvest off our shores.

In the 1400s, ships from the Hanseatic League were working as a cartel-combine. Banded together in a self-protective association, merchants and bankers from sixty cities in the Germanic states tried to monopolize foreign trade. They financed fishing trips to the fishing banks off Maine, where Vikings had fished before them. As the grip of the Hanseatic League was weakened, a few tough sailors from Cornwall and Devon began fishing off Maine in the 1480s. By the 1580s, a fishing boom was in full swing. Captains of fishing boats from England, Spain, Italy, Portugal, and France had heard the news of huge catches along the banks of the Gulf of Maine. They flocked here. By the 1600s, three hundred fishing boats from Europe were off our coast. This was where the fish and the money were.

The fishing world hasn't changed much in all these centuries.

Leap ahead in time to a day in late June 1975, and join me aboard a Coast Guard plane on a surveillance mission over Georges Bank. The account of what we saw on that flight is taken from my column in the *Maine Sunday Telegram*, July 6, 1975:

Aboard Surveillance Flight—Two signs show they are Soviets: The hammer-and-sickle emblem on their smokestacks, and the Russian letters of the alphabet which precede the identification numerals amidships.

Lt. Jim Holland, U.S. Coast Guard pilot, banks our 22-year-old Grumman amphibian into a turn, so we can fly back to circle, inspect, identify each vessel in the Russian fishing fleet, two hundred feet below our wings. We are seventy miles off the U.S. coast, over Georges Bank.

It is an eerie feeling to see so many huge Russian fishing ships so close to American shores. It is an infuriating feeling to see them harvesting enormous catches of fish in traditionally American fishing grounds—and to recall the American draggers left behind in Portland and Port Clyde, in New Bedford and Gloucester. These Americans can't afford to leave port. "The price for fish is too low or the catch is too small," they say.

But below our surveillance plane are the Soviets, the Bulgarians, the Poles, the East Germans, and others. They have millions of dollars worth of fishing vessels manned by up to 17,000 fishermen, working just off our shores. They catch and process millions of tons, here on the spot; load them onto refrigerator ships which head home to Russia. The fleet stays here and keeps on fishing, fishing, fishing. They will be here six months before going home for overhaul, after steaming over 30,000 miles.

In one day of flying surveillance over only one area, of Georges Bank, we have seen ninety ships. But only one ship has been an American.

Behind the copilot sits Charles L. Philbrook, eyeballing each ship through special binoculars. Philbrook has twenty years experience in this surveillance business, tracking and identifying foreign fishing fleets off our shores. His card reads: "Senior Resident Agent" of the Law Enforcement Division of the National Marine Fisheries.

Herring by the millions come to spawn on Georges Bank during July and August. Then, says Philbrook, there are usually 250 or more foreign vessels on the northern edge of Georges Bank.

"Fly over, and you'll see the crew waist-deep in herring on the decks, filling up the holds below."

The West German stern trawlers are three hundred feet or more of extremely modern and efficient fishing machinery. "Last year fifteen such vessels took 29,000 metric tons in 75 days' work," says

Philbrook, shaking his head.

For the record, in 1972 the foreign catch of finfish totaled 925,000 metric tons compared to a U.S. catch of only 175,000. In 1973, the comparison was 990,000 metric tons for foreign fleets and under 200,000 for United States ships.

The sea below is so calm that Soviet fishermen, who work through the night purse seining, are rowing skiffs, visiting each others' ships, 75 miles out in the Atlantic. Out here, water depths in the Georges Bank shallow to forty feet in places, then at the edges plunge to a thousand feet or more.

These big foreign fleets are run with the discipline of a navy task force. There is a fleet commander in over-all charge, and under him are nine group commands, going down to skippers of individual vessels. Scientists in "brain ships" decide where to fish and at what depth; production chiefs set quotas and schedules for deliveries of fish to the processing ships and refrigerator vessels. Other officials decide crew rotation. There are fleet doctors and hospital rooms. There is even a police vessel for dealing with disorder.

Philbrook's pencil fills up sheet after sheet with names and numbers of Russian ships. He adds other notes about the fishing gear, and activities aboard. The information goes to Washington to be collated with other reports from other surveillance. He adds up the sightings after we land back at our base. "Eighty-three Soviet ships in this sector alone this day; plus other foreigners fishing."

We picked up the first big Soviet fleet about 50 miles offshore. The next fleet about 80 miles offshore; and the third fleet about 125 miles off Cape Cod.

Smallest are the purse-seiners, 125 to 145 feet long, carrying 30 to 45 crew members. Scores of these seiners work to supply big processing ships. By the smoke coming from the stacks far aft, we detect when the processing ships are cooking.

The biggest ships, in separate fleets, are the Soviet stern trawlers. They can do their own processing as well as catching. These ships are some three hundred feet long. They carry up to 350 in crew. Many of the crew are women. We see the women sunbathing in bikinis as we fly over. We see helicopters on the larger vessels.

There is recreation for the crew of these big ships. We fly low over their volleyball courts, enclosed in wire mesh so the ball doesn't go out of bounds into the sea.

"The ships stay on station. The crews change," Philbrook tells me. "They take the forty-five people cooped up on a 145-foot ship off after forty-five days or so, and bring a new crew in. On the larger, more comfortable vessels, the crew changes every ninety days or so."

East German crews, changed every ninety days, are taken by transport vessel to Cuba, then flown home. By way of stark contrast, only a few of the seventy-five draggers in the Maine fleet regularly stay out fishing for more than three nights. Most dayfish only.

The Coast Guard runs other patrol missions along the coast. The findings are distributed monthly. I quote from one typical report:

"In the Northwest Atlantic a total of 334 individual foreign fishing and support vessels were spotted this month ... Soviet Union 204; Poland 40; East Germany 13; Bulgaria 8; Japan 13; Spain 48; Italy 7; Ireland 1 ... The Soviets were by far the largest fleet ... They had 156 large factory stern trawlers; 19 medium stern freezer trawlers; 10 medium side trawlers; 16 factory base ships and refrigerator fish transports, two fuel tankers and one research vessel."

This flight was made a few months before the revolutionary law was passed in Congress in 1976 which extended U.S. fisheries jurisdiction to two hundred miles off our coasts. The law finally reduced the massacres of our fishing grounds by foreign fleets. The U.S. now has a measure of control over our Continental Shelf.

Why do these New England waters contain some of the richest fishing grounds in the world? Why did fish congregate here in huge quantities five hundred years ago? Why are they still here today, after five hundred years of constant fishing over Grand Bank and Georges Bank? Today, though, the U.S. Marine Fisheries Department has imposed strict limits and regulations for fishing the banks to preserve dwindling fish stocks.

The answer lies in the nature of the ocean bottom. It is no digression to take a look here at the hidden, astonishing world of the ocean bottom; for in it lies the reason why white men first came to fish from the Maine islands.

On one wall in the office of the admiral commanding Fleet Wing Atlantic at Brunswick Naval Air Station, Maine, I saw a terrifying, three-dimensional map of the bottom of the Atlantic. It hangs there because the prime mission of P-3 Orion search planes under his command in Brunswick, Jacksonville, Florida, Bermuda, Iceland, the Azores, Spain, and Sicily is to maintain surveillance of Russian submarines. These submarines hide deep in the strange, mountainous world beneath the surface of the Atlantic.

The Atlantic, covering $33\frac{1}{2}$ million square miles, has three main parts; the Continental Shelf, the Slope, and the Abyss. The Continental Shelf, which was dry land many millions of years ago, is the shallowest and smallest part, averaging just over 400 feet deep, compared to an average of over 12,000 for the Atlantic as a whole. It occupies only about 7 percent of the ocean bottom.

The Shelf deepens slowly, at the rate of about 15 feet per mile, into the Slope. This Slope occupies only about 15 percent of the total ocean area. But in it are terrifying cliffs, escarpments, precipitous gorges, and jagged mountain peaks.

The rest of the ocean is the Abyss. Here is the pitch-dark, totally silent, unknown, and alien world. Yet the Abyss part of all the oceans of the world is the largest part of our planet Earth. Oceans cover 70 percent of the Earth's surface; the Abysses are 73 percent of the oceans.

Four and 5 miles down in that blackness, pressure is 7 tons per inch. Down there may be more secrets of our world than we have found in outer space. No rage of storms on the surface causes a ripple down there. Scientists who probe the Abyss with seismic soundings report that much of the bottom is covered with soft sediment, miles thick. They estimate it takes 2,500 years for 1 inch of this sediment from the Earth's surface to accumulate on the bottom of the Abyss.

That weird underwater map of the Atlantic hanging on the wall of the submarine hunter shows that the biggest mountain range in the world lies under the Atlantic Ocean. The mountain range is ten thousand miles long and 500 miles wide, reaching from Iceland to Antarctica. One of its biggest peaks shows to our eyes as Mount Pico, in the Azores. From an ocean depth of 20,000 feet, almost 4 miles down, the mountain races up, breaks the ocean surface, and keeps rising till it tops out as Mount Pico, which towers 7,613 feet above the Atlantic Ocean's surface.

Not far off the coast of Maine lies another gigantic underwater mountain, some 13,000 feet tall, but invisible to our eyes. It rises up out of the Atlantic Abyss into the Slope near Newfoundland. As it rises, the water depth shallows, going from 13,482 feet to 9,000 feet to 6,000 feet. Then the Slope changes into the Shelf. Here, the underwater mountain keeps rising higher and higher and the ocean depth gets shallower and shallower, until it is 400 feet—and sometimes less than 200 feet—deep. This forms that huge flat underwater plateau called the Grand Banks. Here is one of the world's richest fishing grounds.

Shallowness is the reason fish by the billions are here over the Grand Banks and the other banks off the Maine coast, such as Georges Bank, Jeffrey's Bank, Platt's Bank, the Monhegan Banks, Three Dory Ridge, Bank Comfort, the 45 Fathom Bunch, and many others.

Sunlight can penetrate right to the shallow ocean bottom, and work its magic of photosynthesis through which plants can grow down there. These plants make possible the best kind of feeding ground for "bottom" fish. They are the magnets that have been attracting haddock and cod by the billions here to the Banks for centuries.

Other fish such as herring, mackerel, and porgies feed closer to the surface, eating plankton and algae. The Maine waters over our Continental Shelf are rich in these fish foods, too, thanks to the mingling of cold and warm currents.

Finally, these fishing banks are very big. The Grand Bank covers over 40,000 square miles. Georges Bank, to the south, spreads across 10,000 square miles. These are the reasons why fishing fleets of many nations have been off New England shores for five hundred years.

Today, when fishing is good, word spreads fast due to radio telephones, spotting aircraft, and even reports that fishing boats must file with government agencies.

Hundreds of years ago, news about "where the fish were at" traveled by the fishermen's grapevine.

On May 17, 1605, two years before 105 English cavaliers landed to form their "first settlement" at Jamestown, Virginia, the ship *Archangel* dropped anchor off Muscongus Bay, under the command of Captain George Weymouth. Aboard was a writer, James Rosier, whose job was to keep a running diary of the trip for the financial backers home in England.

Rosier wrote ecstatically about the fishing. In England, where fish was money, these words of his must have jumped off the page. Rosier wrote:

> Thomas King, boatswain, cast out his hook when we were but thirty leagues (ninety miles) from land, with sails down ... and hauled up an exceeding great and well fed cod. Then there were cast out three or four more hooks, and the fish were so plentiful and great that when our captain would have set sail, we all desired him to permit them to fish a while longer because we were so delighted to see them catch such large fish as soon as the hook went down ... One of the mates with two hooks on a lead at five draughts together hauled up ten fish; some measured to be five feet long and three feet about.

In 1614, Captain John Smith was in the anchorage at Monhegan Island, writing enthusiastically about the fishing. In April that year, Smith reported he was drying and salting 40,000 fish and corning another 7,000 on the beach at Monhegan. He took one shipload of fish home to England, sent another to Spain, and cleared 1,500 pounds sterling profit from that trip alone.

The fishing harbor at Monhegan was busy. A Captain Michael Cooper was back the next year with four fishing vessels. Then, in 1616, came Richard Hawkins, son of the slave trader and pirate Sir John Hawkins. He sailed in with two fishing vessels. Ten more fished close by. Sir Ferdinando Gorges had other boats there. Captain John Smith came back and had seven boats built on Monhegan between 1615 and 1618. The Pilgrims would not set foot on Plymouth Rock till 1620.

Still other evidence of the profitable fishing around Monhegan Island comes from an affadavit by Thomas Piddock. He swore, in connection with a legal dispute, that in July 1617, 173,700 dried fish, weighing 300,000 pounds and valued at $10,000, were shipped from Monhegan to Bordeaux, France, aboard the vessel *Jacob*.

Ships' logs of the time report that during "stormes a full thirty to forty fishing vessels may be found taking shelter in the small harbor" at Damariscove Island, 10 miles westward of Monhegan.

The entrance to that harbor, guarded by submerged ledges well-named "The Motions," can be hazardous. To anchor thirty vessels would mean very little swinging room. Today, if a dozen boats were inside, the next arrival would seek shelter elsewhere. If, in the early 1600s, thirty boats crowded in, it indicated so many fishing boats were in these waters that other harbors were already full.

If these quotes seem suspect as exaggerations to which some fishermen are prone, the Reverend Francis Higginson, who saw the scene from a different angle, wrote:

> "The abundance of sea fish are almost beyond believing, and sure I should scarce have believed it, except as I had seen it with mine own eyes. I saw great store of whales and grampuses and such abundance of mackerels that it would astonish one to behold ... and an abundance of lobsters ... For my own part, I was soon cloyed of them, they were so great and fat and luscious."

Early in the 1600s, the New England fishery was so extensive that more than ten thousand men and boys were making their living exporting fish to England and Europe. Before the 1600s ended, 10 million pounds of fish were being shipped annually from here. Hundreds of fish ships were carrying big cargoes of 300,000 fish each to England, Europe, and the West Indies. Their cash earnings topped $500,000 a year.

In those days, months would elapse between the time fish were caught here and the time they were eaten in England or Europe.

The way those fish were cured, or preserved, for the trip back to market may have had a lot to do with the beginnings of the first semi-permanent settlements.

English vessels did not carry nearly as much salt as Spanish, Portuguese, and French vessels because, to the English, salt was expensive. Salt beds were mostly around Cadiz and the Algarve in Portugal, which made salt cheap to fishermen from those regions. But the English had to import salt; had to pay more for it, and so used less. Therefore, the English cured their fish differently. They used the "dry" method. The French and Spaniards used the "wet" method.

Under the wet method, fish were gutted on board as soon as they were caught and immediately packed layer upon layer into barrels with heavy doses of salt between layers to preserve them. No shore station was necessary.

Using the dry method, which needed far less costly salt, English vessels cured their fish on shore. Half a ship's crew worked on shore. Their first job was to cut timber and build a large wharf. The half of the crew that was fishing from the big boat and from six or seven smaller boats carried aboard, would come alongside the wharf and throw out their fish, fresh and whole. The shore party would gut and split the fish on the wharf. Then they carried the fish up the beach to the "flakes" to dry. Flakes, made from brushwood and branches, were the "drying lines." Split fish were only lightly salted, then hung on the flakes, where they were cured by the sun and dried out until they were hard, stiff and slightly cooked. To prevent them being dampened by fog or rain, the fish on the flakes were covered with brushwood or old sails. This process took several weeks. Then these fish were piled in nearby storage sheds and thousands more fish were hung to dry.

Shore duty was surely preferred by many farm boys from the West Country of England: Devon, Cornwall, Somerset, and Dorset. Working on shore, on a Maine island, where a fellow could stretch his legs, get a sweet smell of spruce trees, snare an animal or kill a bird for dinner, and pick wild berries, was better duty than hauling up cod all day. When night came, the shore crew preferred to bunk down in a shack on the island rather than go aboard ship to the dank, smelly fo'c's'le, crowded with men who'd been thigh-deep in fish all day.

When the time came in September or October for the fishing vessel to head home, loaded with dried cod, I suspect that there were some among the shore crew who chose to stay behind on a Maine island. A month-long crossing of the North Atlantic in October gales, in a ship loaded with 300,000 cod, was not much to offer men who had enjoyed summer on a Maine island. Some chose to stay until the boat came back in the spring. They might be able to make good money in the winter, too, through trapping and fur trading with the

Indians. The market for beaver pelts in London was high. Thus, with no intent of founding a colony, the first, unknown semi-permanent settlers began living on the Maine islands—left behind with a supply of fish, biscuits, salt pork, fish lines, and a small boat. And maybe some rum.

4

Men and Boats
Rugged Atlantic Pioneers

On the north side of Allen Island, in Muscongus Bay, is a cove where I love to anchor. Most often we come to it in *Steer Clear* through that sweet body of water called George's Harbor. The harbor, really a narrow passage crowded with lobster traps, between Allen and Benner islands, has weatherbeaten shingled cottages, barns with gaping holes, and small wharves. Meadows reach down from the high ground on each island to the fish house and wharf on each shore. In summer there may be a few sheep, some laundry drying on a line, swinging in the summer breeze, signs a fishing family is on each island for the summer. There may be a skiff or two on the moorings in midstream, where the lobster boats will lay when they come back from hauling. But in winter there is no sign of life.

The cove I like is just to the east as you come out of George's Harbor. At high water, all of it looks innocent and inviting, but when the tide drains, two sets of ledges are exposed. We discovered them the hard way one summer. We'd dropped anchor fairly far out in the cove, in the lee of the north tip of Allen, and taken the dinghy to the crescent-shaped stone beach to enjoy a swim and a walk. As we rowed back to *Steer Clear*, we found our boat safe but almost encircled by ledge. So we made the best of it, by rowing back to shore and exploring the island further, until the tide came in again.

We walked to the Weymouth Cross, on a hill beside George's Harbor. It is a big granite cross that commemorates the first church service held on these islands by Captain George Weymouth in 1607. The cross was erected more than three hundred years later.

The picture we envisioned of his tattered crew gathered on this empty island, 3,000 miles from their homes, on the verge of an unknown land, celebrating with a Sunday service, made us wonder what kind of men they were, where their roots lay, the kind of boat they sailed here, how they navigated, how they ate and lived and endured; and, above all, why they came, why they left the safety of England.

We wondered not just about the men with Weymouth, but the men who sailed here earlier with Martin Pring in 1603, who saw foxes between North Haven and Vinalhaven and first called the water separating the two islands the Fox Thorofare; the men who sailed with Humphrey Gilbert and Bartholomew Gosnold earlier; with the Frenchmen De Monts and Champlain, in 1604, and scores of others before and soon after them.

These were among the very first white men to set foot on Maine islands. It was they who built the first shacks, dried the first fish, first met the Indians, ate the first lobsters. Among them were a few who chose to stay behind when their ships sailed home. They were the lonely men who built the first winter camps and waited for the return of their ships the next fishing season. They were the men who started the early rough settlements of New England.

Who were they?

The accounts of the early voyages make almost no mention at all of the crews.

Physically, they were certainly small men by our standards today. They stood only about five feet tall, or less: for the headroom below decks was never higher than five feet. Most were fairly young; with ages running from a boy of twelve or so to "mariners" in their twenties and thirties. Almost certainly none of the crew could read or write.

It would be a mistake to think all of them were real seafarers. No more than a handful of each crew were true sailors. When Bartholomew Gosnold sailed for Maine from England in March 1602, a contemporary wrote, "he was attended by thirty-two persons, only eight of whom were mariners." When Martin Pring sailed in the *Speedwell* in 1603, he had a crew of "thirty men and boys." William Browne, accompanying Pring in *Discoverer*, a bark of only 26 tons, had "thirteen men and a boy."

The captain was often highly educated, sometimes blue-blooded; certainly a man trusted by the financial backers in London, Plymouth, or Bristol; a man who could read, write, make reports, and extract money from merchant bankers or land grants from the court. Just below him in rank was a "pilot"; a man who had proven experience in navigation, in crossing the Atlantic on other voyages, a kind of "executive officer." Then, if lucky, the crew contained a mate or two who knew the tricks of sailing and how to handle men well. On larger crews, there might be a carpenter, who could make repairs, build small boats, and keep the food and wine barrels from leaking.

The rest of the crew were usually "picked up" from the waterfront wharves, taverns, jails. Often they were willing to go because the law was after them, because of shrewish wives, because creditors were about to have them thrown in jail. Some, as in every generation, sailed for the hell of it; adventure—or escape—was in their blood. Some were "pressed," kidnapped by a "press gang" who got paid to round up men and dump them aboard.

Life aboard a fishing boat then had few good days. Most of the time the life was hard, miserable, cold, and wet. Men slept on decks or in passageways, wherever they could. They wore the same rough clothes day and night, for months on end. When they finally reached their destination at a Maine island, no city port, no tavern, no female company would be waiting to make life worth living, even for a night or two. Just an island, uninhabited except possibly by Indian "savages." Once they had reached the coast of Maine, there was more work. Shore parties would tote water from cold streams, carrying heavy barrels back to the ship. Others would cut wood for the cookstove or for repairing and building boats. The big boat would be gone, catching fish. Men with shore duty would spend the day handling the earlier catch, gutting and splitting fish, then drying the stinking mess in the sun, on rocks, and drying lines.

After two or three months, when the vessel was abrim with smelly fish, they'd set sail on the long trip home, perhaps another month in the stormy North Atlantic during October or November. Back in Plymouth or Bristol, the catch would be unloaded, sold; and when the money came in, deductions would be taken from their pay for the food, the fishhooks and lines they had used, and the fines they had incurred for breaking discipline. For six months' hard, dangerous, comfortless work, the pay might amount to twenty pounds.

Seamen in the Royal Navy in the 1600s were paid five shillings a month; in the merchant marine the pay was ten shillings a month. So the crew of a fishing vessel, who went "shares," apparently made twice as much money, even after deductions, provided the fishing was good and they were still around to collect when the shares were divvied up.

However, there were compensations. First, there was likely to be plenty to drink and to eat, at least on the outbound trip. The best account of this comes from Samuel Eliot Morison's book, *The Northern Voyages*. Morison quotes from the record of Frobisher's voyage to Newfoundland in 1577 and the food he put aboard.

> The ration was one pound of biscuit and one gallon of beer per man per day; one pound of salt beef or pork per man per day for flesh days; one dried cod for every four men on fast days; with oatmeal and rice if the fish supply gave out; a quarter pound of butter, and half a pound of cheese per man per day; honey for sweetening; and a hogshead of "sallet oyle" and a pipe of vinegar to last 120 men for four months.

In beer alone, that amounts to 14,400 gallons. In salt beef, it adds up to more than 7 tons.

But the food on long voyages went moldy. Ferdinand Columbus says that on his father's fourth voyage: "What with the heat and the dampness, our ship biscuit had become so wormy that, so help me God, I saw many who waited for darkness to eat the porridge made of it, that they might not see the maggots; and others were so used to eating them that they didn't even trouble to pick them out because they might lose their supper had they been so nice."

The smells aboard those early fishing and exploring vessels might have been unendurable to a 20th-century nose. The bilges filled with garbage, urine, vomit, defecation, food scraps. The ballast became impregnated with "pestilential funkes" and the stench was so overpowering that the ship was hauled ashore, the ballast thrown into the tide for cleansing, and the horrible gunk on the inside of the hold washed down with strong solutions of salt water and vinegar.

A description of "a sayler" 350 years ago is contained in Richard Braithwait's book, published in 1631 and called *Whimzies: or a New Cast of Characters.*

> A Sayler, is an Otter or Amphibium that lives both on Land and Water ... His familiarity with death and danger, hath armed him with a kind of dissolute security against any encounter. The sea cannot rant and roar abroad worse than bee within, fire him but with liquor ... In a Tempest you shall heare him pray, but so amothodically, as it argues he is seldom vers'd in that practice ... He makes small or no choice of his pallet; he can sleepe as well on a Sacke of Pumice as a pillow of doune. He was never acquainted much with civilitie; the Sea hath taught him other Rhetoric. He is most contant to his shirt and other of his seldom wash'd linen. He cannot speak low, the Sea talks so loud ... He can spin up a rope like a Spider and down again like a

lightening ... Death hee has seen in so many shapes, as it cannot amaze him.

Aboard a seventeenth-century boat, discipline was brutal, swift, and undisputed. Captain John Smith, who sailed to Monhegan in 1614, wrote, "The Marshall (or mate) is to punish offenders and see justice is executed according to directions; as ducking at the yard arme, hauling under the keel, bound to the capsterne or main-mast with a bucke of shot around his necke, setting in the bilbowes."

It would be hard to exaggerate the hardships and perils endured by the early explorers; the early fishermen and settlers. Equally it is almost impossible to re-create the ships, their daily lives aboard.

Their ships were strongly built, seaworthy; and, except for the captain's quarters, totally without comfort of any kind.

In size, they ranged from about 50 to 100 feet long, sometimes 125; in tonnage from 25 to 50 or 60 tons. In those days, tonnage was measured in "tuns" and usually spelled "tunnage." A tun was a double hogshead, the outsize barrel in which wine was shipped. Tunnage of a ship meant how many tuns of wine it could carry. From this developed the modern maritime ton, 40 cubic feet.

The fishing boats most often had two decks; the main inside deck laid over the holds and ballast, and the spar deck, outside, open to the weather. The seamen slept wherever they could find space to curl up on the main deck. There were no bunks and no hammocks for crew in most vessels. Only the officers had bunks. Sailors wrapped an old bit of sail or blanket over their wet clothes and made do, month after month.

At the forward end of the open deck was the galley or cook-box. Usually it was just a box with a hood to fend off the wind and sea, with a few inches of sand at the bottom of it as a base for a wood fire. One huge stew pot plus a few smaller pots and pans were all the equipment used to feed a crew of up to fifty men. In foul weather, the cook box was moved below, with a makeshift smoke pipe to carry off part of the smoke.

The ship was steered by a helmsman, out in the weather. Usually he got his steering orders from an officer who sat inside with the compass. This compass was probably a dry card type on a pivot, floating in a bowl and enclosed in a waterproof binnacle, lit by a small whale-oil lamp.

The science of navigation was still new. Celestial navigation had been used for centuries, but most navigators had only the experience of sailing the western shore of Europe and the Mediterranean.

Coming across the empty Atlantic however, the North Star and the sun became the best way to fix their latitude.

Even in summer, the North Atlantic can be a nightmare to sailor and navigator alike, especially in a sixteenth-century boat. Westerly gales would batter the little bark, forcing it to drop sail and lay-by, weathering out the storm for days and nights on end. Easterly gales drenched the sailors on deck with cold rain and the water seeped throughout the cold, dank ship. Northerly gales would rip sails and tear masts out of the deck. Between fronts of foul weather, fog would blot out the sun, or dead calms would put the ship in "irons," wallowing in the slow rolls of the Atlantic for day after day. Men died often. They died from storms, died from fights, died from drink, boredom, and scurvy. It was not a pleasant journey to an unknown fishing ground.

Maybe this was what induced the first settlers to stay behind. Men and boys from West of England farms may have preferred to risk a winter on a secure but lonely island rather than go back aboard their fish ship for a November crossing and a winter on the docks.

5

Sir Ferdinando Gorges

Father of Maine

We Americans are fascinated by the men who built our country.
We're intrigued by legends of the men who plotted the Boston Tea
Party; by Paul Revere and his midnight ride; by Lewis and Clark and
their hard journey west; by pioneers who opened the West in their
covered wagons; by the Indian fighters; by the cattle drivers, cow-
boys, badmen, and sheriffs of the Wild West; by the aviators who first
flew the mail; by ruthless money barons who built the transcontinen-
tal railroads; and by the astronauts who flew to outer space and
walked on the moon. We know about all of them.

Yet we draw blanks about the men who first sailed among these
islands of Maine, and about their backers in England and Europe.
Who financed those risky ventures? Who were the backers? Why did
they risk their money to send ships to an unknown land?

Let's look at Sir Ferdinando Gorges, the man with the Spanish-
sounding name who, as much as any single man, was the father of
Maine.

Gorges was for forty years the one man in all of England who
kept faith with his dream of colonizing Maine. From the time he was
thirty until he was past seventy, he master-minded and financed expedition after expedition; he spent more than 20,000 pounds of his own
money when 1,000 pounds could outfit a trans-Atlantic expedition;
he involved his sons, nephews, and other relatives in his schemes and
sent many of them on voyages. He was granted king's charters, only
to fight investigations before the House of Commons that would have
canceled his precious land patents. Through it all, Georges clung ob-
stinately to his dream.

A royalist to the end, Georges backed Prince Charles instead of Oliver Cromwell. Cromwell stripped him of his influence and most of his lands. He was "banished" to a small village in Somerset in his old age, where he died broke and broken hearted.

Gorges was indeed the Father of Maine. Yet in Maine today, all that bears his name is Fort Gorges in Portland Harbor, a dirty, disused, granite fort on a tiny island. He deserves better.

Ferdinando Gorges (1566–1646) was born in Somerset, in the West Country of England. His Spanish-sounding name came from ancestors who'd arrived in England from Spain during the reign of Philip and Mary. Early in his twenties, Gorges received inside knowledge about the conspiracy of his friend, the Earl of Essex—discarded lover of Queen Elizabeth—to overthrow the Queen. Gorges decided to tell the Queen all he knew. Essex was disgraced and executed. As a result, Gorges became a court favorite. The Queen made him a navy commander in her last war against Spain. He fought bravely and was knighted for gallantry during the battle against the Spanish Armada. In gratitude, the Crown made him Governor of Plymouth in 1604, an important post much to the liking of the 31-year-old Gorges. For Plymouth, long a front-line defense port against the Spanish, was also becoming the jumping-off port for voyages to the New World. Gorges was already intrigued by the New World. His imagination had been fired by an Indian birch-bark canoe, brought home to England by Martin Pring from his voyage to the Fox Islands (North Haven and Vinalhaven).

In 1605, Captain George Weymouth returned to Plymouth from his voyage to Monhegan, the Georges River, and the islands of Muscongus Bay. With him, Weymouth brought back five Indians kidnapped from the New World, the first ever seen in England. He presented three of them to the Governor of Plymouth, Sir Ferdinando Gorges. Gorges took the Indians into his home for three years, treated them as honored guests, learning their language so he could question them better about their country. He arranged for them to be presented to the Crown at Court and to get the red-carpet treatment accorded visiting royalty. In a nation already captivated by the stories of the New World, these Maine Indians became the adulated Lindberghs of their time.

These kidnapped Indians not only excited the imaginations of Englishmen at Court and in commerce to hurry along their dreams of an English colony, but also were to have a telling influence on the good and the bad receptions by the Indians of future voyagers to Maine.

It is worth looking at the Weymouth encounters with the Indians, as told by James Rosier, the writer aboard Weymouth's ship, *Archangel*. In his account, Rosier says:

> The Indians visited us on board, lying upon deck with us, and we ashore with them, changing man for man as hostages. We treated them very kindly, because we intended to inhabit their country. And they readily traded with us, the exchange of their furs for our knives, glasses, combs, and toys, being of great profit to us; for instance, one gave forty skins of beaver, otter, and sable, for articles of five shillings value.

Somehow, after these first exchanges, a quarrel broke out. Rosier, perhaps trying to cover up, says little about the details. But Captain John Smith, in his *Description of New England*, written a short time later, tells this story.

> The natives came aboard Weymouth's ship and desired the captain to go and trade with their Bashaba, on the main, who was their chief lord; and he accordingly manned the yawl with fourteen men for this purpose. Yet the Natives would row faster with five oars in their canoe than could our men in their boat with eight oars. At the shore was exchanged one Owen Griffin, for a young fellow of the savages. Griffin discovered their treachery, finding 283 savages, armed with bows and arrows, and without any such articles of trade as they pretended to have.

This trick "gave umbrage" to Weymouth and when natives came to his ship, he seized three of them and took two more on shore, along with two canoes, bows, and arrows. Four of these unhappy natives were called Tisquantum, Manida, Skidwarres, and Assecomoit, one being a Sagamore and three of the others "persons of rank." The first three were those delivered by Captain Weymouth to Sir Ferdinando Gorges when they arrived at Plymouth.

In part as the result of new eager interest stirred by the first Indians seen in England, two corporations were formed under patent from King James I on April 10, 1606. Both had the goal of establishing colonies. One was called The London Company or the First Colony of Virginia. The other was called the Plymouth Company or "The Second Colony." The land patents for both extended from the 34th to the 45th degree of north latitude and included all the islands within 100 miles of the coast, the whole being called under the general name of North and South Virginia.

The two corporations or colonies were carefully separated from each other, so there would be less chance of conflict between them. It was stipulated that the North Virginia Colony could colonize north of the 38th degree; and the South Virginia Colony below the 41st degree. But whoever established a colony first should have at least 100 miles breathing space; the second colony could not establish a settlement within that hundred-mile limit.

Gorges, a key member of the Plymouth Company, was determined he would be the driving force to start the first colony. The patent had been granted only in April. But by August, Gorges and the Plymouth Company were ready to start. They outfitted a ship named *Richard of Plymouth*, put Henry Chalons in command of thirty-one men. Sir Ferdinando also put aboard two of his native Indians, Manida and Assecomoit, to act as guides and go-betweens with the native tribes after Chalons arrived to start his colony. The third Indian, nicknamed Squanto, went home to Maine on a later voyage. There, in the islands of Muscongus Bay, Squanto taught the English words he had learned to Samoset, the Wawenock chief. He must also have told Samoset he had been well treated by the English. For in 1621 and 1622, Samoset welcomed and helped the Pilgrim fathers in their struggle to survive the bad winter at Plymouth.

But Chalons and his ship never reached their destination in Maine. Chalons was blown off course on his way across the Atlantic and wound up near Puerto Rico. There his ship was captured by Spaniards and all the crew was taken prisoner. The London Company, better financed, moved more slowly in a more ambitious way. On December 20, 1606, four months after Gorges' expedition sailed, the London Company sent out three ships and one hundred would-be colonists, plus mariners, and equipped them well. In April 1607, they landed at Jamestown.

But the disaster of the Chalons voyage was not much of a deterrent to Sir Ferdinando Gorges. He just raised his sights, played for higher stakes. This time he went to his illustrious neighbor in Plymouth, Lord John Popham, Chief Justice of England, and persuaded him into active partnership. The Plymouth Company did it right this time. It outfitted three ships, gathered 120 men as colonists, and equipped the expedition with a splendid array of supplies, even including cannons to fortify and defend the colony-to-be. Only two ships eventually sailed, filled with promise and hope, and backed by power and money at home. In overall command was an illustrious name—George Popham, son of the Lord Chief Justice. Second in command was Raleigh Gilbert, nephew of the famous Sir Walter Raleigh. They were determined to beat or at least equal the efforts of the London Company at Jamestown. On May 31, 1607, with bands playing, they sailed out of Plymouth harbor, made a fair crossing, and, by August 8, the expedition touched at Monhegan Island. By the 11th, they were ashore on Stage Island, which turned out to be a poor choice. Quickly they moved to the mouth of the Kennebec River and there established Popham, also called the Sagadahoc Colony.

This, too, proved a poor choice. It was too exposed to the combined perils of the sea, the river mouth, and the worst a Maine winter could throw. The sad failure of the brave Popham colony is told in the next chapter.

The failed colonists arrived back in England early the next year, with terrible tales of how no Englishman could survive winters in Maine. Their discouraging reports dampened every ardor except that of the stubborn, optimistic, determined Gorges. Although now he could raise no money from others, he financed single-handedly another expedition in 1616. He forced sixteen of his tenants and servants to sail under Richard Vines, in a small ship. It was a pitiful and meek departure from Plymouth compared to the great Popham sailing. This time Gorges at last had the good luck in men and weather that he deserved. This tiny colony succeeded at the mouth of the Saco River. Vines sent home enthusiastic reports. But since he had been hired only as the navigator, Vines returned to England, where he spread the good news in person. Enthusiasm for making a new start in the New World boomed. A bevy of new settlements began to thrive along the coast of Maine, now called New Somerset, at Kittery, Isles of Shoals, Richmond Island, Wells, York, Saco; as well as at Pemaquid, Damariscove, and Monhegan Island. Gorges' fame, popularity, and acclaim grew apace in England.

Outside of the book he later wrote, there is little first-hand information about Gorges. I like to imagine Sir Ferdinando at home and at business. He was fifty years old when Vines settled the colony at Saco. Because he was Governor of Plymouth, his working days must have been spent close to the harbor, concerned with maritime business. He'd surely oversee all military and naval defense aspects of the busy port. This would keep him in contact not only with local commanders, but also with Admiralty officials in London. As men o' war, merchant ships, exploring ships, or even fishing vessels, freebooters, and raiders sailed home to Plymouth, their captains would pay their first calls on Gorges. They'd talk the day and half the night through, with Gorges firing questions about where they had been, what ships, what people, what weather, what strange shores they had encountered. Together, he and the skippers would pour over charts. Voyaging was his business and his avocation.

Yet Gorges was probably regarded as a bit of a crackpot; at best an eccentric. For this man had a fixation about the New World 3,000 miles away. In his home, probably one of the grandest in Plymouth, Gorges surely had a workroom crowded with all the information he could get about the New World, particularly Maine and New England. He brought returning captains into that room and pumped them for all they knew; showed them reports from other captains, the courses they had sailed, the charts they had drawn, and asked for comments and comparisons.

In London business circles and at the Court, first of Queen Elizabeth, then of King James I, then of Charles I, Gorges must have had a mixed reputation. He was a good-looking ladies' man. He'd been knighted for gallantry in battle. He'd been wounded and briefly captured at Lille. He'd been a navy officer. Yet, at the same time, Gorges was a West Countryman; his job was far off in the provinces, as Governor of Plymouth. Above all, he was, to the courtiers and financiers, a man with a dream, a fixation on colonizing almost unknown places across the Atlantic. Given a chance, he'd bend anyone's ear for hours, trying to persuade them to invest in yet another expedition. He had persuaded such big names as Sir Humphrey Gilbert, Lord Chief Justice Popham, and the Earl of Southampton to put up money. Gorges, and they, had once had clout at the Court, too. They had quickly obtained royal charters and patents from the King for their risky ventures. And Gorges knew how to promote his wild schemes; the way he had paraded those wild Indians about London, even had them wined and dined at the Palace, was an example of what his enthusiasm and persistence could accomplish.

But ... what did he have to show for it? Not money, certainly. No gold, no silver mines, no rich cargoes of spices and jewels as had come from Cathay, the Levant, Mexico, and Peru. Just a few boatloads of fish and some furs. He'd lost his own shirt, along with the shirts of others, in backing that disastrous attempt to colonize at Popham. His people had hugely suffered there in the first winter. They had come home with stories of terrible cold in a cruel land. Yet the obstinate man wouldn't learn; he had gone ahead again, alone, because he could no longer obtain partners. The dreamer had mortgaged his property and gone into debt to send out still another expedition. A tiny affair of one small boat with sixteen of his own tenants as colonists, this time their reports trumpeting their success under an unknown leader called Vines. Vines was, in fact, a tenant farmer of Gorges'.

Gorges, too, must have had moments when he felt like giving up his dream. He had sunk money into expeditions, waved good-bye to his ships, and then waited; waited impatiently and anxiously for some word back. At best the wait lasted three or four months. Then, when the news finally came, it was often dismally bad.

But this time, the news from Vines was good. What would it lead to? Weymouth, back in 1606, had brought home glowing reports from Muscongus. Those had persuaded Gorges to form the Plymouth Company, which had hit disaster at Popham and gone broke. Then Gorges had backed three expeditions by Captain John Smith, best of all the captains. All three had failed. The first failed almost before it began, with Smith's ship wrecked off Land's End, just down the English Channel from Plymouth. A second hit the skids when ship and crew were captured by French pirates. The third, a sizeable venture with three ships financed, was locked into port so long by bad weather that the other investors gave up and canceled the effort. The list was depressingly long; the Nicholas Hobson expedition had been driven off by attacks from Indians; mutiny aboard ship had ruined the effort by Captain Edward Rocrafot; plague had decimated yet another try.

But now, with Vines, there was good news at last. Small as the colony was, it was enough to keep alive Gorges' dream, to fan the flame of hope and adventure in others. There followed a minor boomlet during the 1620s, with scores of ships coming to Maine to fish, to trade trinkets for furs, to establish small settlements. But, as is often the case, when public interest peaks, the politicians get involved. By this time, Gorges was the target of political infighting, some of it from the financiers, some in the House of Commons.

The problem was that as settlements in Maine grew, so did bickering among them. New authority had to be established for the orderly conduct of business between the settlements and England. The revived Plymouth Council sent over a new team of "managers." Robert Gorges, son of Sir Ferdinando, went to New England as governor-in-chief. Under him was Christopher Levett, as governor of the New Plymouth area; and Francis West was made Admiral of New England, with orders to make even small fishing vessels pay $100 for licenses to fish. (He was never able to enforce payment from the independent fishing-boat captains.) And to make a neat package of politics, commerce, and church, the Plymouth Council sent an Episcopalian minister to supervise all the churches. The local churches in the settlement were even more obstinate against supervision than were the local fishermen. The minister met no welcome and returned home in disgust.

Complaints from the growing settlements poured into Parliament. As head of the Plymouth Council and the long-time expert, Sir Ferdinando was hauled to the bar of the House of Commons. The charge against him was that he and the Plymouth Council were running the New World for their "own private gain" and were usurping the powers that properly belonged to the government. He was told to surrender forthwith the patent, or charter, of the Plymouth Council.

Gorges did a commendable job, according to contemporary accounts, of defending himself and the Council. But the political heat was on. Within a year, his son, Robert Gorges, was recalled from his position as Governor-General of New England. The effort at establishing an overall government, controlled from London, collapsed. (Not until March 4, 1628, was a Royal Charter issued by which a full-fledged colony was established under the name of The Massachusetts Bay Colony, and civil government truly established.) Maine, though it had no such name then, and was part of The Massachusetts Bay Colony, was in the news. Money was being made there. The fish and the fur and the timber businesses were all showing a profit. The number of boats, of settlers, of settlements along the coast and among the islands was increasing every year.

Sir Ferdinando, now sixty, had a tiger by the tail. But the administration of it was chaotic.

The House of Commons hauled Gorges before the bar again in 1634. Like Congress today, the English politicians of 1634 reacted to public complaints and accusations by staging an investigation. They ordered Gorges to appear as a major witness. Furthermore, the House of Commons was jealous. Altogether too many Englishmen were leaving for the New World. So many were emigrating that, in 1633, the government acted to stop the exodus. Several ships, loaded with passengers and cargoes and ready to sail, were held in the Thames. Members of Parliament were personally jealous, too, of the vast tracts of land held by Gorges and other Plymouth Council members under grants from the king. In small England, the size of those land grants—some as big as England itself—were grounds for jealousy. According to parliamentary records of the time, the investigation of the Plymouth Council by the Commons must have been similar to some present-day congressional anti-trust hearings. Their goal was to break up the holdings and the monopolies of the Plymouth Council.

Gorges, in his testimony before them, must have sounded much like today's conglomerate executive defending himself and his corporation against accusations of making too much money. Gorges reminded the Commons of his long, untiring, often unrewarding efforts against odds to advance England's interest in America.

> I have spent well in excess of 20,000 pounds of my own estate and thirty years, the whole flower of my life, in promoting new discoveries and new settlements upon a remote continent, in the enlargement of my country's commerce and domains; in the carrying of civilization and Christianity into regions of savages.

Gorges emphatically denied that he and his associates had run a monopoly or grown rich doing it. "Disbursements have far exceeded receipts," he cried. He said that his colonists had too often proved "indolent and wasteful" and as for mismanagement, he claimed "no superintendent could control their erratic dispositions or prevent their changes of abode from place to place." He sought sympathy from the investigating politicians by recounting how the French and the Indians were "creating mischief" and "encroaching upon our rights."

But the Commons was determined to dissolve the Plymouth Council, and did. In an anti-trust measure, it divided the Council's huge original holdings into twelve Royal Provinces. On February 3, 1635, Gorges and others, who earlier had been granted enormous lands, would have to give them up and draw lots for smaller holdings in the presence of the king—something akin to the way the United States today auctions off rights to oil exploration in the offshore banks. In each Province, each previous owner was to be entitled to only 5,000 acres in lieu of his previous far greater holdings; and in each Province, 4,000 acres were to be set aside for a capital city for the new governor and government of that Province. Each landowner would send over ten men at his expense to help build the city and, in each Province, 10,000 acres were to be set aside for the foundation of churches and the maintenance of clergymen.

On April 25, 1635, with Gorges and fifteen other members present, the Plymouth Council held its last meeting.

> We have been bereaved of friends, oppressed with losses, expenses and troubles, assailed before the Privy Council and the House of Commons again and again with groundless charges, weakened by the

French and other forces without and within, and what remains is only a breathless carcass. We therefore now resign this Patent.

Sir Ferdinando, though head of the Council and a prime target, was above all a survivor. He stayed close in his loyalty to King James, while fighting the Commons. He remained, to his later peril, a staunch royalist. And in return, the King now appointed Gorges his Governor-General over all New England.

For the aging Gorges, this was the highest honor. At last he would sail to the New World as the ruler. Exulting, he made all preparations to depart. He would sail in splendor, too, with the King's blessing and aboard a new man o' war.

At its launching, his new ship met disaster. She flipped on her side and was crushed.

Gorges, who had devoted a full forty years to his dreams of colonizing this coast, was destined never to set foot on Maine shores. He died in 1646, at age seventy.

Gorges' first book, *Discovery and Plantation of New England*, published in 1622, read like a sales prospectus.

> The place is not only seated in the temperate zone but, as it were, in the middle part thereof, standing twenty degrees from the fiery tropics and as much from the freezing Arctic Circle, yet under the same course of the sun as Constantinople and Rome ... The maritime parts thereof are somewhat colder ... for the beams of the sun are weakened partly by ... being laden with the moisture it exhales out of the vast ocean.
>
> Indeed the hot countries yield sharper wits but weaker bodies and fewer children ... But this country is so temperate that it seemeth to hold the golden mean ... The people there are tractable, if they be not abused, to commerce and trade with all ... The seas are stored with all kinds of excellent fish. The country aboundeth with a diversity of wildfowl, such as turkeys, partridges, swans, cranes, wild geese of two kinds, wild ducks of three sorts, many doves, especially when strawberries are ripe.
>
> There is also a certain beast that natives call a moose. He is big-bodied as an ox, headed like a fallow deer, with broad antlers, which he sheds every year ... He hath a great bunch of hair hanging down under his throat, his skin maketh very good leather, and his flesh is excellent good food ... There is hope that this beast may be made serviceable for ordinary labor with art and industry ... We have succeeded in bringing ourselves into familiarity with the natives, which are in no great numbers along the coast for two hundred leagues (six hundred miles); and we have now dispatched some of our people of purpose to dive into the bowels of the continent, there to search and find out what port or place is most convenient to settle our main plantation in.

The salesman's optimism is gone from his later book, written in his old age and published ten years after his death. Here, his writing is tinged with the melancholy of a man who dreamed so persistently, worked so hard, but never saw the land he'd helped to father 3,000 miles across the Atlantic.

We have been endeavoring to found plantations in a wilderness region, where men could hardly be hired to stay, or induced to become residents ... We have made the discoveries and opened the fields for others to harvest. Trade, fishery, lumber, these have been the phantoms of pursuit.

6

Popham, 1607
Why the First Colony Failed

Popham. The name is unknown in most classrooms and history books of America. But the Popham colony in Maine was the first effort at establishing a permanent English colony in this nation after the Lost Colony of 1585.

Before colonists went ashore at Jamestown, and almost fourteen years before the Pilgrim Fathers set foot at Plymouth, the first American colony was begun on the bank of the Kennebec River, near the little town now called Phippsburg.

The Popham colony was a full-fledged, well-financed, well-planned undertaking involving some 124 people, two ships, and some of the foremost names in England.

The Maine colony began well enough in August, 1607. A fort, defended with cannon, was quickly built; homes, meeting houses, and warehouses were built within its walls. Friendly contacts were made with nearby Indians. During its early months, the Popham colony was off to a good start, better probably than the start of the later colonies at Jamestown and at Plymouth.

But thirteen months later, the Popham colony was abandoned. Had this brave first effort succeeded, American history might be different. Popham, instead of Jamestown and Plymouth, would be featured in every history book. Throngs of Americans would be visiting this remote peninsula in Maine to see where their nation began. Instead they make their pilgrimages by the millions to Plymouth Rock and Jamestown, and Popham is known only to a few; and then largely for the magnificent white-sand beach and state park that bears its name.

What went wrong? Why did the Popham colony fail?

The strange fact is that all the first European colonies were pitched on some of the worst possible sites: Douchet Island on the St. Croix River, Roanoke Island, Plymouth, and Popham. Hindsight soon told all the early colonists they had chosen badly. But as they approached little-known land after hard voyages, their sites looked as good as any other bit of unknown territory.

Certainly the site of the Popham colony was not the best choice. A few miles upriver from the mouth of the Kennebec, the site was on an open bluff that may have looked splendid in August and September when they landed, but during winter it was exposed to bitter weather and biting winds. This caused suffering and the colonists later complained that winter was their downfall. Indeed, that winter of 1607 was a severe one, even in England. But if the weather had been terribly bad, the colony could have moved further up the Kennebec, which they explored as far as Augusta, or to the sheltered islands in Muscongus Bay, which Weymouth had suggested. The site near the mouth of the Kennebec, however, offered a good location for trading with the Indians and good fishing grounds.

The prime reason for failure lay not with weather or sickness or site, but with the character of the colonists and their leaders. They were not of the right stuff. They failed to form themselves into an effective, pioneering community.

George Popham, the leader, was described by Sir Ferdinando Gorges as "an honest man, but old and of an unwieldy body, and timorously fearful to offend or contest with others that do oppose him." Popham was to die of ill health before the winter was out. No one else there died from illness.

His second in command, Raleigh Gilbert, then took the leadership. Gorges described him as "desirous of supremacy and rule, a loose life, prompt to sensuality, little zeal in religion, headstrong and of small judgment and experience, but in other ways valiant enough."

Whatever his qualities, Gilbert, too, left the colony a year later to return to England because of his brother's death there.

As to the 120 "landsmen and sailors," they were a mixed bunch: Some good men, some adventurers, some men who headed out to a new world because they were in trouble in the old world. Bickering broke out early aboard ship on the voyage. After they went ashore, according to Gorges, discordant elements caused trouble "by the want of understanding of some to perform what they were directed ... from whence did proceed confusion and faction." Captain John Smith, in his book *General History of New England*, wrote that the colonists "were glad to send all but forty-five of their company back to England" before they'd been at Popham even four months. According to writers of the time, "the company was comprised of the vagrant and the dissolute."

If you sail by that Popham colony shore today, or walk the ground near Phippsburg where the first fort stood, there is little to mark the first American colony. In a nation that adulates success, we bury failures. The Popham colony is buried in most history books. Yet it should not be forgotten.

Preparations for the Popham expedition began in 1605, in a wave of enthusiasm and optimism. Entrepreneurs in the West of England had read the glowing account of Weymouth's voyage the year before, as told in Rosier's *True Relation*, and they were eager to finance a major effort to start the first colony. They formed the New Plymouth Company. In the forefront was Sir Ferdinando Gorges and his powerful neighbors in Plymouth, the Popham family: Sir John Popham, Lord Chief Justice of England, his seafaring relative, Captain George Popham, and Raleigh Gilbert. The Popham influence cut through Royal red tape at the court of King James. Within eight months after Weymouth returned from his voyage, King James had granted a new charter to New Plymouth Company. This document, dated April 10, 1606, was the king's permission to establish a northern colony in Maine. Six months after the king had signed it, a ship was on its way on a mission to reconnoiter the best site. This ship was under the command of Thomas Hanham, son-in-law to Sir John Popham, and aboard as pilot was the experienced Martin Pring, who had sailed the Maine coast three years earlier. By the time Hanham and Pring were back, Gorges and the Pophams were far along with the organization of 120 men willing to blaze a new colony and with equipping the three ships that would carry them to the Maine site recommended by Hanham and Pring. The spot they urged was on the bank of a broad, navigable, pleasant river called the Sagadahoc or Kennebec.

The New Plymouth Company, with Gorges and the Pophams at the helm, spared no expense in preparations for the first colony. They obtained three ships—*Gift of God*, *Mary and John*, and a third unnamed pinnace. The leader, Captain George Popham, kin of the Chief Justice, picked his second-in-command, none other than Raleigh Gilbert, an experienced sailor and nephew of the famous Sir Walter Raleigh. Together they recruited their key subordinates. Edward Harlow was chosen as master of ordnance, in charge of twelve cannons and other firearms; Robert Davis was sergeant major and in command of the militia, which would protect the colony; Ellis Best was marshal. John Scammon was the scribe and lawyer, and secretary of the colony; James Davis was named to command the fort; Gome Carew was "chief searcher," in charge of exploration and mapmaking; and John Digby was master carpenter and shipbuilder.

The ships were well provisioned and carefully stocked with guns, cannon, utensils of all kinds, and knives, beads, and mirrors for trading with the Indians. Everything money and planning could do to establish the first permanent colony was done.

On May 31, 1607, the *Gift of God* and the *Mary and John*, with more than a hundred sailors and settlers, sailed from Sutton's Pool in Plymouth, the very place from which the *Mayflower*, with her company of 102 Pilgrims, was to sail thirteen years later.

The Atlantic crossing went well. The ships reached the Azores in twenty-four days and the crews landed to stock up on fresh water and firewood. Soon thereafter the two ships got separated. Popham in the *Gift of God* sailed to Matinicus. Gilbert in *Mary and John* made Nova Scotia at the end of July, and went ashore to again replenish fresh water and firewood. Then Gilbert coasted through the Maine islands and on August 5 the two ships rejoined near Allen Island, as advised by Captain Weymouth, who recommended George's Harbor there. (Frequently it has been reported the ships anchored off Monhegan, some 4 miles further out to sea. But the discovery in 1875 at Lambeth Palace, London, of a ship's journal kept on the trip by James Davis, indicates the true anchorage was in George's Harbor, the rendezvous recommended by Weymouth, who had held his first church service there.)

This was home territory to Skidwarres, an Indian aboard Gilbert's *Mary and John*. Skidwarres was one of the five Indians who had been captured by Weymouth. He'd been taken to England and given to Gorges, who was now returning him to Maine with the expedition.

Skidwarres immediately wanted to make contact with his tribe. Anxious to please him and to get off to a good start with the native Indians, Gilbert lowered one of the ship's small boats, even though it was already after midnight. A few sailors rowed Gilbert and Skidwarres to wherever the Indian would guide them.

An account written at the time says they rowed "past many gallant islands" that August night and finally landed at the spot where New Harbor stands now. Skidwarres led the party across the peninsula "for near three miles" to the Indian encampment at Pemaquid.

Now the story becomes almost too good to be true. The chief of the Indians at Pemaquid was none other than Nahanta, another of Weymouth's captives, who had been returned home the year before by Hanham and Pring on their voyage. The reunion of Skidwarres and Nahanta around dawn that August morning must have amazed Gilbert.

With Skidwarres as interpreter, Gilbert met for two hours with Nahanta. Then Skidwarres led them back to the boat at New Harbor and they rowed the long 8 miles back to George's Harbor at Allen Island, bursting with the news of the encounter with the Indians.

Next day, being Sunday, August 9, the crews went ashore to hold a thanksgiving service for a safe crossing. For most of the men, it was the first time on dry land in more than two months.

On Monday, Popham and Gilbert left in a shallop, with thirty men, to pay a joint official call on Nahanta and the Indians at Pemaquid. But the meeting was not cordial. The Indians, remembering well that white men had captured Nahanta, Skidwarres, and three other Indians, gave Popham a chilly welcome. The whites spent the night well removed from the Indians on the Pemaquid shore and rowed back to the ships the next day.

The men aboard had rested from the Atlantic voyage. Summer was nearing its end. So on Wednesday, the two vessels upped anchor and headed closer to their destination, Sagadahoc, an older name for the Kennebec River.

That night, they were hit by a bad storm off Seguin—a nasty piece of water even to those who know it well. The next days were filled with local reconnaissance in various directions by Popham and Gilbert and crews in small boats. They made their first camp on Stage Island, found its 6 acres too small and the supply of fresh water unreliable. Finally, a location on the west side near the mouth of the river was chosen for their new home.

On August 19, the entire company assembled on shore. The preacher held a religious service, asking blessings on this first colony. Then the formal articles of government, as issued by the King and by the Plymouth Company, were read. They are long and were undoubtedly boring for the colonists to hear, but they symbolized the formal beginnings of the first colony.

Immediately work was begun on building a fort. Other work crews began unloading the ships. A flag was raised. A plan for location of cannons, storehouses, and dwelling houses was marked on the ground.

By now it was September. In those early days of autumn 1607, supplies were toted ashore. Men hauled cannons off the ships, rafted them ashore, and wrestled them into position on the new fort. Others in small boats scouted the nearby islands and up river, making contact with Indians through their own Indian interpreters. Within a few weeks, the fort was roughly in place, a central meeting house, a warehouse, plus numerous outbuildings and barracks were completed. Ship's carpenter Digby and a crew set to work building the first vessel made by white settlers in North America, a 30-ton pinnace, which they christened *Virginia*. They built her well, for she sailed back and forth across the Atlantic for twenty years, often hauling supplies to colonists in Jamestown, Virginia.

By early December, the colony was in business, with a fort, a big new boat, numerous small boats, storehouses, dwelling houses, and water wells. The firewood was stacked and the cannons were in place. The mother ships had been fully unloaded.

On October 8, the *Mary and John*, one of the ships that had brought them, sailed home to England. She arrived back in Plymouth December 1, with news and a daily diary of the colony's doings, kept for Sir Ferdinando Gorges.

Before the second ship left on December 13 to return home to Plymouth, the colony's leader, George Popham, wrote a letter to King James, to be hand carried to Court by the ship captain. That letter and the writing of it is worth recalling. Popham's letter was the first state document written from an American settlement to the King of England. Popham made the most of the occasion; he wrote the letter in Latin. But he filled it with white lies and embroidered it with outrageous compliments to His Majesty: all, perhaps, in the cause of getting continued support from the Crown.

It is a curious picture ... Popham in a crude hut on the Maine coast in cold December, penning his letter in Latin to the King of England.

> I have thought it should be made known to your Majesty that here among the Indians there is none on the world more admired than King James ... My well-considered opinion is that ... the empire of your Majesty may easily be enlarged and the welfare of Great Britain speedily augmented in these parts. So far as relates to commerce, there are in these parts shagbarks, nutmegs, and cinnamon, besides pinewood, Brazilian cochineal, ambergris, and many other products of great value, and these in the greatest abundance.
>
> Besides, they positively assure me that there is a great sea, large, wide, and deep only seven days journey from our fort. This cannot be

other than the Southern Ocean, reaching to the regions of China, which unquestionably cannot be far from these regions.

George Popham filled his Latin phrases with more flattery than truth and dispatched them with Captain Robert Davis, who was returning to England with the second ship that had brought the colonists here. That ship, *Gift of God*, also carried home fifty or more discontents or troublemakers from the embryo colony.

Then came winter. That winter of 1607–08 was one of the meanest and coldest. The houses built by the novice colonists were ill-equipped to withstand the ice, snow, sleet, and raging winds and storms from the ocean. The shivering colonists found how big a mistake they had made by choosing to settle on one of the most exposed spots along the coast, rather than a snug cove further up the Kennebec or in Muscongus Bay, as Weymouth had advised. Food became short. The ill-dressed, hungry, cold settlers began to get scurvy, which further weakened them.

According to some contemporary accounts, perhaps only forty-five men were left at Popham by Christmas 1607, out of the hundred and more who had sailed. The others had gone home on the *Gift of God* when she left on December 13.

It was quickly apparent to Gorges, when he read the daily diaries brought home on the first returning ship, that all was not well with the colonists. The news brought back by the second ship and the discontented returning colonists in February was worse. As for "return on investment," there was nothing in the cargoes beyond some furs, some fish, and some sassafras to kindle hope of wealth.

Clearly there had been trouble between the colonists and the Indians, though accounts differ in detail. In a winter of bad weather (it was a freezing-cold winter in England, too), this meant that Indians would not be a source of food supplies needed by the colonists.

Purchas, in his book *Pilgrimmes*, published in 1614, reports "a quarrel fell out between the colonists and the Indians," wherein one colonist was killed and others driven from the fort. The Indians took over the fort briefly. They broke into barrels of provisions and supplies. One barrel contained gunpowder, which caught fire and blew the fort to pieces, killing several Indians. Clearly such a fearsome accident would have created mistrust and suspicion on both sides.

Another incident, reported in the book *King Philips' War*, caused more Indian death and injury. A number of Indians came to the fort to trade. The colonists asked them to help drag a cannon up an incline. They agreed. As they were doing this, the cannon fired by accident, killing one Indian and wounding others.

It does seem certain that from whatever cause, the Indians turned hostile, fire destroyed the main building, and the colonists lost a great part of their supplies in midwinter.

But despite bad news, despite the return of discontents aboard the *Gift of God*, Gorges and Popham planned to send out fresh supplies promptly to the Popham colonists. They laid plans for more men, ships, and provisions.

Then misfortune hit in a series of deaths. First, the leader of the colony, George Popham, died. He was an elderly man with a physique unsuited, at best, to a cold first winter in a new, rough fort on the Maine coast.

In England, Sir John Popham, Chief Justice of England, and a major backer in the Plymouth Company, died, too.

Then Sir John Gilbert died in England. He was the brother of Raleigh Gilbert, who had succeeded George Popham as leader of the Popham Colony. When this news reached Gilbert in the summer, he felt he had to hurry home to England to take care of his brother's estates, to which he was heir.

This was the final blow to the Popham colony. They'd had a tough winter, they'd had skirmishes with Indians, their first leader had died, and their next leader was leaving. They could see no future but more trouble and more hardship in their outpost. One year and one month after they had landed, the Popham contingent left. The first colony in America had failed.

7

Isles of Shoals

A Stern and Lovely Scene

The islands of Maine begin and end with names of sea magic. Cross the water boundary from New Hampshire and the Maine islands start immediately with Appledore, Duck, Cedar, and Smuttynose, in the Isles of Shoals. Cruise east among a thousand islands, in and out of coves and inlets of Maine's rugged coast for almost 3,000 miles and you end up at Campobello, just across the water boundary with Canada. From the Isles of Shoals to Campobello—could there be more beautifully named beginnings and endings?

The Isles of Shoals is the magical, mysterious name for those nine small islands, 9 miles out to sea from Kittery, which rise weirdly, wonderfully white from the ocean. They came close to being stuck with the name "Smith Islands." Captain John Smith, that insatiable seafarer who'd helped settle Jamestown in 1607 when he was 26 years old, spent years voyaging the Maine coast, exploring and charting its islands. He never involved his own name in any of his charts until he sailed to these bare little islands. Their strange and wild white-rock beauty won his heart and stirred his ego; and he named them Smith's Islands. The name didn't last.

Early fishermen changed the name to Isles of Shoals, not because of its pretty sound but because the ocean becomes suddenly shallow, or shoals, here. Nine treacherous ledges surround the nine islands. The only harbor is Gosport Harbor, bordered and protected by Star, Cedar, Smuttynose, and Malaga islands. The boundary line between Maine and New Hampshire runs through Gosport Harbor, giving the five northern islands to Maine—Appledore, Duck, Cedar, Malaga, and

Smuttynose; and the four southern islands to New Hampshire—Star, Lunging, Seavey's, and White.

God must have loved these strange, stark islands, for He made them from a white, shining, banded, metamorphic rock, in startling contrast to the dark granite of most Maine islands. Birds love them, for more than 140 species have been sighted here. So do plants and flowers, with over 250 varieties finding places to bloom here, even though the islands are bare, rocky, almost barren of trees, but thickly covered in places with low bushes. Herring gulls and great black-backed gulls by the thousands, six kinds of herons, guillemots, snowy egrets, eider ducks, song sparrows, yellowthroats, red-wing blackbirds, cormorants, and spindly legged sandpipers abound. Because there are so few trees, the islands seem barren at first, but the meadows of Appledore sprout clover, stitchwort, and ox-eye daisies. Iris bloom among the duckweed, loosestrife, and arrow-grass in the swampy areas. In summer, wild roses, wild strawberries, bachelor buttons, buttercups, lilies of the valley, morning glories, and tiny scarlet pimpernels flourish on these rocky, inscrutable islands.

Early in the 1600s, fishermen from England began using the Isles of Shoals regularly. In 1623, Christopher Levett, commissioned by Sir Ferdinando Gorges to start a settlement and a church in the Province of Maine, wrote of the Shoals: "The place is found to be a good fishing place for six shippes, but more cannot well be there; for want of a good stage-roome, as this yeares experience hath proved. The Harbor is but indifferent good. Upon these Ilands are no Savages at all."

By 1628, so many fishing crews were using the Shoals, they were able to support two tavern keepers. The needs of the spirit as well as the flesh were catered to. The Reverend Jedediah Morse wrote that a meetinghouse was built before 1640, with the Reverend Joseph Hull as its minister. The good minister was sued by Gorges in 1646 for possession of a 20-acre marsh. Three Kelly brothers, the Oliver brothers and the Seeleys, and the three Cutt brothers from Wales, were all established fishermen who were playing active roles in life on the Shoals during the 1640s.

Men have always loved the Isles of Shoals. But women have not. The early settlers, all male, banned women from setting foot in their Eden. A strange court record of 1647 contains a lawful complaint from Richard Cutts and John Cutting, settlers on Hog Island (now prettily changed to Appledore), against their neighbor, John Reynolds.

Contrary to an act of court, which says that no woman shall live on
the Isles of Shoals, John Reynolds has brought his wife hither with
the intention that she live and abide here ... He has also brought
upon Hog Island a great stock of goats and swine, which by destroy-
ing much fish, do great damage ... and spoil the spring water ... Your
petitioners therefore pray that the Act of Court be put in execution
for the removal of women from inhabitating here; and that said
Reynolds also be ordered to remove his goats and swine from the
island without delay.

The court ordered Reynolds to get rid of his goats and swine
within twenty days, "but as to the removal of his wife, she may remain and enjoy the company of her husband, if no further complaint
be brought against her."

That was the end of the ban against women. They came. Soon
they had the upper hand on the Isles and in court. Later court
records show many men from the Isles were being sentenced to the
lash for abusing their wives. Further, the Isles of Shoals women
forced their men to ignore a court order requiring them to build a
"ducking stool for scolds and brawling women."

One of the first big fortunes made in Maine began in the Isles of
Shoals. A young immigrant from Cornwall, England, named William
Pepperrell settled on Appledore in 1676 and began curing and dunning fish on its sweeping rock ledges. His specialty was to cure them
the Appledore way—light on the salt and heavy on the sun, then
bury them in salt hay until the flesh turned the color of brown sherry
wine.

This trick—called dunning—tickled the palates of the wealthy in
Europe and Pepperrell's dried fish fetched premium prices in Spain.

His son, another William, was born at Kittery Point in 1696 and
grew up to lead three thousand Maine men in battle, to storm and
capture the French fortress of Louisburg, on Cape Breton, in March
1745. He became a hero and was invited to sail to England for a
hero's welcome, where he was the first American to be created a
baronet by the King of England. The boy from the Isles of Shoals was
made Sir William Pepperrell by King George II. For a hundred years,
the Pepperrells prospered in Kittery, amassing a great fortune.
Colonel William Pepperrell built the Pepperrell mansion in 1682.
Lady Pepperrell built her house in 1760.

In the American Revolution the Pepperrells lost their wealth,
estates, and deer parks in America because they picked the wrong
side and stayed loyal to King George III of England, largely because

the king's father had made their grandfather the first baronet in the New World.

There is an interesting conflict in the contemporary records about how poor or how prosperous the Shoals were during the early 1700s. A French vessel visiting the Shoals in 1702 reported prosperity: "There are at these islands about sixty fishing shallops, each manned by four men. Besides these are the masters of the fishing stages, and as they are assisted by the women in taking care of the fish, there may be in all about 280 men." The Reverend Jedediah Morse reported the Shoals were curing up to 4,000 quintals of fish (about 448,000 pounds) in the 1730s and were selling many big boatloads of their famous dunfish to Spain and cod to the West Indies market.

The islanders, however, told a different story. They cried poor, especially when threatened by a new tax. In a petition of April 22, 1721, the inhabitants of Gosport protested: "The people here are very few in number and most of them are men of no substance, live only by their daily fishing; and near one third of them are single men who threaten to leave if taxed, which will prove our utter ruin ... They live on a Rock in the Sea and have not any privilege of right in common lands, as other Inhabitants in the respective Towns have ... "

In 1761, it was Kittery's turn to cry poor, to plead for a reduction of taxes, saying of the Isles of Shoals: "There was seldom more than ten or fifteen persons ratable there, and they were all poor, had about three or four boats for fishing, and they never paid half the rates and taxes that was added to the Town ... "

The Reverend John Tucke, a Harvard graduate, became minister on the Shoals in 1732 and he introduced a new orderliness to life. Tucke was the first to record marriages, births, baptisms, and deaths among the islanders; and he began the first town meetings. Under him, a new ordinance was passed that made liable to fines any fisherman "who spelt any fish above hie warter marck and Leave their heads and bonese ... " Tucke ministered to the Shoals for forty years, until his death there in 1773. An indication of how much the islanders liked and respected him is the fact that they paid him his salary in quintals of the prized dunfish.

The death of the Reverend Tucke marked the end of an era for the Isles of Shoals. Within two years, the American Revolution began and its repercussions hit the Shoals hard. Almost everyone living on the islands was evacuated during the Revolution. A government order said "the islands afforded sustenance and recruitment to the enemy"; and commanded all islanders to quit their homes and move to the mainland. Some floated their homes by raft to Kittery or Portsmouth.

This was no minor evacuation. About six hundred families were crowded on these small, lovely islands before the Revolution. Today there are no year-round inhabitants.

The Shoals enjoyed more than a hundred years of growth from the early 1600s as one of the nation's early island settlements. But at the time of the Revolution, the islands hit the skids. With the hundreds of Shoalers now scattered to new homes and with new ties along the coast, few returned after the Revolution. The islands became a rough hangout of bad repute. The rag-tail population that drifted back was considered depraved, drunken. The men were suspected of setting out false lights to entice storm-driven ships onto the rocks and then looting them.

By 1820, however, a big effort was made to bring Appledore back. The burned-out church was rebuilt; town meetings were begun, and improvements in living, fishing, and schooling were started. New settlers came.

The big change took shape in 1839, when Thomas Laighton, a New Hampshire politician, obtained appointment as lighthouse keeper on White Island. Laighton, who had a good nose for real estate, bought half of Appledore and three other islands on the Maine side of the state line: Smuttynose, Malaga, and Cedar. Laighton took his wife, Eliza, their four-year-old daughter, Celia, and infant son, Oscar, with him and moved to his job as keeper of the White Island Light.

Laighton was a hustler. Keeping the light was not work enough to occupy him full time. He was elected to the New Hampshire legislature in 1841 and to the Portsmouth Board of Selectmen. He worked to revive the fishing business. Then he took the wild, bold step of building a small hotel on Appledore in the 1840s. Summer people filled it. By 1848, Laighton built Maine's first island resort hotel, called The Appledore House, which in time became a famous trend setter, a magnet for artists, authors, and the whole "culture crowd" of 19th-century New England. This transformation of the Shoals was due in great part to his daughter, Celia Thaxter.

Young Celia, who came as a baby to White Island Light, moved with the family from White to Appledore and the little Mid-Ocean Hotel when she was twelve. After the bigger, grander Appledore was opened, she became the hostess. An attractive girl as hostess in a Maine island hotel made news. She began writing poetry about the life, the plants, and the birds on the Isles of Shoals. Her poems were published and well received in the *Atlantic Monthly*. Celia, who at six-teen had married Levi Thaxter, attracted the lions of the literary and art worlds—the movie stars of their day—to stay at the Appledore. Soon the hotel register was signed by Nathaniel Hawthorne, James Russell Lowell, Richard Henry Dana, Harriet Beecher Stowe, Franklin Pierce, Samuel Longfellow, William Dean Howells, Sarah Orne Jewett, and Frances Burnett (of *Little Lord Fauntleroy* fame). Artists such as Childe Hassam, A. T. Bircher, Olaf Brauner, and William Morris Hunt came to paint.

The Appledore House was constantly enlarged, with two wings, a dance hall, billiard room, a huge verandah, and heating and lighting systems. The Reverend A. M. Coulton in a letter dated July 23, 1873, described it:

> Appledore House is a finer hotel than can be found elsewhere on or near these eastern shores ... It is a first class house, and will compare favorably with the United States and the Grand Union in Saratoga ... abundance of sofas ... bible in every bedroom ... billiard-saloon, bowling alley, ball-room, a band of music and bar ... this last in the rear basement ... Our company at this hotel now number three hun-dred—from St. Louis, Chicago, Philadelphia, New York. They are the choicest ... representing millions in wealth.

The Shoals, once a rough fishing settlement, was now prominent on the social map. Boston promoters even staged illegal prizefights on Smuttynose, with steamers bringing the bloods of the sporting world up from Boston and New York, much to the fury of Cedric Laighton, the great hotel keeper at Appledore House.

Competitors built new resort hotels, the big Atlantic House and the Oceanic, nearby on Star Island. By 1875, Celia's brothers, Cedric and Oscar, bought them out. The Laightons ran the Star Island hotels until 1916, when, for $16,000, they sold Star Island and the hotels and cottages to a religious group. The Unitarian-Congregational Star Island Corporation soon transformed the Isles again—this time into a kind of religious retreat.

Then this era on the Shoals abruptly came to its end. The Apple-dore burned to the ground in 1914. Cars, rather than trains and boats, became the summer transportation for vacationing families. Bigger, newer resort hotels lured away the summer trade from the islands to the mainland. The Laightons died. Father, mother, Celia, and her brothers (Oscar lived almost to his one-hundredth birthday) are all buried in the Laighton family cemetery on Appledore. A museum in Celia's memory was built on the ruins of the famous

Appledore hotel. The garden in front of her cottage, made famous with her book in 1893 called *An Island Garden*, has been recreated, with plantings based on her text and the Childe Hassam illustrations in her book.

Cottages from the days of the hotel have been restored, after years of vandalism. They are used by the Shoals Marine Laboratory, established in 1973 by the University of New Hampshire and Cornell University.

Part of Appledore Island is now a heron rookery and the great nests of helter-skelter twigs mark where generations of long-stemmed herons hatch.

Smuttynose

Across a narrow channel lies Smuttynose Island, smaller than Appledore and named for the black ledge that sticks like a landmark into the sea. Seamen gave it this apt descriptive nickname when they first came to the Isles of Shoals some 370 years ago. Official records from 1684 show the Court of the Western Islands sat at Smuttynose and tried cases here.

Pirates supposedly buried treasure on Smuttynose. That pirate and killer, Edward Lowe, so brutal and bestial that his men mutinied and set the rascal adrift in a small boat, committed murder at Smuttynose in 1722. The beautiful fair-haired girl whom he murdered is said to haunt the island, guarding the hidden treasure of Blackbeard. Many have searched but none have found much treasure. However, Captain Samuel Haley, who lived on Smuttynose early in the 1800s, did find four bars of silver buried beneath a rock. The captain used the money to build an expensive breakwater to provide shelter for the fishermen on his island and nearby Star Island. Today, you can safely anchor there at Gosport Harbor and see to the bottom, 20 feet below. Elsewhere, the bottom is solid rock, sometimes deceivingly covered with kelp, neither of which will hold an anchor.

Horror struck in the upright life of Captain Haley on a winter's night early in 1813. The Spanish ship *Sagunto* headed for a light, which they thought was a beacon, burning in a window above Captain Haley's mill, and hit hard on rocks and ledges on the eastern shore of Smuttynose. The shipwrecked sailors, freezing in the winter gale, struggled ashore and tried to crawl through deep snow to the light in Haley's mill. But they collapsed and froze to death, while Captain Haley slept nearby, unaware. In the morning, Haley found the bodies of the fifteen Spanish sailors. He gave them all he could give them—a decent burial on Smuttynose. Their graves can be seen today, marked by one of Haley's mill stones. Walk by the graves and down to the shore on a winter's night and you may see the ghosts of the Spanish sailors, hailing passing ships, seeking one that will carry them home to Spain.

Murder of the foulest kind was committed on Smuttynose on the night of March 5, 1873. A man named Louis Wagner knew the island men were away fishing and Smuttynose was deserted except for two women, Karen Christensen and her sister-in-law, Anetha Christensen. Wagner had heard the women had a strongbox filled with money. He stole a dinghy from the waterfront at Portsmouth and rowed the 9 miles out to Smuttynose. He murdered the two women with an axe. But a third girl, Maren, and her dog escaped through the snow and hid in rock crevices by the shore. Wagner, his foul murders done, rowed the 9 miles back to Portsmouth in the nighttime. At daybreak, Maren and her dog climbed out from the hiding place and she screamed and waved to attract fishermen coming down to the shore on Appledore, across the channel. They rowed across and she led them to the bloodstained house. They saw and never forgot the sight of the bodies of the two dead women, hacked by Wagner's axe.

Wagner was caught, tried, and sentenced to death, the last man hanged in Maine. His story is an interesting episode in Maine history.

Wagner's trial took nine days. But the jury took only fifty-five minutes to bring in a verdict of "guilty of murder." Yet many in Maine contended Wagner could not have committed the murders. They thought no man could row 9 miles out to Smuttynose, commit two murders, and then row 9 miles back to Portsmouth in the time for which Wagner had no alibi.

The law of Maine on the statute books then was clear and curt: Anyone found guilty of murder should hang by the neck till dead. But to minimize chances of hanging the wrong man, the law also required that the hanging should not be carried out for at least one year. Wagner's lawyer appealed the sentence, asking for life imprisonment instead of death. Opponents of the death penalty added their pleas. A two-year delay followed. Wagner waited in his jail cell in the Maine prison at Thomaston.

Another prisoner in Thomaston, named Gordon, awaited execution along with Wagner. Both men were in their thirties. Finally, Governor Dingle signed both death warrants. Gordon tried to commit suicide by stabbing himself on the day of the hanging. But he was carried to the gallows, bleeding and unconscious, side by side with his fellow prisoner, Louis Wagner. The hangings were carried out under supervision by the sheriff, his deputies, twelve witnesses, the prison doctor, and other state officials who, by law, had to witness the executions. The bodies, with no relatives to claim them, were sent to the Maine Medical Society for dissection. In 1887, Maine outlawed the death penalty, in part because of the outcry against the hangings of Gordon and Wagner. The Smuttynose murderer was the last man legally executed in Maine.

No one lives in winter on the Isles of Shoals today, except the caretakers on Star Island. Today, the little islands are only a summer paradise. But for more than 370 years, families lived through terrible winter storms which bombarded the Shoals. The storms, as much as the summer flowers, are part of the Isles of Shoals.

Celia Thaxter, who went to the Shoals with her father as a four-year-old in 1840 and died on Appledore in 1894, describes a Shoals storm in a letter to a woman friend.

I know you thought of us in the terrific storm yesterday ... Had it continued another twenty-four hours, it would not have left a stick or stone on the Shoals. It is utterly indescribable. All of the islands were lost in clouds of flying foam. Our yacht, the *Lone Star*, sank at her moorings and is lost. The wind and water were blown through the house ... You remember Londoners' Island (Lunging Island), where you and I went for morning glories? ... A brig lies there smashed to atoms, eight men drowned, but one alive to tell the tale. She struck at 8 a.m. in broad daylight, but thick fog, on the outlying rocks of White Island; a breaker carried off part of her stern and drowned five men. Then she rolled and wallowed to Londoners' and went ashore there ... There the brig was smashed in two ... three more men were drowned. I have been over to see the wreck ... the huge vessel lay not far from our morning-glory garden. Crushed like an eggshell ... her huge beams snapped like sticks of macaroni; such a total and gigantic destruction is not to be described ... Her sails strewed the whole beach, she was one heap, of splintered fragments. Eight men dead, lying about the ledges; everywhere I feared to see a ghastly face, a hand, a foot. One thick grey vest lay in a pool and stared up at me with ghastly white horn buttons. Iron bolts four feet long were twisted like hairpins. The brig was forty days out of Liverpool to Boston, loaded with salt.

It has stormed five days, wearily, wearily. The face of the gale was awful to behold—the sea black, swollen, angry, streaming with hoary vapor from the cold and flinging broadsides of freezing spray all over the island; snow falling, hissing, whispering, lashing the windowpanes; the noise of the breakers booming and thundering; and the voice of the wind wailing, howling, expostulating, shrieking.

Tonight the world is calm in comparison. Just before sunset, I ventured out. Solid ice about the island shore; wharf and crane a mountain of solid saltwater ice; snow everywhere; the sea dull olive green and black; a rift of stormy grey in the sky. A huge black shag rose from the rock opposite me and flew ponderously away. The gulls soared and shrieked. I ran back and crept to the fireside.

At times, close to a thousand people lived happily on these Isles of Shoals. During 370 years, scores of ships have wrecked here. Today, old headstones in the island cemetery tell the story; the graves of sailors shipwrecked and drowned here; and the tiny headstones of infant children who perished from some forgotten plague. Yet poets and artists have written and painted paeans of praise to the strange, hypnotic beauty of these remote Isles of Shoals. Robert Low described them:

> A heap of bare and splintery crags
> Tumbled about by lightning and frost,
> With rifts and chasms and storm-bleached jags
> That wait and growl for ships to be lost.

Legends and ghosts abound on the Isles of Shoals. Where the sea pours onto Appledore is a ghostly spot named Betty Moody's Hole. The legend is that Betty Moody fled here with her little children during an Indian attack on the Shoals. They hid in this cleft in the rocks. Through the long night, Betty Moody heard the Indians on the rampage. Her children, cold and frightened, would break out crying. When a band of scalp-hunting Indians came searching for survivors among the chasms on the shore, one child cried out, and kept crying despite Betty Moody's efforts to stifle the cries that would lead the Indians to her children. In a desperate move, to preserve the safety of their hiding spot, Betty Moody is said to have slit the throat of her wailing baby. That wail can be heard some nights now, if you walk the shore.

The pale ghost of Constable Babb also walks the moonlit shore of Appledore. Babb, island constable when the Court of the Western Isles convened here in the 1680s, had witnessed such fearful crimes that now, 320 years later, wearing a bloody butcher's smock and wielding a long knife, he walks the Isles of Shoals in an eternal round of vigilance against more crimes.

The U.S. Navy began close to the Isles of Shoals. In 1776, the Continental Congress ordered the new nation's first frigate, *Raleigh*, thirty-two guns, to be built in frantic haste at Badger's Island, 9 miles from the Isles of Shoals. Within sixty days, she was launched. No sooner was she off to war than the famous sloop of war *Ranger* was laid down on her blocks at Kittery. *Ranger* was launched in May 1777, with Captain John Paul Jones in command. *Ranger* was followed by *Congress*, seventy-four guns; then *America*, also commanded by John Paul Jones. Then, in 1798, *Crescent*, thirty-two guns, and *Portsmouth*, twenty-four guns, were launched there.

In 1800, the government bought Dennett's Island for $5,000. Ever since then, the Portsmouth Naval Shipyard in Kittery has been prominent in American naval history. The keel of the first steam sidewheeler, the USS *Saranac*, was laid here in May 1847. Old Ironsides, officially the USS *Constitution*, was rebuilt at Kittery. She is now anchored at Boston, the oldest ship in the Navy.

During the Civil War, more than 2,000 men worked at the Portsmouth Yard; in World War II, more than 25,000. Portsmouth built the first submarine, the L-8, launched in April 1917. Before 1941, Portsmouth had built 33 submarines. During World War II, it built 75 submarines, cutting construction time from 469 days down to 173 days. Portsmouth built the early nuclear-powered submarine *Swordfish*, launched in 1958. Today, more than 3,000 civilians and military personnel work there on the Los Angeles–class submarines and on deep-diving submersible research and development.

Coming in from the Isles of Shoals on my boat, I sometimes stop at the town wharf at Frisbee's store for supplies. This fine old store in a seafaring town still serves customers from the wharf as well as from the road on Kittery Point.

This is the oldest family grocery store in the United States. In 1981, I spent two hours talking with Frank Frisbee and his brother, David, and their children—the fifth generation of Frisbees to work here in 150 years.

Frisbee's was first opened by Daniel Frisbee in 1828, when John Quincy Adams was President and Maine was just eight years old as a state. The family store is run by successive generations.

Frank Frisbee kept a library of Frisbee memorabilia.

"The stock in trade of the store in 1828 included skunk oil, gunpowder, flints, ox yokes, bear grease, and lots of rum … Great schooners, home from voyages across the world, unloaded their cargoes at this wharf. We had barrels of molasses, rum, spices, and all kinds of drygoods and dress materials to sell, straight from the ships.

"Frisbee's was a ship chandlery then, as well as a grocery and drygoods store. Our great-grandfather did a handsome business in stocking outgoing vessels."

Today, a corner of the grocery is filled still with boat supplies—
marine paints, caulking compound, nails, and rope. Frisbee's still has
one foot in the sea, supplying food, drygoods, wine, beer, and fuel to
the boats that come to their float.

"When we were putting in new foundations in 1954, on the site
of the very first Frisbee store, we found six bottles of rum, carefully
and safely hidden. We sniffed the rich old rum but didn't have the
courage to drink it," says Frank Frisbee. Nearby is the Frisbee
School, named for their great-grandfather, Frank Frisbee.

From the wharf in back of Frisbee's, you can look out to the Isles
of Shoals. Stand quietly and in your mind's eye you may see the old
sailing vessels of the first settlers in the early 1600s. Now there are
moorings out here for hundreds of boats—sailing craft, pleasure
cruisers, and lobster boats.

"Each morning up until World War II, the store sent a man with
a horse and wagon to knock on customers' doors. He'd take their
orders and deliver the goods later in the day," said Frank. "I helped
make the deliveries as a boy."

The old ways have, of course, changed. But despite changes, Frisbee's still has a very special atmosphere that rightfully clings to the
oldest family grocery store in the United States. Frank and David
wore neat short-sleeved shirts and ties. They wore the long white
aprons that have been the traditional hallmark of grocers.

David explained how they've been making Frisbee's corned beef
for one and a half centuries.

"We start with cold, fresh, clear water. Add salt and keep adding
until it is salty enough to float a potato. Sometimes we use an egg instead of a potato. Then we put in first-quality beef, about four pieces
weighing 10 pounds each. We put the beef into the brine on Monday
and by Thursday it is ready—Frisbee's famous corned beef."

The famous and wealthy who used to summer in vast rambling
summer cottages were customers at Frisbee's. Old account books tell
the story of enormous orders from the estates of John M. Howells, de-
signer of New York skyscrapers and son of William Deal Howells, the
19th-century writer; and from the homes of Mrs. Decatur Wright,
Mrs. Anna Payson, Ambassador Edward Crocker, and dozens more.
Theodore Roosevelt, Margaret Truman, Mark Twain, and the great
eagle carver John Bellamy have all been customers of Frisbee's.

Across the road from the store is a headstone, in memory of Sir
William Pepperrell, 1696–1759, a leading figure in the colonial days
of Kittery Point. His birthplace, his mansion, and his tomb are close

to Frisbee's store—a store built on land confiscated from the Pepper-rell family at the time of the American Revolution.

"We take care of his marker and his tombstone now," said Frank Frisbee.

Here on the southernmost tip of Maine, Frisbee's Store is a comforting sign of continuity in a rather rootless world.

Before I went to Frisbee's, I'd seen a small lobster boat hauling traps off Appledore and had done a double-take. Clearly a woman was running the boat and doing the hauling, single handedly. I made it my business to talk with her. Yvonne Sullivan was a brown-eyed blonde.

"Lobstering is a great job for a girl," she told me. "I paid for my new 22-foot boat in two years, thanks to my lobstering. I wish I had started fishing a long while ago. I've been married to Rodney Sullivan fifteen years and helped him lobster often. But I didn't start going on my own till twelve years later. I began small, in a skiff with just a few traps, and gradually added more. Then I got my own 22-foot fiberglass boat and I'm setting out 250 traps. Hauling 100 traps a day."

Dozens of women go lobstering along the Maine coast. Most go with their husbands, as helpers on fine days. Others have a skiff and an outboard, and fish a few traps close to shore. Very few have their own lobster boat, their own traps, and go alone several miles off the mainland as Yvonne Sullivan does.

"She is a darn good, serious lobsterman," I was told by her neighbor, J. Russell Smith, who retired after thirty-six years building submarines at the Portsmouth Naval Shipyard. "There are not many as good as her."

Yvonne talked about lobstering from the Sullivan cottage out on Appledore Island in the Isles of Shoals.

When it comes to lobstering, the Isles of Shoals are a bit like Monhegan, farther down the coast. By tradition, the Shoals are sovereign territory. "You don't set traps close in to the Shoals unless your family comes from one of these islands."

The Sullivan family does indeed belong on Appledore Island.

"Rodney's father fished from there. And his father before him. On back through generations, Sullivans have fished from Appledore. Now Rodney and I live on Appledore and lobster out of here from May till November," said Yvonne Sullivan.

Rodney goes in a bigger 37-foot boat and fishes more traps farther out.

"I only lobster in summer, from Appledore, and my traps are

within 2 miles of the island. I make all my own traps. Built fifty new ones this winter. Rodney hires men to build his for him. But I have to buy the heads. I plain can't knit the heads."

There are only three cottages and a Cornell University marine research station on Appledore now. On nearby Smuttynose, the Foys are the only family there. Again it is their fishing territory, because generations of Foys have lobstered from Smuttynose.

One man had bad luck fishing in the waters around the Isles of Shoals. In President George Washington's diary for November 2, 1789, he wrote: "On my way to the mouth of the harbor, I stopped at a place called Kittery, in the Province of Maine ... Having lines aboard, we proceeded to the fishing banks a little without the Harbor and fished for cod; but it not being a proper time for tide we caught only two."

Scientists share Appledore with fishermen today. Cornell and the University of New Hampshire have been operating research laboratories on the Shoals in summer. From time to time, the Shoals Marine Laboratory publishes its technical research into marine organisms, plant, and bird life. The northern end of Appledore has been declared a Critical Natural Area by the State of Maine, to protect the natural heron rookery there. Botantists have reconstructed the 1890s garden with the same types of plants, flowers, and shrubs that Celia Thaxter tended with so much care and so much success.

Star Island has for over eighty years been a center for summer meetings of religious groups. The tradition started in 1896, when Thomas H. Elliott, of Lowell, Massachusetts, proposed bringing a large group of Unitarians to the Shoals. Oscar Laighton was cautious. "What's a Unitarian?" he asked.

"Are they good people? It won't do to introduce any rough element."

The coming of the Unitarians to Star Island, and their subsequent purchase of the hotel properties there, has added an entirely new dimension to the Shoals, turning Star Island into an island almost totally devoted to religious teaching. More than three hundred people, engaged in various religious conferences and retreats, are on Star Island every summer month.

The worst shiver and shock to hit the Shoals came in the winter of 1973. It was not a storm of nature, but a scheme by oil men that shook the Shoals. Olympic Refineries, then controlled by Aristotle Onassis, proposed bringing supertankers to a docking station they would erect near the Shoals; then unloading crude from them by underwater pipeline to a 400,000-barrel-a-day refinery, to be built on the mainland at Durham, New Hampshire. Each supertanker would have been as big as two or three of the islands. The supertankers, plus their support vessels and equipment, would have occupied much of the ocean near the Shoals. For ninety days, a battle was waged between those who wanted the jobs and money promised by the refinery and those who feared the possible consequences of supertankers and oil refineries. When the critical vote was taken at the Durham town meeting, the town refused to grant the required rezoning permit by a vote of 1,254 to 144. The oil project was dead.

The Isles of Shoals, which can be easily reached by sightseeing boats from Portsmouth, are now on the National Register of Historic Places. In rather dry and musty words, the Historic Register states: "The Isles of Shoals, though small in area, barren in appearance, and possessed of an inhospitable winter climate, have exerted an historic and cultural influence that is disproportionate with their modest area and resources."

Indeed they have.

8

Casco Bay Islands
Cinderellas of Maine

Certain tribes of American Indians can be very discriminating in island real estate. One tribe sold Manhattan Island cheap, but another fought hard to hold onto the islands of Casco Bay. The Indians who loved Casco Bay islands christened this glorious huge bay "Ancocisco," which means "Place of the Herons." White men, unable to twist their tongues around that word, corrupted and shortened it to "Casco."

Like many places with name origins obscured by history's mists, Casco Bay has proponents for another name source. They say Spanish explorer Estaban Gomez named it "Bahia de Casco" because of its shape resembling a helmet. Take your choice.

Indian Chief Madockowando was top man on Chebeague Island when the first white settlers came in the 1600s. Each June in those days, Madockowando led his people from the inland forests to the bay. In a long line of birch-bark canoes, the Indians would paddle down river and cross the open water to Great Chebeague to make their summer headquarters on its shores. All summer, the men caught fish in tremendous quantities from Casco Bay, while their squaws on shore dried much of the catch for eating during the inland winters; the men hunted porpoises and turned the hides into a winter necessity, snowshoes; they killed seals and a whale or two, extracting oil for their cooking and for use as medicine. Like Chebeague Islanders today, the Indians enjoyed summer on the islands, lying in the sun and swimming from the beaches. On feast days, Indians from other islands gathered on Chebeague over four hundred years ago for days and nights of games, visiting, and partying. Dig in the island soil today and you may still spade up tools and cooking utensils those Indians used here.

Indians sold Manhattan Island in 1624 to Peter Minuit for $24. But as late as 1870, a small group of the Maine tribes still summered on Great Chebeague.

Today, no Indians come to Chebeague. But some two thousand whites summer here; and four hundred live here year-round. If you go down to the island wharf and wait there for the ferry to bring its load of supplies and passengers out from Portland, you'll probably meet Doughtys or Rosses, Seaburys or Rickers, Bennetts or Webbers, and a Johnson or two. These families have been on Chebeague and other islands of Casco Bay for hundreds of years. Their names are synonymous with good pilots and good fishermen. Their roots go deep into Chebeague's past. That is a long way back.

Great Chebeague, the biggest of some 180 islands in Casco Bay, is $4\frac{1}{2}$ miles long and a mile wide, with a land area of 2,800 acres. The recorded history of the island dates back to before the Pilgrims landed at Plymouth Rock. Then Chebeague was listed as a "colony of the Royal Crown of England" and its first white proprietor was the father of Maine, Sir Ferdinando Gorges. But not for long. In 1650, he sold out to a Boston merchant named Merry, thereby starting a trend of island selling. Merry never set foot on the island, but he boosted his ego by changing its name from Chebeague (Indian word for cold spring water) to Merry Island. However, money spoke louder than vanity to Merry. He sold the island at a profit for $500 to another Boston businessman named John King. Then King sold at a profit to Walter Gendall of Yarmouth. He held it despite the inconvenience that he was charged with treason at the time by a Massachusetts court, and had to pay more than twenty pounds to buy his pardon. But the Indians didn't pardon Gendall; they killed him. And soon Chebeague's name changed again, strangely this time. The island was given to two deacons of the First Church of Boston as "recompense for their goodly deeds," and was renamed "Recompense Island."

But only briefly. On shore, where Stroudwater stands now, between downtown Portland and the Jetport, big money was being made in cutting and shipping tall pines for the masts of the English navy. Since 1691, all white pines with a diameter of 24 inches at 1 foot above the ground were reserved for the English Crown and marked with the King's Broad Arrow. Colonel Thomas Westbrook was one of the men making small fortunes from shipping out the tall white pines. A mast tree 120 feet tall was worth $500. A 75-foot tree for a bowsprit fetched $200, and a spar fetched up to $100. In 1772, Maine shipped 382 masts, 69 bowsprits, and 451 spars to England and earned more than $200,000, a very big sum in those days. With some of those profits, Colonel Westbrook bought Great Chebeague. But business on the mainland was too hectic for him to settle out on an island. None of the early owners had the good sense of the Indians to really enjoy this lovely island. That had to wait until Scotsman Ambrose Hamilton arrived.

Hamilton built a log house on the north end, fathered twelve children and became grandfather to seventy-one. Hamiltons built and made famous the Chebeague stone fleet. By the 1850s, more than thirty Hamilton stone sloops, the Mack truck of their time, were hauling heavy loads of granite from Maine quarries to be made into some of the greatest buildings of their time. One Chebeague stone sloop, the *Addie Snow*, is believed to have sent the 291-foot passenger ship *Portland* to the bottom in the great storm of 1898, one of the worst tragedies at sea. The theory is that the *Portland*, in zero visibility, heavy seas, and a howling gale, collided with the granite-laden *Addie Snow*, caved in from the impact, and sank with the loss of 175 lives.

Exactly how or where the *Portland* was lost had been a mystery for half a century. Then, in November 1944, a scalloper out of Rockland was dragging off Cape Cod and brought up the *Portland*'s bell in her net. With the ship's bell as evidence of exactly where the *Portland* sank, Edward Rowe Snow, who has written fine books on New England's coast, sent down divers to find out if any more of the *Portland* lay on the bottom. The divers found the bow of the *Addie Snow* embedded in the side of the Portland, indicating a terrible collision and immediate sinking. All lives on both ships were lost. In another tragedy in a winter sea, ocean spray froze on the masts and decks of a Chebeague stone sloop outside of Boston Harbor. Tons of ice weighed her down till she became helpless in the breaking, freezing seas. Captain John Ross and his two sons, John and Walter, were found aboard, frozen to death, encased in ice on the rigging.

A gentler side of Chebeague, the summer cottage colony, began a hundred years ago. Hotels, a golf course, swimming beaches, boat slips, and yacht moorings in Chandler's Cove multiplied as the summer folk arrived. One of the earliest was Dr. L. L. Hill, who came to the island to practice medicine in 1884 and doctored island families for thirty-one years. Early in the 1900s, Ellis Ames Ballard, a wealthy Philadelphian, built a splendid summer house on Indian Point, spent

some $40,000 (a big sum a hundred years ago) on it, and called it
"Khatmandu."

Ballard lavished special care on a great oak tree that stood alone
on Indian Point, a seamark for generations of fishermen in the Bay,
The story goes that, in 1791, when Wentworth Ricker came to settle
on Chebeague, he found a tiny oak growing in his garden plot on Indian Point and nursed it along with loving care. When Ballard bought
the land, over one hundred years later, the tiny tree had grown into a
massive oak. A survivor of a century of hard weather, age was taking
its sad toll on the great tree. Ballard brought tree experts to the island
to doctor the massive lone oak. It recovered and lived to survive hur-
ricanes that demolished younger trees in more sheltered spots.

Great Chebeague is only a few miles away from the heart of Portland, yet it has managed to retain qualities of a remote island of special beauty. But that was threatened in the 1950s, when some
Chebeague Islanders started a campaign for a bridge to link the island
closer to the prosperity and business of downtown Portland. Howard
Beehler and F. E. Repetto, strong advocates for a bridge, argued that
there were too few ways for young people to make a living on
Chebeague, except as caretakers for summer folk. They pointed out
that a bridge already linked nearby Cousins Island to Littlejohn
Island, and thence to the mainland. They argued that, since only a
sandbar separates Littlejohn from Chebeague, a causeway with only a
couple of spans could link Chebeague to Littlejohn and thence to the
mainland. With a bridge like that, they said, Chebeaugue could grow
from a year-round population of four hundred to one of four thousand. The Chebeague bridge lobby succeeded in persuading one state
legislature to authorize such a bridge, only to have the proposal defeated in a statewide referendum. Today, it is still a ferry that links the
island to the mainland. You cannot drive your car to Chebeague yet.

The island the Indians loved so well for so long is still a true
island. But the pressure for a bridge is likely to be revived. As Portland more and more becomes a favorite, expanding city, the urge to
live on a nearby island and drive to work will become more powerful.
The pressure for such a bridge may come not only from people on
Chebeague. Just across the channel from Great Chebeague lies Long
Island, the 650-acre 'oil' island. Already there are hundreds of houses
and buildings on it, with an assessed valuation topping $4 million.

At low tide, a sandspit connects Great Chebeague to Little
Chebeague. One summer night we anchored off the magnificent
beach at Little Chebeague and spent the night aboard *Steer Clear*.

Almost half a mile long, shaped like a shallow crescent, the beach uncovers as the tide drops, until it is 200 feet wide from dunes to low-water mark. I've gone back in the log of *Steer Clear* to refresh memories of that day and night.

> Anchor down by 3 p.m. Elmore Wallace, who is cruising with us for the week as the expert with local knowledge, says when he was a boy fifty years ago, he used to row over here from his home on Long Island and get milk from the cows the farmer kept in the meadows on Little Chebeague. It was a big farm then.
>
> We rowed ashore in the dinghy and wandered those meadows. The grass is shoulder high now. Small mice scuttle in it. Young birds who can't yet fly seek shelter in it, after crashing from wobbly take-offs. The warm smell of hot summer lies fragrant on the meadow this afternoon. Ancient shutters creak on broken hinges in a vandalized house as the breeze from the sea stirs up a moaning through the gaping walls. But it is not eerie or ghostly in these abandoned meadows, and there is no meanness in the tumbled down porches; just a whisper of sorrow that the joy and happiness which once filled these houses and the young people who once lived in them are gone.
>
> Two kids have been laughing and playing on the beach all this afternoon. Now their father rows in from his sailboat and fetches them. They up anchor and depart. Little Chebeague is ours. We sit in the cockpit and watch the sun sink, then the moon rise, and feel the cool summer air, and hear the bell buoys clank. The night is so quiet and still that we can hear voices of youngsters on Long Island, across the water, calling goodnights to each other.

Below this entry in the log, a sheet of paper has been pasted in. On it are notes made after I'd gone to City Hall to find out more about Little Chebeague.

The island, empty and vandalized in the summer of 1970, was loved and cared for in 1890. Over a dozen fine homes stood here; today we see only their sad skeletons or their foundations and remnants of once lovely gardens of roses, lilacs, and day lilies. For a while after World War II, the island was used as a training camp for prizefighters. Before that the navy, which had installations and men on nearby islands, used Little Chebeague for rest and recreation. The navy set up a firefighting school for training sailors to become firefighters on aircraft carriers. The strange steel hulk on the beach was where fires were set, only to be put out in practice training.

City Hall Records show that anyone could have bought this gem of an island for a song in the 1950s. The federal government offered it for a dollar to the State of Maine, then to the City of Portland. Neither would take it. So it went on the auction block. Mainers didn't think enough of it then to buy it. So this 200-acre island beauty was sold in 1951 for $6,250 to John Absmeier of New York. He did nothing with it. But in 1965 the Press Herald told of plans to put in an air strip, a summer theater, a hotel complex ... part of a scheme for big money development of Little Chebeague and part of Jewell Island, farther out in Casco Bay. But, thank heaven, nothing came of it.

After John Absmeier died, his estate sold the island in 1972 for $155,000, making about $149,000 profit. Guess who bought it? The State of Maine, which had refused it twenty years earlier when the price was one dollar. John Absmeier of New York was smarter than Mainers. He bought it for $6,250 when no Maine resident thought a 200-acre island, ten minutes from Portland, with a magnificent beach, was worth $31 an acre!

But now this beauty of an island is a Maine State Park for everyone to enjoy."

Maine woke up very late to the value of its precious islands. From the time Maine became a state in 1820 until the 1960s, the State of Maine and the towns along the coast hardly gave a damn about the islands. Often nobody knew who owned them. Often when the state or town had title, they were eager to be rid of them and sold them for a song.

In Casco Bay alone there are plenty such instances.

The same John Absmeier who bought Little Chebeague also bought 160 acres of Jewell Island, further out in Casco Bay. Again he bought it from the federal government after the State of Maine and various Maine towns had refused it as a gift. Absmeier paid $10,240 at auction for these 160 gorgeous island acres ($64 an acre). His estate sold his 160 acres on Jewell in 1972 to the State of Maine for $200,000; and they are now part of the Jewell Island State Park.

On Great Diamond Island, David L. Lukens of New Jersey and Michael Montalbano, also of New Jersey, bought 200 acres and fifty buildings at auction from the federal government for about $40,000. The same David Lukens in 1956 bought 125 acres of Cushing Island, once the site of Fort Levett, for $33,750, complete with fifteen brick army buildings. Another little 8-acre island, called Overset, close to Portland, was offered to the City of Portland for just $500 by the federal government. By a vote of five to three, the City Council refused it. In 1965, a private buyer got the island at auction for $3,300.

The State of Maine and the City of Portland both turned down the chance to take for one dollar the spectacular, spacious military reservation on close-in Peaks Island. So, in 1958, Peter Cioffi of Massachusetts bought it for $14,671 at auction and later sold it off as subdivisions for cottage colonies. Today one small oceanfront lot costs more than Cioffi paid for the entire parcel.

Why did the state and the city turn their backs on these

bargain-priced islands? Of course, it's fun to blame the bureaucrats for lacking foresight. But private Maine people had no more foresight than the bureaucrats. No Maine residents made winning bids at the public auctions. The fact is, islands in Casco Bay were unwanted Cinderellas as late as 1960.

Casco Bay has been unappreciated until recently. When city, state, or federal funds were available, they went for the development of the Portland airport, not to the Port of Portland or the islands. Millions for air, not a penny for harbor and sea.

Why? One reason may be that, in the years from World War II until the 1970s, Casco Bay meant little to most people. More than 100,000 people live near Casco Bay today; yet perhaps not more than five in a hundred have had a chance to set foot on the islands from which Portland sprung. We have cared little about these precious islands because we have known little about them.

I was lucky that my job as a Portland newspaper reporter put me in working contact with the bay and the islands.

For seventeen years I looked at Casco Bay from the windows of my newspaper office. I've looked up from the typewriter to glance with joy at sunsets, storms, fog, sea smoke; seen the passage of ships winter and summer, spring and fall, night and day. Over the years, I've been out on the bay on rescue stories with Coast Guard boats; in pilot boats in storms; on an ocean tug, towing an oil barge 678 feet long behind it; in my own small boat, spending days and nights on and among the islands; on a racing yacht in the Monhegan race; ridden the Portland–Yarmouth cruise ferry, with its dance bands and gambling salons; flown in helicopters to hover over the islands where Indians feasted and the first settlers fought for a toehold; seen them from the bridge of a supertanker arriving in port from the Persian Gulf. But the more I learn about Casco Bay, the less I feel I know. These islands are so filled with history, romance, adventure, with terror and hardship, scullduggery and kindliness; and each is so different from the next that no man in a lifetime could know more than half there is to know about them. I can give only part of what there is to tell.

9

Casco Bay Islands
Part Two

There's a catchy story that there are 365 islands in Casco Bay, which are sometimes, therefore, called "the calendar islands." Untrue. The man to blame for this convenient mistake is Colonel W. Romer, His Majesty's Chief Engineer for the Colonies. In 1700, the colonel made a quick inspection trip of Casco Bay and reported to his bosses: "Said Bay has a multitude of islands, these being reported as many islands as there are days in the year." However, there are actually some 758 islands, islets, and exposed ledges.

Biggest of the islands is Great Chebeague, over 2,800 acres; the most heavily populated is Peaks Island, 720 acres, close to the city and linked to Portland by commuter ferries. But Peaks is no modern-day suburb of an island. Peak's was first settled more than 350 years ago by the Palmers and Bracketts, whose families were massacred in a bloody Indian raid in October 1689. The name changed as ownership changed, from Munjoy's Island to Mitton's to Michael's; finally the name of Peaks Island stuck, although Samuel Peak's greatest claim to fame may have been that he married the widow of the previous owner, George Munjoy (whose name stuck to Munjoy Hill). Some of the small islands, with such grand names as Pound of Tea, Junk of Pork, and Pumpkin Knob, were probably christened to commemorate the price paid for them.

Casco Bay is huge; more than 200 square miles. The entrance is 18 miles wide; the average width is 12 miles; and the tides run 12 feet or more. The depth in the channel is deeper than the shipping channels of Boston, New York, Philadelphia, and Baltimore. The harbor is unobstructed by bridges. Anchorages in Hussey and Luckse sounds are sheltered and spacious enough to hold half a hundred ocean-going vessels. When the Navy in World War II operated a refueling depot on Long Island, as many as sixty warships waited with room to spare to take on bunker oil. In 1891, half a million passengers sailed through Casco Bay. Freight trains a mile long used to bring wheat from the Canadian prairie to be shipped out of Casco Bay to Europe. In the 1970s, 438 big tankers from the Persian Gulf and Venezuela unloaded six billion gallons of crude oil at Portland, making this just about the biggest oil port in the East.

In 1623, young Christopher Levett, age twenty-seven, became the first permanent white settler in the Casco Bay islands. For his anchorage he chose the protection of four islands, now called Cushing, Peaks, Diamond, and House. Three years after the *Mayflower* reached Plymouth, Levett and his ten men went ashore at House and built a stone home there, the first permanent white settlement in Casco Bay. In his journal, Levett described his chosen spot:

> It lyeth about two leagues to the east of Cape Elizabeth … There are foure Ilands which make one good harbor, there is very good fishing, much fowle, and the mayne as good ground as any could desire. On the mayne I found one good river wherein the Savages say there is much salmon … The river I made bold to call by my owne name Levetts river, being the first that discover it. (Poor Levett, it is now called Fore River).

Island buffs today still argue over which island Levett settled on; some say House, some say Cushing, some say York. Levett, like the Indians, himself called his settlement Quack (the Indian word "Maquack" means the red-colored earth. On these islands there is still plenty of "Maquack"). But in his written reports he called it York, after Yorkshire in England, his home county there.

Levett had earned the favor of King James through his earlier work as His Majesty's forester. As a reward, King James gave Levett membership in the Council of New England and a land grant of 6,000 acres in Maine. Levett sailed the coast from the Isles of Shoals to Cape Small, making friends with the Indian chieftains and examining sites where he might settle. In the winter of 1623, he chose the sheltered island harbor in Casco Bay. Levett was the first settler to take pains to get along well with the Indian tribes, to write about their way of life, to stay with them, and invite them to eat and visit at his settlement. Levett wrote extensively about the Indians he knew and liked in his book *Voyage into New England*, published in London in 1628.

I find them generally to be marvellous quick of apprehension and full of subtlety; they will quickly find any man's disposition and flatter him and humor him, if they hope to get anything of him. And yet they will count him a fool if he do not show a dislike of it ... They are slow of speech, and if they hear a man speak much, they will laugh at him and call him 'mechecum,' a fool.

They have no apparel but skins. In winter, they wear the hair side inwards, in summer outwards. Sometimes you will not know the men from the women but by their breasts, the men having no hair on their faces.

When their children are born, they bind them on a board and set it upright against a tree. They keep them thus bound until they are three months. You will see them take their children and bury them many times in the snow, all but their faces, for a time, to make them the better to endure cold. And when they are above two years old they will cast them into the sea, to teach them to swim. Their houses are built in half an hour's time, being only a few poles stuck in the ground and covered with the bark of trees.

I find they have two gods; one they love and one they hate. The god they love they call Squanto; and to him they ascribe all their good fortunes. The god they hate, they call Tanto, and to him they ascribe all their evil fortunes.

Thus when anyone is killed, hurt, or sick, or when it is evil weather, they say Tanto is angry. They say that no one can see Squanto or Tanto except their "pawwaws," or medicine men, and then only when they dream. Every sagamore or chief has a 'pawwaw' in his company and is altogether directed by him. One time I was at a sagamore's house and saw a martin's skin, and asked if he would sell it. The sagamore told me no; the pawwaw used to lay that under his head when he dreamed, and if he was without that he could do nothing. Thus we may perceive how the devil deludes these poor people and keeps them in blindness. I have had much conferences with these savages about our one and only true God and have done my best to bring them to know and acknowledge Him. But I fear all that labor will be lost and no good will be done, except it be among the younger sort.

The sagamores will scarce speak to an ordinary man, but will point to their men and say: "Sanops must speak to sanops, and sagamores to sagamores."

They are very bloody-minded and treacherous among themselves. One will kill another for his wives; and he that hath the most wives is the bravest fellow. Therefore I would wish no man to trust them, whatever they say or do, but always to keep a strict hand over them, and yet to use them kindly and deal uprightly with them."

Because of his friendship with Indian chiefs, Levett was able to get Indian help in making many trips in small boats up the rivers around Casco Bay and to report in detail on the natural wealth of

fish, timber, game, and fresh water. Enthused about the possibilities
of turning his 6,000-acre land grant into a flourishing colony, Levett
returned to England in the spring of 1624 to spread the word and
drum up new backers and new settlers to establish a new colony on
the mainland, which he hoped to develop as the town of York, close
to where Portland now stands.

Levett left ten men behind on his island when he sailed home to
recruit new settlers in England. He never returned. He died at age
forty-five, in 1631, probably drowned at sea. His men and his headquarters were abandoned. Had Levett come back with the support
from the Crown and the Church, that he sought, this able, educated
leader, who got along unusually well with the Indians, might have
begun the diocese and the City of York, which he envisioned where
Portland is today.

Today, people driving in and out of Portland and its suburbs cast
a passing glance out to the islands of Casco Bay, seeing them as scenic
but unimportant appendages of the city and the mainland.

When the nation began, it was the other way around. Three hundred years ago, Cushing and Peaks, Chebeague, Diamond, Long, and
Jewell islands were the hub of living, of trade, of work; the islands
were the population centers and the Portland mainland was the
rough and dangerous land.

If you put yourself in the shoes of those first settlers of Maine, it
is easy to see why they chose the islands for their homes and farms.
First, they were safer from Indian raids. Second, an island seemed far
more tamable than the vast forests of the unknown mainland. The job
of clearing land, building a house, keeping sheep or cows from stray-
ing, seemed easier to a settler if he had the shoreline as a natural
boundary. The first, most plentiful food supply was, of course, fish
from the ocean; and it was handy to have that at your door and your
boat only a short walk from your cabin. The ocean was the road, far
safer than woods trails on the mainland, where it was easy to get lost
or get attacked, and hard to travel on foot or horse.

At first, when the settlers were few, each island was the fiefdom of
one family. But they were not isolated. They visited back and forth;
they helped each other in "raisings," the building of houses and
barns, exchanged seeds for planting, swapped vegetables, and the
men and boys teamed up to go on fishing and hunting trips together.
In disasters, such as the loss of boats or men at sea, or in defense
against Indians, or in dealing with the courts and the government of
the Massachusetts Bay Colony, the island families worked together.

Naturally they inter-married. The same family names crop up on many different islands. And the names of the islands changed often in the early days, since they were generally called by the name of the principal family settled there. The mainland developed through families who decided to move off islands that were getting crowded. As island families grew in numbers, there was not always space enough for more farms and fish houses, or enough trees suitable for turning into new homes, outbuildings, boats, firewood, wharves, and barrels, without disputes and quarrels.

Disputes and quarrels over land titles on the islands, and then the mainland, pockmarked the first 150 years of settlements in Maine. Little wonder. For in England, different companies kept being formed to milk the wealth from the New World. They obtained land grants to ill-defined areas throughout New England, marked upon maps that differed from each other and that had little accuracy when it came to "marking the bounds" on the actual territory. In New England itself, some jurisdiction over land lay with the governors and deputy governors, sometimes in Plymouth, sometimes in Boston. Sir Ferdinando Gorges and others gave away or sold off parts of their original land grants to settlers, whom they sent out to colonize the region. The story of who owned what island, and when, is tortuous. But a few thumbnail sketches of these islands give an idea of the changes in ownership.

Cushing Island

Christopher Levett, after he'd sailed home to England and never returned to his little colony in Casco Bay, sold his 6,000 acres of land grants, which he had obtained from Sir Ferdinando Gorges. He sold to a number of different buyers. A merchant in Plymouth, a Mr. Wright, got title to some of the Casco Bay land, including Cushing. He never set foot on it. In turn, Wright sold Cushing Island to George Cleaves. Cleaves, a wheeler-dealer of prominence and persistence in the early days of Casco Bay, gave the island to his daughter, Elizabeth. Elizabeth married a boy from nearby Peaks Island, Michael Mitton. And it became known as Mitton's Island. They, in turn, gave Cushing to their daughter, Sarah, who took it as her dowry when she married James Andrews. Andrews kept the island from 1667 to 1698 and it was known as Andrews Island. But even during these thirty-one years, the island had three different names; Andrews, Portland, and Fort Island. Andrews built a small fort there when he first married Sarah. When Indians attacked the islands, which happened often in the 1670s, many settlers on nearby islands fled to Andrews' fort. The men, working together, expanded its defenses and their families hunkered down in safety on Fort Island (Cushing) when they saw war canoes heading their way. They built a fine protective fort. But they had too little food for all the families to eat while they kept out of the way of the Indians for prolonged periods. After living on berries and fish for three weeks, George Felt, one of the men who'd fled to the island fort from Indians, recruited six other men and they rowed over to nearby Peaks Island. There they planned to round up and bring back the sheep that had been left behind when George Palmer's family and other frightened Peaks Islanders fled for safety to far off Boston. But the Indians, who had earlier attacked and laid waste to Peaks, were still on that island. They let Felt and his party land, let them round up the sheep; then the Indians attacked, killing them all.

The murders took place within earshot of the hungry men, women, and children waiting on Cushing for their meal of mutton.

Andrews' fort must have been large and well-built, for traces of it existed until the Civil War; eight hundred soldiers were stationed on the island as Indian fighters in 1754, more than eighty years after Felt's party was murdered.

After thirty-one years on the island, Andrews sold to John Rouse of Marshfield, Massachusetts; who, in turn, sold to his neighbor, John Brown; who, in turn, sold it to John Robinson of Newbury, Massachusetts; who, in turn, sold to Nathaniel Jones; and by 1735, Jones sold the island to Captain Joshua Bangs. Again, the name of the island changed. For the next hundred years, it was called Bangs Island. But Bangs himself did not stick long. Soon after he got ownership, Bangs sold to another Massachusetts man, Ezekiel Cushing. Cushing paid $2,300 for the island in 1762, more money than some of the Casco Bay Islands were sold for in the 1960s.

Ezekiel Cushing, like many a minister's son after him, grew up to be a money-making, fast-trading, luxury-loving business man. He made a sizeable fortune in trade with the West Indies, largely from rum. He spent money lavishly on the island, building himself a big home, which he called "The Homestead in the Willows." There he entertained in grand style and his guests drank from the finest wine cellar in Maine. (During the War of 1812, this house was used as a hospital.) Cushing, who held the high rank of colonel and became selectman of Falmouth (as Portland was called then), tired of this island; sold it back to Joshua Bangs, and bought nearby Long Island. There he built another, even grander "Homestead in the Willows," and lived a life of fabled luxury as a feudal overlord until he died. He left Long Island, Overset Island, and Marsh Island to his children.

This time, when Joshua Bangs came back to Bangs Island, he lived there until his death. His daughter, meanwhile, married an island-raised man, Brigadier Jedediah Preble, who had once owned Richmond Island, and Preble became owner of Bangs Island. His son, the famous Commodore Edward Preble, father of the U.S. Navy, inherited it. The Commodore's heirs split and sold off much of the property. By 1812, Simon Skillings had moved into "The Homestead in the Willows" and set about acquiring as many of the island parcels as he could buy. In 1856, Skillings and the last of the Preble heirs left on Bangs Island agreed to sell the whole island to Lemuel Cushing, a distant cousin of Ezekiel. Once again, the name of the island changed.

Bangs Island now became Cushing Island. And this Lemuel Cushing, who came from Canada, went into the resort hotel business, perhaps the first man to try it in the Casco Bay Islands.

He made a success of it, too. First he built a large brick hotel for a mere $10,000 in 1858, on a high granite cliff overlooking the bay. He named it "The Ottawa," and wealthy Canadians came in great numbers to spend their summers there, traveling on the newly completed railroad from Montreal to Portland. But fire burned the hotel in 1886 and Lemuel Cushing spent $75,000 to build a new one. This, too, burned, in 1917, but was never rebuilt.

Military men instead of vacationers took over Cushing. The fort, first begun by Andrews in the 1670s and rebuilt at the time of the Spanish American War, was expanded again in World War I, and yet again in World War II, when it was equipped with 12-inch and 16-inch guns. This fort was named Fort Levett to honor Christopher Levett, who'd built his stone house in 1623.

To buy the land, construct Fort Levett, dig underground tunnels hundreds of feet long, build fifteen brick residences and barracks, and install and maintain the great guns, the federal government spent untold millions of dollars.

Then in 1956, the federal government put it all up for sale— buildings, docks, fort, roads, tunnels, and 125 acres of island close to Portland. A New Jersey man, David Lukens, bought it all for $33,750. A few years later, at the time of the Cuban Missile Crisis, Lukens sold his part of historic Cushing Island to the United States Safekeeping Corporation, supposedly for $90,000. This outfit planned to modernize the huge underground tunnels into a vast vault and rent out sections of it as safekeeping havens for the precious documents of banks and corporations in the big cities that felt insecure in the face of a possible missile attack. At the time, it was reported that $100,000 were spent in pursuit of the idea, which, with the ending of the Cuban Missile Crisis, died a quick death. The precious, historic island finally came back into Maine ownership, bought by a group called The Cushing Island Associates, Maine residents with strong ties to summer homes on Cushing. Sidney Thaxter of Cape Elizabeth led the group, which included Farrars, Meachams, Hammonds, Quinns, Coles, Hitchcocks, Hales, and Gignouxes.

In 1970, Cushing Island underwent another milestone change. Four men from the Portland area, Martin Johnson, Peter Murray, Richard Balser, and Howard Dana, organized Whitehead Associates and bought the old fort and 50 acres around it for $25,000 from Cushing Island Associates. Buyer and seller agreed to deed an additional 75 acres to The Nature Conservancy, thus ensuring the scenic land would remain unspoiled and undeveloped. Further, Whitehead Associates agreed to limit the buildings on their 50 acres to eighteen units, including the twelve buildings already there and built by the military; barracks, NCO and officers houses, a hospital, jail, and mess hall. Each of the original six partners (Peter Colli of New Jersey and Peter Lincoln of New York City joined the original four Maine partners) took one house each and sold the five other original buildings to friends, who agreed to renovate their properties within two years. This has been done. Even the six-cell jail has been turned into a summer cottage, with bars on the windows left in place. The only vehicle now permitted on the island is a service truck belonging to the year-round caretaker. A daily ferry serves the island in summer, so the Portland people can commute to and from work.

Great Diamond Island

Bangs Island got its name changed to Cushing, an improvement in connotation caused by change in owners.

Hog Island got changed to Great Diamond—a still bigger change in connotation for a smaller reason.

Great Hog Island earned its name because originally the island was used as a 230-acre hog pen. Tons of hay were later harvested on the island farm and cut and shipped to Portland stables in the horse and buggy era. Horses gave way to autos, hogs gave way to summer residents on the island, and the summer people—wanting a more mellifluous address—changed the name from Great Hog to Great Diamond Island. They justified the new name because of the way the sun glinted on pockets of quartz, mica, and crystal in the rock ledges. Great Diamond is one of half a dozen islands within Portland city limits. City tax records show Great Diamond in 1981 had sixty-eight homes on its 230 acres, with its land valued at $570,000.

The first land transaction known regarding Hog Island was in 1635. Then Sir Ferdinando Gorges (a man of long vision) gave a 2,000-year lease to George Cleaves and Richard Tucker for "one is-land known by the name of Hogg Island." Thereafter the land trans-fers came fast and frequent. Cleaves sold Hog to Thomas Kimball of Boston in 1658; and Kimball sold it five years later, in 1663, to Edward Tyng of Boston for 25 English pounds. In the next hundred years it changed hands many times until, in 1756, Deacon James Milk, who lived on Exchange Street in Falmouth (Portland) bought it. The island soon became ideal housing for the big family he was to acquire. In 1762, Deacon Milk married his second wife, the widow Deering of Kittery. She came to the marriage with eleven children, he with five; and the eighteen people in the Milk family moved out to live on Hog Island. The property passed through parents to children, to grand-daughter Mary, who married the famous Commodore Ed-ward Preble; and the Preble family, which also had an interest in Cushing Island and Richmond Island, kept possession of Hog or Great Diamond for a century.

By 1882, this island was a rather exclusive resort. A Great Dia-mond Island Association bought 97 acres of land by raising $7,679.55 overnight and paying it over immediately to Francis and J. D. Fes-senden, who needed to raise that specific amount within thirty-six hours. Seven years later, in 1889, the Association reported fifty-seven cottages (only eleven fewer than in 1981) and a population of three hundred. Great Diamond had become a summer resort for Portland's upper crust. The Portland Club built a summer clubhouse on the high knoll. Steamboats and ferries landed at three sides of the island, even then shuttling commuter's back and forth to work in Portland. The trappings of urban life quickly developed: roads lit by kerosene streetlights; a 140,000-gallon reservoir; an acetylene gas plant for home lighting.

The smell of real-estate development began to permeate the is-land air. The firm of Ilsley and Cummings surveyed the island and presented a plan that showed room for 506 cottage lots covering 126 acres, to be served by thirty avenues and streets. Some 76 acres of the most desirable waterview lots were earmarked as the property of the Great Diamond Island Association. Members built and operated a nine-hole golf course, two tennis courts, and their own steamboat, *Isis*, to carry them back and forth to Portland. The harbor blossomed with moorings for their pleasure craft. The threat of World War however, put a crimp in the idylls of summer life on Great Diamond.

The government built Fort McKinley, as part of the Portland Harbor Defense System, and the exclusiveness of the resort declined. The War Department took the northeastern part of the island by eminent domain, paying $149,850 in damages for it. Soon there was a year-round military population of more than a thousand men, dwarfing the summer colony of 350. The former summer island became the site of a great building program of massive gun emplacements, barracks, roads, ammunition dumps, warehouses, stables, and hospitals. Target practice for the 12- and 16-inch guns ruined the island's quiet. Cottages were sold or rented to the military.

But Portland Harbor was never attacked in either World War I or II. By the 1950s, the military decided it had no further use for the multi-million-dollar installation on Great Diamond. The great brick buildings, wharves, and warehouses stood empty. In 1961, it was all put up for auction. The once-powerful association sent a representative to the auction, but without money or authority to bid. Michael Montalbano, a developer from New Jersey, and David L. Lukens (who had bought 125 acres and military installations at Cushing Island for $33,750) made the winning bid. They bought 200 acres of Great Diamond plus Fort McKinley's hospital, theater, barracks, brick homes, paved roads, sewer systems, and power and water plants for $42,350. In 1970, they sold it for a reported $225,000 to King Resources, an oil company that had bought the Navy Oil Depot on nearby Long Island. King Resources, however, went into bankruptcy in 1972. Fort McKinley and 200 acres of Great Diamond Island went into the hands of the receivers.

What you see depends on where you sit. The first time I saw Great Diamond up close was from *Steer Clear* when cruising for a few days and nights with photographer Donald Johnson, and the perspective then was different. I turn back to the log of *Steer Clear* to recapture a night in Diamond Cove.

> Near seven o'clock on this July night, we dropped anchor in Diamond Cove. We have the cove to ourselves, except for one unoccupied power boat tied to the wharf on Great Diamond Island. We decide to cook a steak on a nearby island, a precipitous hump of rock and scrub brush, inhabited only by nesting gulls and an automatic navigation light.

At the water's edge we watched the summer sun go down, cooked an epicurean steak and fed scraps to angry gulls as payment for disturbing them when Don photographed their nests. Through a cut between Crow Island and a tip of Great Diamond we see cars darting between Falmouth and Portland on the mainland. The world ashore seems a thousand miles away from our peace and isolation. Etched against the evening sky out here are unlikely telephone poles and drooping, broken wires, strung and abandoned long ago by the military along the ridge of nearby Crow Island's fourteen acres. A rotted military wharf lies twisted and broken, drooping into the quiet sea.

We douse the embers from the hibachi and stretch out, warming our backs on the ledge which has baked all day in the splendid sun. I wonder how many Indians, how many explorers, how many early settlers, how many G.I.s have lain warming their backs on these same rocks, watching the same sun go down. No Mainer lives on Crow Island now to relish its island beauty, so close in to Portland. John A. Richardson of Brookfield, Massachusetts, was smart enough to buy the fourteen-acre island in 1958 for the sum of $2,656.

The night is balmy. We stay on the ledge until the moon is high and the water turns velvet black. Then we row back to *Steer Clear* and read old books about the Indians, the first settlers, the fishermen-farmers, the pirates, and the treasure-seekers who once roamed the islands we have seen and loved today. We feel a kinship with that ghostly company.

Little Diamond Island

Ted Rand has been making Little Diamond Island run since 1954. He was twenty-five then and bought the old Coast Guard buoy station atop the hill for $2,500 and came to live here winter and summer. A University of Maine graduate and one-time teacher, Ted Rand has fathered two boys and three girls on this island. He is busy. He has been island policeman and fireman, lobsterman (450 traps), runs the wharf, and has built up a flourishing boat-storage, marine gas and waterfront store business. Between times, he has served as president of the Casco Bay Island Association.

He knows the islands must change with the times. He is a realist. But his goal is to see that development of them benefits all; that the islands are neither raped to enrich a few nor held back, unnaturally keeping the clock standing still, to make a special sanctuary for those rich enough to maintain summer retreats here. He knows the past and present of these islands and intends to safeguard their future as best he can.

When the tide is out, you can cross the sand bar from Great Diamond and walk over here to Little Diamond. Yet in feeling, the two islands are many miles apart. There are a few dozen houses on Little Diamond now. But until 1900, this little, lovely island was one working farm. Then it began to change, in the footsteps of Great Diamond, into a summer colony, until by 1910 the open farmland was dotted with twenty-five cottages on the south side. The north side was owned by the Catholic Diocese of Portland, which ran a summer camp for girls from the St. Elizabeth's Orphanage in Portland. Busiest cottage on the island in those days was the Nissen cottage, run as a boarding house. Charges were four dollars per week, all meals included. This Nissen family later become the prosperous and famous bakers of Maine and New England.

George W. Brown bought 40 acres of Little Diamond in 1908 with the idea of creating a fancy summer colony. He put in a water system, roads, even promoted sun-heated saltwater baths, and began an attractive restaurant. But within four years his company ran out of money and the members of the Little Diamond Association took over. General Frederick Keating, British vice-consul in Portland, bought the restaurant and under his management it flourished until he left Portland after World War I. He sold the restaurant, casino, and bathing beach facilities to the Association and in 1924 the old Keating cottage was turned into the new casino. (Nothing so exotic as gambling! "Casino" is what the Little Diamond Island Association called its prim and proper clubhouse.) Two years later, electricity came to Little Diamond and drove out "Old Charlie" the lamplighter, and his pet pig who accompanied him on his nightly rounds.

Peaks Island

Peaks is the only island in Casco Bay to have developed into a bedroom suburb of Portland. There are more than a thousand homes here built on fewer than 700 acres. Morning and evening ferries are filled with commuters who go daily to jobs in the city, and with youngsters who go to school in Portland. Peaks is only a 15-minute boat ride from the city.

The Casco Bay Lines ferry is a focal point in the lives of Peaks Islanders; its fares and schedules are issues that bind all Peaks Islanders together in a running battle with the ferry line. In frustration, they often threaten to operate their own private line.

Peaks Island, so close to the mainland, was settled 350 years ago by the Bracketts and the Palmers, and later the Sterlings, Trefethens, Mittons, Munjoys, and Trotts. The name of the island changed often, depending upon who was living here. The busy hand of George Cleaves is imprinted in its history. Cleaves held title, then gave it to his son-in-law, Michael Mitton. Two Brackett brothers married two daughters of Michael Mitton and sold out to B. Trott.

Peaks' problem was that it was in easy striking distance of the Indians. They raided in 1689 and wiped out many of the settlers. Only the presence of Major Benjamin Church and his soldiers, stationed there to help guard Falmouth (Portland), kept that fight from becoming a total massacre. The next year, a second battle drove the brave remaining souls from the island. Yet soon a few settlers came back. The island was too handy, too big, and too lovely to leave totally empty. But even one hundred years later, at the time of the Revolution, only three major houses stood on Peaks Island named after Samuel Peak.

By 1850, William Jones had begun to turn Peaks into a tourist island for day visitors from Portland. Jones turned his boarding house into a restaurant specializing in shore dinners. Canadian visitors coming into Portland on the Grand Trunk Railway would take the boat out to Peaks and eat lobster, clams, and corn at Jones' restaurant. By 1851, the tourist traffic was big enough for Horace G. Cook to put a fast steamer, *Antelope*, into service out to Peaks Island.

In the next thirty years, Peaks became Casco Bay's great summer attraction. Amusement parks, boarding houses, hotels, skating rinks, and theaters dotted the island. A huge building, first used as the Forest City Skating Rink, became the Gem Theater, run by a Portland entrepreneur named Bart MacCullum. He staged musical comedies and Broadway tryouts on this Maine island. A kind of Coney Island amusement park, called Greenwood Park, attracted thousands of families on a day's outing. A famed balloonist named Prince Leo was a top-drawing card. The Prince would climb into his balloon, ascend hundreds of feet into the air, then parachute down to Peaks Island. A Professor Oldwie astonished visitors by walking on water. He wore two outsize floats as shoes and plowed across the water rather like a cross-country skier over snow.

In summer, a fleet of steamers able to carry several hundred passengers each plied between the island and Portland.

The day's outing was offered at a bargain; only twenty-five cents, which included the boat ride plus a chance to see the open-air vaudeville shows.

That great figure of Broadway, George M. Cohan, produced some of his first hits at the Gem Theater on Peaks Island. John Ford, the Portland boy who became one of America's greatest film directors, started on his theatrical career by being an usher at the old Gem.

Peaks Island enjoyed fame as the supposed site of Longfellow's *Wreck of the Hesperus*. It wasn't. Longfellow wrote *The Wreck of the Hesperus* in Portland, in the year 1839. But the shipwreck of the *Helen Eliza* on Peaks Island, on which the poem was supposedly based, did not happen until thirty years later, on September 8th, 1869.

The *Helen Eliza* was wrecked off Peaks Island with eleven persons aboard, ten of whom drowned. Here is the story, told by the sole survivor, Charles Jordan. But first, a word of caution. Jordan was a colorful character, prone to embroidering facts; he'd been taken prisoner in the south in the Civil War, supposedly the sole survivor of a company of eighty men. At war's end, Jordan was released from Libby Prison and boarded a schooner headed north. That schooner was wrecked off Cape Cod—and Jordan was, supposedly, the sole survivor of that, too. He then took passage aboard the *Helen Eliza* and became the sole survivor again when she met her end at Peaks Island.

Now, for Jordan's account of the wreck of the *Helen Eliza* at Peaks Island.

During the afternoon of September 8, 1869, thick fog set in, followed by a perfect deluge of rain, and wind increased till it blew a regular hurricane. Both anchors were let go, but the cables parted and there was little doubt the vessel would go aground on Peak's Island. Captain Miller at the helm probably received his death blow from the main boom ... The vessel struck heavily, killing instantly five persons with me in the forecastle ... I was swept into the raging water ... Seeing an empty barrel floating by, I was fortunate enough to secure it ... The waves ran fearfully high. I was swept by George W. Clark and Benjamin Lurvey who were clinging to a plank ... I decided I must not make myself known to them, for the chances of three clinging in safety to my barrel were slim ... The undertow was very powerful, but I managed to get to a ledge of rocks. I heard Clark hailing. I answered the call, enjoining him to hold on to his plank and get to the ledge. I did not hear him again and probably the two men were swallowed up in the undertow ... I soon found the ledge did not form part of an island, but would be covered at high water. I plunged again into the seething waters. Another terrible contest with surf followed ... Moments seemed like hours ... My strength was fast failing ... Making one last desperate effort, I neared a shore and made a landing ... Now it was nine in the evening and the past two hours of exertion told on me. I could scarcely lift one foot before the other, but I persevered and came to the house of Mr. Smith Hadlock ... When rested, I joined the men of the island in a search for my shipmates. Mr. Jones, landlord of the hotel, secured me a free passage home. The inhabitants of the island, mostly poor fishermen, made me up a purse of $18.

Jordan swore he'd never come close to water again. So he went inland and took up farming in New Hampshire, far from the sea. There he slipped on a log crossing a stream. And drowned.

Jewell, Stave, and Outer Islands

The many islands of Casco Bay can be grouped into three rings, inner, middle, and outer. Here is an account of a visit to Stave Island, one of the smaller, unspoiled islands in the Outer Ring.

"Seal pups," says Elmore Wallace, as he slips *Steer Clear* between sea-covered ledges and creeps into the sheltered cove at Stave Island.

At first glance the baby seals look like silvered logs of driftwood, floating atop the blue water. Now they lift their heads in curiosity, twitching their long hard whiskers, gazing at us with their bulbous eyes. While they are pups, their hide is white and furry. The approach of *Steer Clear* rouses them from lazy sunbaths on a ledge barely above water.

With a splash, a dozen seals that had looked like silver logs now move, slide into the water and vanish.

"We'll tie to this mooring," decides Elmore. He has been cruising these waters for fifty years, fourteen of them as a marine warden. "You don't want to miss going ashore on Stave. Go for an hour. I'll stay with the boat. Then we'll move over to Jewell before you head out of the Bay and home to New Harbor."

Thousands of years ago, when the Ice Age created the islands of Casco Bay, it left three tiers of islands; the Inner Ring of Mackworth, Clapboard, Cousins, Bibber, and others closest to the mainland; the Middle Ring of Cushing, Peaks, Long Island, Great and Little Diamond, Great and Little Chebeague, and others a little further out into the Bay; and the Outer Ring of Cliff, Stave, Jewell, and others to seaward.

Stave Island is as pretty and unspoiled as any. Not as large and magnificent as Jewell; not as close to Portland as Little Chebeague; not as wild as Whaleboat; not as flat and barren as Bangs or Stockman or Ministerial islands. But little Stave has every kind of island beauty mingled in a smaller scale.

Our safe cove is peppered with black rocks for surf to foam upon; there's a small white sand beach for a man to stretch out on and snooze in the sun; there are cliffs to climb and, breathless after racing to the top, to watch the sea and nearby islands from; ripe, salt-savored berries to eat, sweet-smelling bright-colored wildflowers and fresh fern to smell; there are green spruce for the winds to whistle through and birds to nest in and men and girls to lie under.

Abner Harris, founder of The Harris Company, ship chandlers on the Portland waterfront, once owned Stave. The weir and lobster pound he built still stand, tumbled and punished by fifty years of storms. Scores of Casco Bay fishermen sold Abner thousands upon

thousands of lobster here, and he held them in these pounds. Now
the old lobster pound is a grand place to skinnydip, far out to sea;
Abner's old fish house stands by the water and the house he built
atop the hill amid sweet ferns is still there. The doors are open; and
inside are a few survival essentials for a man caught out here in a
storm.

Austin Harris, Abner's grandson, says Abner sold the island in
the 1940s to Charles Olsen, a Cape Elizabeth fisherman. Now, according to tax records of the town of Cumberland, six people own Stave;
and they are all from Maine. "I haven't been back in thirty years,"
mourns Austin Harris. "My grandfather took me out often when I was
a little boy. Those memories come flooding back whenever I hear the
name 'Stave.'"

From atop Stave, we see a huge, immaculate lodge on nearby
Hope Island. Well-to-do Philadelphians, with an eye for beauty at a
bargain price, bought Hope Island and have kept it as a private club,
complete with private power plant, private water supply, and private
boat service. Beyond Hope is the Singing Beach of Long Island, the
beach where the undertow of the Atlantic rolls stones to create a
wild and eerie song. On the far side of Long Island is water a hundred feet deep and the piers where, in the early 1970s, an oil company, King Resources, planned to dock supertankers 1200 feet long
and unload over 2 million barrels of oil from each. That incredible
juxtaposition to the wild loveliness of Stave never happened: King
Resources went into bankruptcy. But it is a good time to look at Long
Island, part of the Middle Ring.

Back in 1640, John Sears of Boston owned Long Island. According to a 1703 map in London, it was called Smith's Island, after the
Boston merchant to whom Sears sold it. By 1763, Colonel Ezekiel
Cushing was the big landowner and he sent his brother Ignatius to
live on it. By 1830, Maine, a state only ten years, took its first census
and Long Island had a population of 146, largest of any island in
Casco Bay. The Godes and the Doughtys, experts in swordfishing,
prospered and multiplied here. Then tourism almost swamped fishing
as Long Island's primary business. Hotels such as Dirigo House, one
hundred rooms; Casco Bay House, sixty rooms; and the grand
Granite Springs Hotel with 150 rooms, offered accommodations from
$1 a day to $17 a week. Only Peaks Island, crowded with twenty-one
hotels and boarding houses, was a busier tourist center a hundred
years ago. Long Island staged the biggest clambake in Maine history.
In 1886, more than 2,500 people came out to Long Island by steamers to celebrate Portland's bicentennial. Records show 16 cords of

wood were needed for the fires and 500 bushels of clams were eaten that day.

Last in the Outer Ring of Casco Bay is Jewell, 221 acres of history-packed and heavenly beauty. It was our last stop in a week spent among Casco Bay islands. If God was in His Heaven on that July day, He was missing a lot by not being on Jewell Island.

George Jewell, of Saco, bought this island gem from the Indians in 1637 for one powderhorn, twelve fishhooks, and a barrel or two of rum. The unlucky man fell overboard in Boston Harbor a few years later and drowned. But his name, a good one for this island beauty, has stuck for almost 350 years. Henry Donnell of York owned the island after Jewell and was lucky enough to live on it for thirty years.

Today, Jewell Island is a Maine state park. The State paid $290,000 for it in 1976. About $200,000 went to the estate of John B. Absmeier for his 130 acres (he had paid $33,000 for them twenty years earlier, buying from the federal government). For the remaining 90 acres, the State paid $90,000 to the heirs of the McKeen family, direct descendants of the McKeen who had been the first president of Bowdoin College. McKeen had bought his part of Jewell in 1894. His whole family enjoyed summers there; some of them spent several winters on the island; and three children were born on Jewell. The McKeen cottage was horribly vandalized in the 1960s and '70s and was in total collapse by the time the State bought Jewell. Where it once stood, there now grow wild roses, wild peas, sweet-smelling honeysuckle vines, and a bold banner of white daisies.

From the new State wharf on Jewell, it is a half-hour walk to Knife-Edge Rock, which towers above a cove where Captain Kidd is supposed to have buried treasure. The Army in World War II installed 70-foot-high watchtowers here, great coastal gun emplacements, together with underground tunnels and bunkers. Now they stand, scarred, rusty, decrepit. But for those who will climb the steep, winding, concrete stairs to the top, the views will remain a spectacular, lifelong memory. The walls are scrawled with graffiti, marks of a moment of beer or love. One—strange echo of a London scandal in the 1960s—reads "Dr. Stephen Ward loves Mandy RiceDavies ... P.S. So does John Profumo."

Deep in the ground beneath the watchtowers are sweating, dark tunnels, 8 feet wide, winding for hundreds of yards. Massive iron doors hang precariously from broken hinges, doors that once guarded 8-inch shells which were never fired in anger.

The blood of Indians and early settlers once wet this island soil. Settlers fled here for safety from the atrocities on Harpswell Neck and closer-in islands. They believed no Indians would paddle out to Jewell, exposing themselves to fire from its high point. The settlers built a fort on Jewell and felt secure. On the second day of September 1676, fine weather blessed Jewell. Richard Potts and all the other men, women, and children who had fled here for safety from Harpswell, sailed over to cut corn on nearby Green Island, where the corn stood high and rich, thanks to regular fertilization by gulls.

Left alone on lookout at the fort on Jewell was nine-year-old Thomas Potts, well-trained to load and fire his father's musket. Suddenly young Thomas spied eight canoes, each carrying four Indians. They were less than half a mile away, paddling fast from Cliff toward Jewell. The boy raised his musket and fired the alarm. At the signal, men cutting corn on Green Island, and women washing clothes in the stream, rushed back to defend Jewell. By the time the Indians reached shore, the settlers were in place, ready and able to fight them off.

It is not known how many settlers or Indians died that day. But the whites were scared enough to leave. Earlier that summer, thirty-five whites had been murdered near Back Cove in Portland. Others had been killed on Casco Neck. Settlements all along the coast were being attacked. So the families on Jewell Island fled that September afternoon, aboard sloops that John Damarell from Richmond Island had led to their rescue. At Richmond, they were safer; but during that long, bloody autumn of 1676, Indians destroyed almost every white man's building between the Piscataqua and Kennebec rivers. In fear, the Potts family fled to faraway Pennsylvania. Young Thomas Potts, when he inherited the family farm on Potts Point at Merriconeag Neck, never returned to live on it. He sold it, without a qualm, to Benjamin Marston.

Today, walking the wild meadows of Jewell Island, looking to sea from Knife-Edge Rock, time plays strange games. Despite gun emplacements and watchtowers from World War II at my back, I feel closer to the Potts family of 1672 than to the G.I.s of 1944. The roots of the old McKeen family cottage seem closer than the new docks installed by the State of Maine in 1976.

Out among these Casco Bay islands there is a strange kinship of feeling that pays no heed to time. From Jewell, I can look at Eagle and feel close to Admiral Peary, as he sat there, planning voyages to the North Pole; to Edna St. Vincent Millay, writing her poems on Ragged Island off to the east ... to the thirty-two men wrecked on the *Oakey L. Alexander* in 80-mile-per-hour winds and 40-foot seas near Cape Elizabeth, across the bay, on March 3, 1947 ... to the holiday crowds who swarmed to see the fireworks on Peaks in the 1880s; and to the men aboard the dragger now heading out to fish.

This wondrous bay, with its hundreds of islands, may sometimes look empty. But stand on an island alone and listen. Casco Bay fills with the ghosts of explorers, Indians, first settlers, men manning forts and massive guns in many wars; and fishermen, farmers, land-grabbers, pirates, holiday crowds, convoys heading out for Murmansk, tankers heading in from the Persian Gulf.

10

Lighthouses
Sentinels of the Coast

I admire the beauty, the toughness, and the duty of Maine's light-houses. Their flashing beams at night can be more welcome than a letter from home. The heroic lighthouse keepers, men and women, who've kept their light burning in the foulest storms wear splendid badges of courage, emblazoned into the sage of the Maine coast. Yet when it comes to downright gratitude, mine goes mostly to foghorns and the whistle buoys. After hours of tension, when fog, vapor, or lashing rain blot out even the bow of the boat, the sound of that deep-throated hoarse moan is like the sound of a friend's voice.

The easternmost light in the United States is at Mt. Desert Rock. Far to sea and brutally exposed to the North Atlantic, the light is anchored to a barren half acre of volcanic rock rising out of the Bay of Fundy. It is now automated. But a special breed of men and women operated this forsaken outpost for 145 years, from 1832 to 1977. Just before Christmas 1977, a helicopter landed on the wave-swept rock and took off the last men to man this light. They were two young Coast Guardsmen—Robin Runnels, twenty-two, of Hyannis, Massachusetts, and Douglas Nute, twenty, from inland St. Louis, Missouri.

From Grand Manaan to Mt. Desert to the Isles of Shoals on the New Hampshire border, sixty-eight lighthouses stand along the coast of Maine and her rivers.

Oldest is the Portland Head Light, begun before our independence, finished by order of George Washington, and first lighted January 10, 1791. Only four lighthouses ordered by the first president still stand today. Portland Head Light is one of them. In 1981, it was featured on a postage stamp.

Two Lights at Cape Elizabeth was the first lighthouse ever featured on an American postage stamp. This light was built in 1828, at a cost of $4,250. The stamp was issued in 1970 and bore the famous Two Lights painting by Edward Hopper, which now hangs in New York's Metropolitan Museum. Only one of the famed Two Lights shines now. Actor Gary Merrill bought the West Light for $30,000 in 1971. He planned to make living quarters on the six floors, with an all-glass living room with a 360-degree view in the tower, but his plans never became reality.

The names of Maine's lighthouses unlock a torrent of history, hardship, heroism, and loneliness. The names alone flash vivid pictures across the mind's eye ... Boon Island Light, where, in 1710, survivors of the wreck *Nottingham Galley* kept from starving by eating one of their mates ... Matinicus Rock Light, where seventeen-year-old Abbie Burgess kept the light burning through a month of horrendous storms while her father was marooned on the mainland and her mother was a bedridden invalid below in the keeper's house; Seguin Light, on the great island rock, where the first colonists in December 1607 headed in to land at Popham; Monhegan Light, run by a woman for eighteen years; Petit Manan Light at the foggiest spot in the nation ... The lights at Goose Rocks, Eagle Island, Burnt Coat, Great Duck, Heron Neck, Isle au Haut, Whitehead, the Cuckolds, Whaleback, Pemaquid. The roll call evokes the perils of the sea.

Lighthouses are as ancient as the times men first ventured far to sea. The first lighthouse of the world was build by King Ptolemy Philadelphus on the island of Pharos near Alexandria. Built 250 years before Christ was born, the light was a marvel of size and beauty. Made of marble, it stood 600 feet tall. At the 400-foot level was a meat and vegetable market. At the 500-foot level was a terrace from which tourists could see the great lamp itself. The wonder of the world endured for sixteen hundred years and its light guided the ships of Caesar and Cleopatra.

By comparison, the Colossus of Rhodes was a pygmy. It stood a mere 160 feet high and lasted a mere fifty-six years, until felled by an earthquake in 224 B.C. While it stood, the fire was kept burning in its eyes, as a beacon to ships of the Mediterranean.

Lighthouses were slow in coming to North America, though our nation was founded by seamen. More than one hundred years went by after the first colonists came here before the first lighthouse was built in 1716, in Boston Harbor. Throughout the whole 18th century, only twenty-four lighthouses were built along the entire Atlantic coast. However, once our nation had broken ties with England, we knew that our destiny lay in the sea, the pace quickened. In the first fifty years after independence, sixty-six lighthouses were built from Maine to Florida and around the Keys to the Gulf Coast and Louisiana, compared to only ten built while we were an English colony.

The ninth bill passed by the First Congress, enacted August 7, 1789, authorized lighthouse construction. So important were lighthouses that presidents themselves appointed the lighthouse keepers. George Washington personally chose Joseph Greenleaf to be the first keeper of the Portland Head Lighthouse, on January 7, 1791.

Portland Head Light

Captain Greenleaf's job carried more honor than money. He received no pay for more than two years, though the government did supply him a house. In July 1793, he got cash, too—a federal salary of $160 a year. He didn't collect it long, for two years later he died of a stroke while crossing the Fore River in a skiff. He was succeeded by a Portland blacksmith, Barzillai Delano, who died on the job in 1821 and was succeeded by his son.

Politics perhaps crept into the appointment of John F. Watts. When the new Board of Lighthouse Commissioners made an inspection of Portland Head Light on July 5, 1852, Watts surprised them all. He said that when he had taken the job his predecessor refused to tell him how to operate the light. He had to hire a man for two days to show him how to run it. The inspectors also found that Watts blew his foghorn only for special steamers, with whom he made private arrangements, in cash, in advance.

The two best-known keepers of the Portland Head Light were the father and son team of Joshua and Joseph Strout, who, between them, kept the light almost sixty years, from 1869 until 1928.

The year Captain Joshua Strout became keeper, at a salary of $620 a year, one of Maine's infamous September gales smashed twenty ships in Casco Bay and claimed scores of lives. Rogue waves tore loose the huge fog bell and tossed it like a tennis ball into a cut in the rocks below the lighthouse. The replacement lasted only three years; then the stronger, louder Daboll trumpet was brought from Monhegan and Portland Head got its first real foghorn. This lasted but two years. The light tower was raised and lowered several times over the years; lowered in response to budget cuts; raised in response to protests from ship captains who could not see it soon enough.

On Christmas Eve 1886, the *Annie C. Maguire* met disaster at

Portland Head. She was a 34-year-old, three-masted bark, British registered, with fifteen in crew, headed from Buenos Aires to Quebec. In command was Captain Thomas O'Neil, with his wife and young son aboard. Some accounts say a blizzard and a windstorm were blowing and that the *Annie Maguire* turned off course for Quebec to seek shelter in Portland Harbor. But weather-bureau records show the weather on Christmas Eve that year was a balmy 49 degrees; seas were moderate; visibility was excellent; that a light rain and southerly breeze were coming off the sea. Whatever the conditions, the *Annie Maguire* hit the ledges by Portland Head Light so hard that the impact shook the lighthouse like an earthquake. Strout and his son, Joseph, raced for the family Christmas tree, rigged lights, and shone them on the still-filled sails and frantic crew of the *Annie Maguire*. The Strouts hurled a line aboard, which the crew fastened to the cross trees, while the Strouts made the end fast to the base of the lighthouse tower. They quickly rigged a bo'sun's chair and snatch block between wreck and light and the Strouts hauled the entire crew, the captain, his wife and son safely ashore. At daylight on Christmas morning, everyone could see the gaping hole in the *Annie Maguire* was so huge that the ship was a total loss. The tides poured into her holds; waves tore asunder her broken frame. So little was left of her that she was put up for auction on December 29 and fetched only $177.50. Before even those remnants could be salvaged, another storm on New Year's Day hit her again and her wreckage was strewn for miles.

There is an odd ending to the wreck of the *Annie Maguire*. Days before she hit the ledge, the sheriff had told Strout to keep an eye out for the *Annie Maguire* because American creditors were trying to attach the vessel for bad debts before she reached Quebec. So, on Christmas morning the sheriff arrived to serve attachment papers. He searched the sea chest for the ship's papers. The captain then discovered the satchel with all his and the ship's money was missing. He whispered his loss to his wife in frantic undertones. She calmed him and told him to shut up and pretend it had been lost in the wreck. She had the money and papers well hidden. Just before going overboard, she had ransacked the strong box, taken the cash, and put it inside her hat box. When she climbed into the bo'sun's chair, her hat box was in her lap.

In the winter storm of February 22, 1864, the almost-new iron steamship, *Bohemian*, out of Liverpool, hit Alden Rock near the Portland Head Light, slid off, and began to sink with 313 souls aboard. The captain called for "full ahead," hoping to ground her out, but he was too late. The sea poured in. The captain ordered his 218 passengers and ninety-five crewmen into the lifeboats. All boats were launched well except for the No. 2 lifeboat. A huge wave hit it, turned it over, and drowned nearly fifty people. Among the survivors was a little boy named John F. Fitzgerald. For years, people said the boy grew up to become the popular leader of the Boston Irish and his offspring became President John Fitzgerald Kennedy. It's a good story; the dates and ages fit, but it is untrue.

In 1914, the Boston-to-Portland steamer hit rocks near Portland Head Light in thick summer fog and blew her distress whistles full blast immediately. The revenue cutter _Androscoggin_ rushed out from Portland Harbor and hauled her off on the flood tide. Still another wreck at Portland Head Light involved a local fishing boat. In the fog on Tuesday evening, October 4, 1932, the schooner _Lochinvar_, with 40,000 pounds of fish aboard, owned by the Willard-Daggett Fish Co. of Portland and skippered by Captain Frank Doughty, a veteran of twenty-eight years experience, hit hard only 100 feet from where the _Annie Maguire_ had met her end. She sank fast. Her thirteen crewmen leaped into dories, but they had a hard time getting Captain Doughty to abandon ship and climb into his dory before _Lochinvar_ sank. For several days thereafter, the tops of her masts and sails showed above water until a new storm demolished her.

The beacon on the Portland Head Light went out on June 27, 1942, in World War II, lest it be a marker for German submarines, and the fog signal went silent July 5. The 200,000-candlepower beacon went out again just after midnight March 22, 1977, in a storm that devastated the Portland area.

Lights of Casco Bay

At night over Casco Bay and Portland Harbor you may see half a dozen lighthouses flashing their signals to the sea ... Portland Head Light, Two Lights at Cape Elizabeth, Halfway Rock Light, Spring Point Ledge Light, Ram Island Ledge Light, and perhaps the Portland Breakwater Light, though it is no longer a navigation aid.

A lot of Portland's story lies in those lights.

President John Quincy Adams appointed the first keeper of the Cape Elizabeth Light. When Elisha Jordan got the job in October 1828, he received a salary of $450 a year, along with strict instructions that it was a full-time job and that he "must make it a habit to be at home."

The monster storm of November 22, 1831 devastated Portland

Harbor, carrying away boats, wharves, and buildings, and flooding the city. The result was the construction of the Portland Breakwater, begun in 1836, but not finished until 1855. A light 25 feet high was illuminated August 1, 1855 by the first keeper, W.A. Dyer, who was paid $400 a year. Next to be built was Halfway Rock, put into operation by Captain John T. Stirling on August 15, 1871. He often rowed 11 miles back and forth to Portland for supplies. A quarter century passed before work was started on Spring Point Ledge Light, activated May 24, 1897 with William A. Lane as keeper.

The last light to be built in Portland Harbor was the Ram Island Ledge Light, where William C. Tapley first lit the kerosene lamp an hour before sunset on April 10, 1905.

Disaster and death and shipwreck, not forethought, triggered the building of each light. Portland was a shipping center for the big lumbering and rum trade during the 1780s, but it had no light and no way of paying for one since all such funds were funneled through the Massachusetts Legislature. In 1784, seventy-four owners and masters of vessels around Portland went to Boston seeking a lighthouse. They got nothing. The next year they tried again and got nothing. But, in 1787 disaster spoke louder than reason. On February 4, a Sunday, a 90-ton sloop bound for Massachusetts was wrecked on Bangs Island. Captain Moses Crane and a boy called John Deane were drowned; five others in crew clung to pieces of wreckage and saved themselves.

The *Cumberland Gazette*, Portland's only paper then, ran editorials asking, "Does not this unhappy accident evince the necessity of having a Lighthouse at the entrance of our harbor?" Portland citizens signed petitions demanding a light, but English officials of the Massachusetts Legislature responded with a mere $750. However, two months later, George Washington became president and the First Congress in New York City provided Portland with $1,500 to resume construction of Portland Head Light.

At Cape Elizabeth, where Two Lights stands, a rubblestone day marker was built. Mariners said it was not much help, but politicians thought it was quite enough—until disaster hit. The lumber sloop *Resolution* was wrecked there on October 24, 1811. Over the next fifteen years, more wrecks raised more public outcry for better lights. They were built, but wrecks kept on happening almost in the shadow of the lights. The 386-ton *Tasmania* was lost in 1857; the *Abigail* met her end the next year. Then the little schooner *Susan*; then the *Catharine Beals*; followed by the *Kate Aubrey*; and next the coal schooner *Australia*, in 1885. Many men and ships had to die first, but by 1900 Two Lights was finally well-equipped.

Before Halfway Rock Light was finished, the Bath-built brig *Samuel* was wrecked there in 1835. So many more followed her onto those treacherous hidden ledges that, by 1837, Captain John Smith of the U.S. Revenue Cutter Service urged his superiors in Washington to spend $300 to erect a marker. His plea fell on deaf bureaucratic ears. Over the next thirty-one years, uncounted wrecks followed. Then, in 1861, after a February storm, a ship's wreckage washed up on Jewell and Inner Green islands. The water was crowded with flotsam, but no survivors were found. The only clues were the letter on a medicine chest *Boadicea* ... a British bark that had cleared New Orleans December 2, 1860, bound for Glasgow, and hadn't been heard from since. Congress appropriated $50,000 in 1869, but the Halfway Rock Light did not get into operation until August 15, 1891.

Even by the time the Spring Point Ledge Light was built in 1897, it took shipwreck, death, and disaster to pry funds for lighthouses. The schooner *Nancy* hit this ledge in 1832, shattered her hull, and the sea poured in over her dangerous cargo of lime. The water and lime mixture caused fire and explosion. She burned to a hulk. The government responded by installing an inadequate spar buoy. It was of little help. The *Mazaltan, Seguin, Solomon Poole, Smith*, and untold others hit Halfway Rock.

Then came the savage gale of the equinox, March 20–21 in 1876, which destroyed dozens of vessels, among them the fine new bark *Harriet S. Jackson*, 393 tons. After six days of trying with numerous tugs, she was hauled off for rebuilding at the Dyer Yard in South Portland.

Wrecks and groundings continued. In 1891, seven steamship companies banded together and presented a joint petition to the Lighthouse Board in Washington. All seven lines served Portland. They said that between them they carried more than half a million passengers every year past Spring Point Ledge. They urged that a light and fog bell be installed without delay, but for years Congress refused to appropriate the needed $45,000. By 1895, money was earmarked and the Spring Ledge Light shone at last on May 24, 1897.

Even after all this, it took more disasters to get a light for Ram Island Ledge. This danger was marked only by a wooden triangle, which storms washed away on at least three occasions. When the 400-ton steamer *California* pulled out from Grand Truck Wharf in Portland just before midnight February 24, 1900, she had twenty-one passengers and $300,000 worth of freight aboard. She hit Ram Island Ledge and it was six weeks before the damaged vessel was pulled off. Her accident made headline news and demands for a light became so strong that Congress earmarked $166,000. However, since the ledge on which the light tower was to be built was under water 70 percent of the time, work was slow to start. Disaster struck again when the three-masted *Glenrosa*, heavily laden with 850 tons of coal for the S.D. Warren Co., tried to enter Portland Harbor in dense fog. She was stripped by scavengers, then broke to pieces where she lay. Shortly thereafter, a fishing schooner, *Cora & Lillian*, met the same fate on the same ledge. After construction was begun, another disaster struck. This time the lime carrier *Leona*, out of Rockland, hit the ledge. The crew abandoned ship in a brutally cold January storm at 3 a.m. Visibility was nil. They rowed for four hours in the dory, not knowing where they were headed, in freezing, stormy darkness. They fired flares. At dawn the Ram Island work crew, sheltered within their shack nearby, spotted the signal and rescued the exhausted rowers. Three months later, an hour before sunset April 10, 1905, the Ram Island Light was officially lighted.

The famous mark, the lightship *Portland*, now an inhuman automated buoy anchored off the entrance to Portland harbor, went on station on March 7, 1903, during the administration of President Theodore Roosevelt. Her name was then *Cape Elizabeth* and did not change to *Portland* for several years. In the early days, there was no communication with land and the only news came when a passing fisherman would draw alongside and throw an old newspaper on deck. Mail arrived only when the tenders would come out to bring water or coal for the lightship. Edward L. Eaton, who served fifteen years on the old lightship, reported:

> "She was a terrible roller" and would shiver and shake in a storm. The ship was anchored in 150 feet of water and pitched and rolled, fighting the cables. "We broke away twice—once on February 14, 1912. The big combers hit us like a ton of bricks. One sea swept the vessel from stem to stern and took everything with it. We steamed ahead all the time and took what pressure we could off the chain; but she was dancing around so and surging back and forth that somehow the anchor chain shackles unshipped. We worked her into Portland and they were some surprised to see us come sailing up the harbor. We got a new anchor and chain and went back again.
>
> "Next time we went adrift was in a fog mull. The old 12-inch fog whistle had been hammering away for twenty-four hours. I was asleep when I was awakened by a motion, and, by johnny, we were adrift. We made soundings and decided we had plenty of water under us and anchored. When daylight came and the fog lifted, scores of fishing vessels were all around us. We were anchored near Cashes Ledge.

"Well, to see a lightship anchored on Cashes with the name *Port-land* on her sides had the old skippers guessing. One old feller in a vessel out of Gloucester stood down to us and shouted, "'Where in the hell am I?' We had twenty-five vessels all around us. I saw one man run below, come back on deck with a chart, lay it on top of the cabin, look at the chart, look up at the lightship."

Thirteen men lived aboard the old lightship, but the pounding of the giant seas took their toll and the old wooden ship had to go. She was replaced with a steel-hulled vessel. She, too, had to go and was replaced by an unmanned light buoy.

In recent years, with almost all the state, city, and federal money spent on highways and airports, it is easy to forget what a busy port Portland has been during the past hundred years. Here are a few figures to put a surprising perspective on Casco Bay and to suggest that this huge harbor, in a fuel crunch, may again become a hub of coastal and international trade.

In 1872, sixty-five trains a day were arriving and departing from the waterfront in Portland. Twice a week, steamers left for New York, and more often for Boston. Ships came and went to Europe regularly. In 1874, 6 million feet of lumber left Portland for the West Indies alone, and on return the ships brought sugar and molasses for Portland's huge rum industry. Along Commercial Street alone, thirty lumber companies flourished. For five months a year, Portland was the winter port for Montreal. The grain elevator on the waterfront had a capacity of 200,000 bushels and the adjacent warehouses could store more than 450,000 bushels of wheat. In 1899, 22 million bushels of Canadian and Midwest wheat poured into Portland and 13 million of them left by ship for Europe. Portland was a human gateway to America. In 1913, more than 26,400 aliens came through immigration on the Portland waterfront. As recently as the mid-1970s, almost five hundred oil tankers a year unloaded here.

While this vital water commerce was going on, Portland harbor became the third most heavily fortified harbor in the United States, dotted with island forts and thousands of troops traveling back and forth to the islands from the waterfront. The lovely islands of Casco Bay were in their heyday summer resorts, with scores of hotels and boarding houses catering to tens of thousands of waterborne visitors each month.

Lighthouses in Casco Bay were as essential as traffic lights are to a city today.

How the Lights Burn

Automation and electricity run most lights today and, therefore, the human bond between ship and lighthouse, seaman and light-keeper is gone. But how did those men and women, frequently far beyond middle age, keep the lights burning before automation and electricity? Ships without loran, radio, radar, global-positioning equipment, or telephones, often without an engine, depended more than we can realize today on lightkeepers and their lamps.

At the beginning, the lighthouse lamp was simply a fire of wood or pitch, blazing in a brazier atop a tower. Later, the fire was fueled by coal, which had to be hauled by hand in small buckets from ground level to tower top. When the first light on the New England coast was lit in 1716, in Boston Harbor, the keeper lit tallow candles. Fifty years later keepers were using spider lamps fueled with whale oil or fish oil, later with lard. Groups of lamps hung together in the tower and the stench was strong.

Maine lightkeepers used these oils at Portland Head (1791), Seguin (1795), Whitehead (1807), Franklin Light (1807), West Quoddy Head (1808), and Boone Island (1812). About 1812, sperm oil in an Argand lamp, newly equipped with magnifiers and parabolic reflectors, began to come into use, but such labor-savers were a long time reaching the Maine coast.

The French were far ahead of us. In France, Augustin Fresnel had invented, and the French government had installed, Fresnel lenses and prisms, which brought new brilliancy and more distance to the beam. They were not installed in all U.S. lighthouses until 1850, thirty years after France; but the basic fuel for the light remained sperm oil (until the price got too high because of the scarcity of whales). Then lard and various fish oils were tried and, finally, by 1880, kerosene. A few lights soon after 1900 got electric power, but not until the 1930s was electricity universal among lighthouses in Maine. After World War II, the automation of Maine lighthouses slowly spread, often opposed by coastal seamen, because when men no longer manned the light, there was no longer a lifesaving service. Today there are no manned lighthouses in Maine.

Fog Signals

In fog, no light could be seen and sound became the guide for seamen. The first fog signal, like the first light, was installed in Boston Harbor. In 1719, cannons were fired to alert the shore that a ship was creeping into the harbor. Bells were rung by hand to reply.

Their sound was feeble, even when bells weighing four thousand pounds were struck by primitive machinery. By 1851, trumpets, sounded by compressed air, were tried. They were somewhat better than bells, but mariners complained they were too hard to hear. Steam whistles were tried at West Quoddy Head Light and at Cape Elizabeth Light in 1855, the first installations of this kind in the U.S. The sound was louder, but it took time to generate the steam and there might be no signal until hours after fog filled a harbor approach. Finally, the air diaphone horn, powered by compressed air, electricity, or steam, was developed and refined until foghorns, too, were automated, triggered into action by the approach of fog and governed by timing devices, so that horns, like lights, had their own identifiable characteristics.

11

Favorite Lights
Heroic Keepers

Behind every lighthouse along the coast there is a story. Almost every seaman has his personal favorites. I have chosen a few of mine. Some because the stories involve a breed of men and women gone forever from our coast; some because I have developed a special love for particular lights that have proved special friends in need to me. I marvel at their beauty or solitude or plain ability to stand there, take punishment, and render service against the worst the wind and ocean can mete out.

Boon Island Light

For twenty-seven long years, stretching from the 1880s to World War I, Captain William W. Williams was the keeper of Boon Island Light, 9 miles out from York Beach. A light has stood here since 1799, on one of the smallest but most battered ledges off Maine, just 700 feet long and not 14 feet above sea level.

For fifty-five stormy years, until 1854, the early keepers had nothing but a hole in the hard ground to crawl into for safety in storms. None could stand the duty for twenty-seven years as Williams did. He was past ninety in 1934, when he told some of his memories to a younger light keeper, Robert L. Sterling. "There were days when I first went on station," said Williams, "that I could not get away from the idea I was locked up in a cell. All we had was a little stone house and a rubblestone tower. When rough weather came, seas swept the ledge clean. I was always thinking what I would do to save my life should the whole station be washed away."

Carrier pigeons carried news and messages to the mainland. The ledge had no natural soil. Williams brought out dirt in buckets to grow a few vegetables and flowers. His wife shared the hard life with him. Together, they rescued shipwrecked crews from December storms. When six men and a fourteen-year-old Negro boy were en-cased in ice, frozen to the thwarts, Mrs. Williams nursed them back to life. "Boon Island derived its name," said Williams, "from a 'boon,' or barrel of provisions placed on the rock for more than fifty years, from 1800 to 1854, by fishermen from York, for the use of ship-wrecked sailors."

No such "boon" awaited the shipwrecked crew of the *Nottingham Galley*, which broke up here in 1710. As storms raged over the ledge for weeks, the crew was dying of exposure and starvation. When one died, the others, to keep alive, fell to cannibalism and ate their ship-mate. Kenneth Roberts wrote a gripping and gruesome novel about the incident.

A heroic and tragic legend persists about one keeper of the Boon Island light in the middle of the last century and his bride of just a few months. The keeper fell ill and died. That night a great storm lashed the ledge. The frantic young widow, alone with the body of her dead husband, climbed the tower and kept the lights shining. In free moments, she'd climb down to stand watch over her dead lover. Night after night the storm continued and the widow climbed between lights and lover. The young widow finally lost her reason and the light failed. Next day the storm abated and fishermen came out to see why the light had gone out. They found the demented, mad girl grieving, wandering the rocks, and took her ashore to York.

Seguin Light

The highest light in the state of Maine, the beacon at Seguin flashes into the night at 180 feet above sea level. This is not because the tower itself is so high, but because Seguin, a giant 22-acre rock, rises 150 feet out of the sea at the mouth of the Kennebec River.

According to one of the endless "pidgin English" Indian stories, Seguin got its name from the words an early Indian guide spoke to an early settler as he piloted him to the mouth of the Kennebec, "Sea-go-in here," said the Indian, supposedly—from which "Seguin" derives.

A more likely story to those who've sailed off Seguin in foul weather is that it derives from the Indian word "sutquin," which means "sea vomits." This is an accurate description when the current from the Kennebec crosses the incoming tide and wind from the ocean. Seguin can be a violent passage, made more disturbing by a magnetic phenomenon that sends a ship's compass spinning.

In 1796, the first keeper of Seguin Light came onto the rock. He was an unusual man and before long an unhappy one. He was Count John Polerecsky, whose first home had been in Alsace. He voyaged to the New World, fought in the American Revolution, and became Major John Polersky of Pownalboro, Maine. As a reward for his military service, he was named the first keeper of Seguin. A bitter reward it turned out to be. Soon Polersky was writing letters of complaint to his supervisors, detailing his desperate living conditions and abysmal pay, and the fact that he was marooned on the island for months at a time. Death relieved him of his troubles before his earthly superiors did.

Three Seguin Lights were demolished by weather before Congress, in 1857, authorized a 53-foot stone tower at a cost of $35,000. Improved and automated, it stands now.

Frank E. Bracey, who'd endured five years rolling and pitching aboard the old lightship *Portland* in the 1920s, became keeper of Seguin in 1926. He spent five years on the rock before transfer to the quieter life at the Eagle Island Light in Penobscot Bay. But Bracey never could get the sound of Seguin's foghorn out of his head.

"That Seguin is the foggiest spot in America, I swear. The horn blew weeks, even months, on end, and it's among the most powerful along the coast. I've seen seagulls flying by get knocked down by the concussion of the sound waves."

Bracey boasted that the Seguin Light had been seen 42 miles away by the Boston-to-Maine boat and that the blast of its fog horn had been heard in Bath, 14 miles away.

Pemaquid Light

This is my home light and so my favorite. Once we have Pemaquid Light in sight, *Steer Clear* can sense her mooring nearby in New Harbor and heads to her stable.

Pemaquid Light is on the mainland, a sweet and luxurious post compared to Seguin or Boon Island lights. And it is newer, built in 1827 for $4,000. Isaac Dunham from Bath, the first keeper, even took up farming on the side. His successor, Nathaniel Gamage, paid Dunham more than $1,000—a big sum then—for his barns. Politics cost Gamage his job in 1841, when newly elected President Benjamin Harrison gave the Pemaquid job and the farm to J.P. Means. Poor Gamage could never collect from Means, despite appeals to President Harrison, then after Harrison's death to President Tyler. In desperation, Gamage tried to get back his job at the light so he could reclaim the farms that went with it. He never got either.

Fourteen men lost their lives by Pemaquid Light on September 16, 1903, aboard the fishing schooner *George F. Edmunds*, skippered by Captain Willard Poole.

The light is automated now. The handsome farm is a parking lot. The keeper's house was rented to strangers. In recent years, friends of ours have lived in and painted from the keeper's house. Now it has been turned into a fine fishermen's museum, a project of local fishing families, and filled with the gear used by local fishermen in generations past.

Monhegan Light

Thomas B. Seavey lit the Monhegan Light for the first time on July 2, 1824 and more males succeeded him. Keeping the light is thought of as a man's job—but not always on Monhegan. A woman, Betty Morrow Humphrey, kept the Monhegan Light burning for eighteen years, including the years of the Civil War, when raiders were sinking ships close to Monhegan.

Betty Humphrey's husband, John F. Humphrey, became keeper in March 1861, two weeks before the outbreak of the Civil War. His two sons immediately enlisted and Humphrey took ill and died in December. From Christmas of 1861 until 1880, the dauntless Betty served as official keeper of Monhegan Light. During her tenure, the government cut her pay from $820 a year to $700.

Besides running the light, Betty Humphrey also took over operation of the fog signal, separately housed on Manana Island, almost half a mile distant across the harbor. The first fog signal was installed in 1854, but on a breezy day nobody at sea could hear it, so in 1870, a Daboll trumpet was tried, without success. Then a steam whistle was tried and it, too, could not be heard. Finally, a firs-class, very loud, new Daboll trumpet was relocated over on Manana Island and a telegraph line was run across the harbor. When Betty Humphrey, high in her lighthouse atop Monhegan, saw fog rolling in far at sea, she pushed a button. That rang a loud electric gong in the bedroom of fog signal keeper Frank Adams on Manana, who would leap from bed and start his trumpet sounding.

When Betty Humphrey retired, men again took over the job; first Sidney Studley, then William Stanley, who ran the light for nineteen years, from 1883 to 1902.

The early keepers burned oil from sperm whales to keep the Monhegan light burning. When that grew too expensive, the switch was made to lard oil. Did the smell permeate the tower? Did the keepers grow accustomed to the reek? How often did they curse as they hauled heavy containers up the endless circular stairs? In 1912, the great modernization was made—a change to incandescent oil vapor. The early fog signal over on Manana was huge—a 2,500-pound bell that was struck by hand in foul weather until, in 1870, an engine was installed to operate the first 10-inch Daboll trumpet. And in the same year of 1912 that the light got incandescent oil vapor, the fog trumpet was replaced by an air siren. Keeper followed keeper—Pierce, Wallace, Orne, Handley, Dyer, Woodward, Hutchins, Robinson, Foss, and Wilson B. Carter.

Today the automated light sends out a 170,000-candlepower beam. The diaphragm horn explodes with two terrific blasts every minute. Despite automation, the indispensable Monhegan Light can still fail. It did, just after midnight during an icy gale on February 2, 1981. Coast Guardsmen William Spencer and Mark Wilson, on duty across the harbor on Manana, got the bad news. They launched their 16-foot pea pod and outboard motor into the teeth of the gale and set off to repair the light. Half way across, their outboard quit, their boat capsized, and the 40-knot winds lashed waves through the narrow harbor and swept the little boat and two men onto an exposed ledge. They scrambled through the storm, drenched and bitter cold. The tide was rising and could submerge the ledge. On their portable VHF radio they called the Coast Guardsmen back at the fog station, who relayed their plea for help to the Coast Guard in Boothbay Harbor, 15 miles away—a risky, many-hour trip in a February gale. On Monhegan, Sherman Stanley and harbormaster Steve Rollins were awakened from sleep about 3 a.m. by a call from the Coast Guard asking if they could rescue the stranded men. Stanley and Rollins went out into the black, storming night, with winds reaching 50 miles-per-hour. The seas were too rough for an outboard, so Stanley and Rollins rowed the 300 yards in a small skiff and took off the half-frozen Coast Guardsmen.

Owls Head Light
Heading east after passing through Muscle Ridge Shoals, the Owls Head Light signals the entrance to one of Maine's best cruising grounds—Penobscot Bay.

Owls Head is one of the most handsome of all the Maine lights. Rising 100 feet above the water, from atop a tree-studded high cliff, it is a joyful landmark. Its horn has been our guide poking through dense fog across West Penobscot Bay. After saluting the light for many years with a toot of our horn, we finally went ashore, met the keeper, and admired the immaculate house, light, and surroundings.

The Thomaston-Rockland lime trade triggered the building of Owls Head Light. When Rockland lime sold for a dollar a barrel, after the Revolutionary War, schooners began carrying lime to Europe and returned laden with salt for Maine fishing boats. Fog and storm wrecked many when they were within only a few miles of home. The need for a light became more urgent when the steamer *Maine* began making Owls Head a regular stop. The light was built and, in September 1825, Keeper Isaac Stearns lit the light for the first time.

In the more than 156 years since Stearns lit the light, Owls Head has saved scores of ships from disaster. But not all. Dozens of dire wrecks have marked the rugged ledges of the outlying islands and there are many tales of shipwrecks.

One of the weirdest occurred in the terrible gale of December 22, 1850, when five ships were lost along the 8-mile stretch between Owls Head and Spruce Head. One of those was a small coasting schooner at anchor in nearby Rockland harbor, with the mate, his bride-to-be, and one deckhand aboard, all asleep. Near midnight, the raging storm snapped her anchor lines and the schooner blew out of Rockland toward Owls Head, was smashed on ledges, but did not sink. Water poured into the hold, but the vessel held fast to the ledges. The mate, his bride-to-be, and the deckhand pulled heavy blankets on deck and sought shelter under them; but coats of ice built up as each wave swept across them. Ice soon encased the three. The deckhand used a knife and his fists to keep open a breathing hole. By 6 a.m., he decided he could get ashore for help. He struggled across the wave-lashed, iced ledges and got half way to the lights shining from the keeper's house before collapsing on the dirt road. His body was seen from the kitchen. He was rushed to the warm house, where he told the keeper, William Masters, of the ice-enclosed bodies still on deck. A rescue party brought the bodies back to the house, thinking they were frozen dead; but Masters poured water over the ice, slowly increasing the water temperature. First the ice fell off from the hands and legs of the man and woman. As it melted from their bodies, the rescue party massaged the frozen limbs. After an hour, both the girl and the mate were revived to consciousness. Weeks later, they were able to walk. Six months later, in June, they were married, but the deckhand never fully recovered.

Brutality laid its early scar on Owls Head, too. The high ground near the light had been fought over by settlers and Indians for many years. On June 7, 1757, thirty Indian war canoes landed. In the battle that followed, Captain Joseph Cox reversed the usual story; he scalped two of the Penobscot Indians.

Mt. Desert Rock Light

It can be a long, long haul from Owls Head to Mt. Desert Rock, most remote of all Maine lighthouses. Between the two are dozens of lighthouses, each with its own beauty, romance and—above all—usefulness, to boats at sea. There is not room here to tell all their stories. For lighthouse buffs who want more, I suggest *The Lighthouses of New England* by Edward Rowe Snow and *Lighthouses of Maine* by Robert T. Sterling, as good starters; and *Lighthouses of Casco Bay* by Peter Dow Bachelder. Town libraries often have local histories giving great detail on the lights of their slice of coast.

Mt. Desert Rock Light is a hard, remote lonesome world and getting to it is not easy. It lies 26 miles out from the mainland, a speck in the fierce Atlantic. The might of the ocean hitting this rock for thousands of years is difficult to conceive. According to federal records, a mammoth stone 18 feet long, 14 feet wide, and 6 feet thick, weighing 57 tons, was hurled from its place in a storm of 1842. In another storm, a 75-ton boulder was moved 60 feet by the gigantic waves. This is not a place keepers stayed long and today the light runs by remote control.

The first known white man sailed by here in late May 1524, the Italian, Giovanni da Verrazano. The light was built more three hundred years later, in 1830. A more difficult, dangerous construction job is hard to name. Men and materials not only had to be hauled 26 miles from the nearest mainland, but, once here, getting the men and materials ashore was a terrible challenge. The rock is barely a half acre; its high point is barely 11 feet above the waves on a calm day and awash or submerged in bad weather. Yet, for almost 150 years, men (and for a while, women) lived here, kept the light, and saved lives in peril.

In 1880, the *Helen and Mary*, out of Halifax, with a deckload of timber and a cargo hold of granite, foundered off here. Captain Jared Parker, after putting his wife, baby, and crew into the first lifeboat, climbed into the second boat with first mate Nelson White. It capsized in the wake of the sinking schooner. When White surfaced, he saw the first boat floating, bottom up, and no sign of any human. White reached some floating wreckage and climbed on it. Then he spotted a bundle of yellow oilskins and grabbed it. Inside was the infant baby of the captain's wife, who was White's sister. White and the infant lasted the day and the night in violent surf. By the next morning, the wild ocean had calmed. The gale had carried the wreckage, to which White clung with the infant in oilskins strapped to his chest, to within 10 miles of the coast. At noon, they were sighted and rescued by the lighthouse tender *Iris*. No others survived.

An ocean tug, *Astral*, towing a big barge, met a strange fate here in a dreadful storm on December 9, 1902. The *Astral* hit hard at five in the morning. Her frantic signal on her whistles was heard by an assistant keeper; but, until the tide went down, there was no possible way the lighthouse keepers could rescue the crew because mountainous, icy seas forbade the launching of any boat. At low tide, the keepers dragged rescue lines to the outer point. From there, they hurled a line aboard and brought seventeen men ashore, one by one. The eighteenth man froze to death. For six days, the keepers and their wives nursed the seventeen injured back to life.

But the barge they towed was still out there. The crew aboard the barge had no idea what had happened to their tug. They could not see it. Ice more than a foot thick blocked the windows of their pilothouse. Sea vapor was so dense that visibility was less than 25 feet. The crew thought the tug had anchored to weather it out. So they lay on the barge from Tuesday to Thursday, held from drifting by a hawser more than 2400 feet long, still tied to the wrecked tug. The length of the hawser allowed the barge to be blown into the lee of Mt. Desert Rock, giving them a little protection from the worst of the storm.

By Thursday, the wind shifted to the south. The barge crew cut the cable, hoisted sail, and were picked up 40 miles down the coast, off Rockland. Once ashore, the captain of the barge called his home office at Standard Oil Co. in New York, which sent a wrecking crew to tow off the remnants of the tug and take ashore the seventeen crew members.

Matinicus Rock Light

The Audubon Society, on calm summer days, runs special boat trips for members to see the spectacular puffins on Matinicus Rock. The trip is memorable and unforgettable for birdwatchers, who can see the colorful, parrot-like puffins strutting and nesting in the volcanic rock and marvel at the huge colonies of Arctic terns, guillemots, and gulls that call this outpost home.

But the Rock carries its tales of tragedy, violent storms, heroism, and amazing human endurance through fearful isolation and terror.

The Rock is a 32-acre volcanic outcrop, barren and vulnerable, 25 miles out to sea from Rockland. The nearest human habitation is 6 miles away, on Matinicus Island. In a running sea, there is no safe way to land a boat here.

More than 154 years ago, on June 26, 1827, John A. Shaw got the job of first keeper of Matinicus Rock Light by appointment of President John Quincy Adams, at a salary of $450 a year. Shaw and his wife moved into the wooden structures that were to serve them, perilously, as home and lighthouse. The North Atlantic seas and gales made short work of those wooden buildings. All that remains to tell of what they endured are the laconic one-line entries from a logbook kept by Shaw, now in the federal archives:

31 Oct. 1829—A savere gail Broak over Rock

9 Nov 1829—A bad storme

24 Nov—A man of war pased hear to Day

25 Jan 1830—A vilant Snow Storm

9 Feb—Trim and set up All night

23 May—The keeper very sick

June—The keeper is Beter and he aught to be.

Keeper Shaw first lit the light on this godforsaken rock when he was sixty-five. He died of sickness in 1831, aged sixty-nine.

Abbie Burgess will forever be one of the great heroines of seafaring Maine. She came to the Rock as a fourteen-year-old girl in the springtime of 1853, when her father, Samuel Burgess, was named keeper. Abbie was later to marry on the Rock, bear children on the Rock, bury one infant there, and tend the light in the direst of times. Half a century after she died in 1892, seacoast historian Edward Rowe Snow found a note she had written: "I wonder if the care, of the lighthouse will follow my soul after it has left this worn out body. If ever I have a gravestone, I would like it to be in the form of a lighthouse or beacon." In 1946, historian Snow arranged for a replica of the Matinicus Rock Light to be placed on the grave of Abbie Burgess at Spruce Head, Maine, where she had been buried in 1892.

Here in brief is the story of Abbie Burgess and her courage and tenacity in single-handedly keeping the light burning on this barren rock 600 yards long, 200 yards wide, and 25 miles at sea.

At fourteen, Abbie became her father's helper. Mrs. Burgess was an invalid, mostly bed-ridden. Abbie had two younger sisters and took care of them, too. Her father also taught Abbie how to care for the light. She spent her free hours reading the old logbooks of earlier keepers and their stories of the storms they had endured. When she was seventeen, Abbie got her first test. In January 1856, her father took Abbie aside and told her that he had to make an emergency trip to Rockland for food and supplies to last through the winter. The supply boat, he said, had failed to come with replenishments in September, as scheduled. So while the weather was good, he would leave the light and the family in her care, while he sailed 26 miles to Rockland for supplies and 26 miles back. But storms stopped him from getting back for almost four weeks.

I quote now from Abbie's story:

> For a month no landing could be effected on the Rock ... we were without the assistance of any male of our family. Though at times greatly exhausted from my labors, not once did the lights fail. Under God I was able to perform all my accustomed duties as well as my father's ... The waves destroyed the old dwelling and swept over the Rock ... The sea is never still and its roar shuts out every other sound, even drowning our voices.

The next winter, her father was on another trip to Rockland and again was cut off for twenty-one days by storms. Again, Abbie was alone on the Rock, feeding herself, her invalid mother, and her young sisters on a diet of one cup of corn meal a day. In addition, the teenage girl had kept the twenty-three wicks in the lights burning, feeding them with thinned-out lard oil through the wild storms.

Almost thirty-five years later she wrote: "Many nights I tended the lights and then could not sleep the rest of the night, thinking nervously what might happen if the lights should fail ... When I dream of the old lamps on Matinicus Rock, I am always hurrying to light the lamps before sunset ..."

Burgess lost his job. It was a political appointment. In 1861, after Abraham Lincoln was elected president, Burgess was fired and John Grant was named to replace him; but Abbie stayed on the Rock with the Grant family, to show them the ropes of running the station. The son of the keeper was attracted to the 22-year-old Abbie. Later that year, Isaac H. Grant and Abbie were married and four children were born to them on the Rock.

An infant, two-year-old Bessie Grant, is buried on the Rock, the only person ever buried there. The little grave was discovered almost twenty years ago by Harriet Buchheister, wife of the president of the National Audubon Society, who went often to the Rock to see the puffin colony there.

Little Bessie died suddenly, almost 120 years ago. The weather was too severe to take her body to the mainland, so the Grants scraped together buckets of scarce soil on the Rock, lugged the dirt to the top of a cliff, away from the waves, and, between two sheltering slabs of weathered granite, made a grave. Remnants of a small wooden cross were found by Mrs. Buchheister. Coast Guardsmen stationed on the Rock forty years ago helped shore up the grave with brick and mortar to stop further erosion. George R. Perry of Rockland carved a little headstone marker which was taken out to the Rock.

Abbie Burgess Grant, her husband, and their children left the Rock in 1875, but the Grants were not finished with lighthouses. Abbie and Isaac went as keepers of the White Head Light, near Spruce Head and over 20 miles closer to shore than Matinicus; but old Captain John Grant stayed on the Rock until 1890. The man who succeeded him as keeper was his grandson, William G. Grant.

Storms lash still at this barren volcanic rock. During the 1970s, lobstermen 6 miles distant on Matinicus Island sent over a Christmas tree to the men on the treeless Rock. At Christmas, Albert Bunker and his wife organized "bakes" to supply pies, breads, cookies, candies to the men on the Rock who, all year long, kept a weather eye on lobstermen. One year the seas were too rough to land a Christmas tree, so the boat fired off a line from a rescue gun. The men on the Rock grabbed the line and hauled ashore their Christmas tree through the towering seas. Today, the lighthouse at Matinicus Rock is automated and maintained by the Coast Guard.

These stories of a few Maine lighthouse keepers have recounted the highlights of storm, disaster, and shipwreck. But a keeper's job has long stretches of routine work, days of gorgeous weather, moments of supreme happiness, and long hours of boredom. Keepers turned often to time-passing hobbies; to reading, writing, music, and attempts at gardening, even farming.

A journalist, Gustav Kobbe, writing in the 1890s in *The Century Magazine*, told of a visit to Matinicus Rock Light and the cow he found there.

> The keeper owns the only quadruped on the rock—a cow. This valuable beast is called Daisy. She was brought over from Matinicus Island on a small boat and a short distance from the shore, the boat was tipped so far over to one side that Daisy lost her balance and fell into the water where she was left to swim ashore. I have often seen her standing upon that mass of barren granite, the only living thing in view, the wind furrowing up her hide. She would gaze out at the waste of wild waters with a driven, lonely look, the pathos of which was almost human ... Often the cow looks over in the direction of

Matinicus Island and moos pathetically ... She formerly found some companionship in a rabbit, with which she was accustomed to play at dusk, but the rabbit died.

The bane of every keeper's life was polishing the brasswork; and the cussedness of having it all shined, only to have the fog roll in and spoil it.

Fred Morong, born Down East in Lubec in 1883, became a keeper and hated the brasswork with a vengeance. He wrote a poem about this hated chore of keepers. Here are a few verses from it:

> O' what is the bane of a lightkeeper's life
> That causes him worry, struggle and strife,
> That makes him use cuss words, and beat at his wife?
>   It's Brasswork.
>
> What makes him look ghastly, consumptive and thin,
> What robs him of health, vigor and vim,
> And causes despair and drives him to sin?
>   It's Brasswork.
>
> The devil himself could never invent
> A material causing more world-wide lament
> And in Uncle Sam's service about ninety percent
>   Is Brasswork.
>
> The lamp in the tower, reflector and shade,
> The tools and accessories pass in parade.
> As a matter of fact the whole outfit is made
>   Of Brasswork
>
> The machinery, clockwork, fog-signal bell,
> The coal hods, the dustpans, the pump in the well.
> Now I'll leave it to you, mates, if this isn't-well
>   Brasswork
>
> I dig, scrub and polish, and work with a might,
> And just when I get it all shining and bright,
> In comes the fog, like a thief in the night;
>   Good-by Brasswork
> And when I have polished until I am cold
> And I'm taken aloft to the Heavenly fold
> Will my harp and my crown be made of pure gold?
>   No, Brasswork.

12

Damariscove Island
Shelter and Sanctuary

If you enjoy going to extremes, leaping quickly from present-day Vacationland to frontier Maine 1581, spend a day in Boothbay Harbor at the peak of summer, and at nightfall sail out to Damariscove Island and anchor there. The contrast is superb, with the best of opposite worlds only an hour apart.

In summertime Boothbay Harbor, not a parking spot is empty. Traffic creeps as drivers hunt for 20 empty feet in which to leave their car. Summer business booms in this hilly, handsome harbor town. Since early morning, tourists have been swarming from cars and buses, some headed for salt breezes on the decks of sightseeing boats, some went off to fish from party boats, some prowled the shops. All day, sidewalks have overflowed with vacationers licking ice cream cones, snapping pictures of fishing boats, nursing sunburns, buying souvenirs and postcards with lobster motifs. Now, with darkness falling, Fisherman's Wharf, Jordan's, Rocktide, The Tugboat Inn, The Thistle, dozens of restaurants, bars, and pizza parlors shine brightly with neon lights. The sounds of music throb across the harbor.

Out in the harbor, cabin lights shine from cruising boats resting here for a night or two on their way Down East. Dinghies visit back and forth. Voices from sailors relaxing on decks come loud and clear across the water. Youngsters in outboards kick up an unwanted and illegal wake as they speed on missions of love or party. The Catholic church shines serene and handsome, bathed in floodlights on the eastern shore. The scene is happy, lively, noisy, frenetic, the essence of a Maine summer resort in the happy throes of tourism.

Leave all this behind. Sail out as I often do, slow and easy on the night breeze, past Tumbler and Mouse and Squirrel islands, leave Ram Island Light to the east and the Cuckolds to the west, sail by Fisherman's Island, and 6 miles from downtown Boothbay, slip past the swells of The Motions and drop anchor in the darkness of deserted Damariscove.

This is where America began, four hundred years ago. Long before the famed early colonists set foot at Popham, Jamestown, or Plymouth, nameless seamen from England and Europe anchored in this cove, dried and salted fish on this island, cooked supper, and passed the rum on this rocky shore.

But on this night, not a soul lives on Damariscove, except perhaps the ghost of a headless man and his barking dog, walking the lonely shore. Their legend lives and will be told. On a lucky night, yours may be the only craft here; but four hundred years ago, scores of fishing boats and crews from England, France, Spain, and Holland sheltered here. Their shouts, their motley of languages, echoed between these lonely ledges. On one night when we anchored in the snug harbor at Damariscove Island, I wrote in the ship's log:

> Black night has fallen, the wind has dropped. The sea is so flat calm that the stars shine back up from the ocean as well as down from heaven. The only night noises are the laugh of a loon, eerie and primeval in the darkness of a deserted island, and the sound of small waves lapping on the shore and the tide gurgling among the boulders. It is warm. I lean over the side of the boat and run a hand through the black sea. The water comes alive with flashes of fire, the miracle: of phosphorescence. Thousands of years ago, thousands of miles away, the Romans gave a beautiful name to these tiny creatures of the sea who cause this light to shine. The name is *notilucci*—lights of the night.

The *Mayflower* sailed into this harbor of Damariscove. Long before she, or her namesake, carried 102 pilgrims into Plymouth, *Mayflower* was a fish boat and this harbor is where she loaded cod. The log of the *Mayflower* during her pilgrims' voyage records that she stopped here, "to take some coddes before sailing on to Maffachufeets Bay" in 1620.

The second winter after they landed at Plymouth, the Pilgrim fathers were threatened with starvation. Edward Winslow sailed from Plymouth to Damariscove to seek food from this flourishing colony of fishermen on this little-known island.

"It was about the end of May 1622," Winslow wrote, "at which time our store of victuals was wholly spent, having lived long before with bare and short allowance." So Winslow sailed here, set his anchor, and asked for food at Damariscove. He wrote: "I found kind entertainment and good respect, with a willingness to supply our wants; and they would not take any bills for same, but did what they could for us freely." Winslow reported in 1622, "there were thirty ships of sail" in the harbor when he came in to Damariscove, all taking on loads of dried fish for markets in Europe.

Damariscove Island proved a safe haven from Indian attacks. In 1675, the Indians staged widespread attacks on white settlements all along the Maine coast. More than two hundred settlers from Sheepscot, Damariscotta, Arrowsic, Pemaquid, and Newagen fled their burning homes, took to their boats, and sought refuge on Damariscove Island, 6 miles at sea.

The island is only 2 miles long, not more than a quarter mile wide, and pinched to a narrow waist in the middle, yet three hundred refugees, fleeing without provisions of any kind, were able to find food and shelter enough from the little colony that had been long established here.

Now, centuries later, we were alone out here, refugees of a kind from the midsummer invasion of Boothbay Harbor. We went below on *Steer Clear* and slept in our bunks with a feeling of being strange intruders into a heroic past. We'd sailed only 6 miles out from vacationing America and dropped our 20th-century Danforth high-tensile anchor deep in the same mud where killick stone anchors had held fishing boats of early settlers almost four hundred years before. But we slept soundly. Soon after daybreak we loaded the dog into the dinghy and went ashore to explore.

The remnant of an old Coast Guard station, built in 1897 and abandoned in 1959, stands dilapidated and vandalized. During its time as a lifesaving station, they averaged twenty-five rescues a year. In World War II, they installed listening devices to detect German submarines that surfaced to recharge their batteries at night. When the lonely Coast Guardsmen heard such sounds, they radioed Brunswick Naval Air Station to send out attack planes.

Far up the little harbor are a couple of rough shacks used by lobstermen to store gear or to shelter in overnight during a storm. John W. Sargent was the last man to live and fish full time out here. He spent many years on Damariscove, but they ended in tragedy. His child drowned here, and twenty-five years later, in 1976, Sargent's own body was found washed up on the shore near the spot where he kept his boat. Someone found his hat later and nailed it over the door of his one-room camp.

On high ground further inland are cellar holes of granite; in fields beyond, the rusted relics of plows and farm tools. Lovely-hued wildflowers grow among them, in soil those plows had once tilled. Obscured and overgrown by salt grass are traces of stone walls, built long ago to keep sheep and cattle out of the planted fields. The only sounds today are the calls of meadowlarks roused by our dog and the mew of gulls following a dragger.

This island land has been farmed and timbered for centuries. Standing on the high ground, you can look back to the harbor and envisage it as a fishing station. Historian Charles K. Bolton, in his book, *The Real Founders of New England*, wrote about Damariscove.

"Here was the chief maritime port of New England. Here was the rendezvous for English, French, and Dutch ships crossing the Atlantic. Here men bartered with one another and with Indians, drank, gambled, quarreled, and sold indentured servants." Then, hundreds of years back, this empty shore had been busy. Wharves, salting houses, sheds, boatyards, makeshift taverns, and perhaps a bawdy house or two for sailors ashore after a long Atlantic crossing, must have lined this empty harbor.

Humphrey Damarill was the first kingpin here, the first major businessman in residence. By 1608, Damarill was operating a busy trading post on Damariscove, catering to the ships and crews, and soon he owned the nearby islands—Fisherman's, Outer and Inner Heron. The harbor was called "Damarill's Cove," and through usage became Damariscove. His influence may have spread further. In some early records, the Damariscotta River is called "Damariscove River." Linguists are confounded in their efforts to decide whether the name Damariscotta is related to Damarill, or whether it stems from the Indian words meaning "river of alewives." In any case, Damarill flourished on his island for close to forty years, then, with money in his pocket, headed to Boston to enjoy the fruits of his labor. There he died in 1650.

Captain Richard Patishall owned the island after Damarill. His headless body is said to haunt the island still. He met his bloody end when Indians captured him aboard his boat at Pemaquid on August 2, 1689. His body was beheaded and thrown into the sea—an Indian tribute to a brave enemy. His dog jumped in after him. Both bodies later washed up on the shores of Damariscove Island, where the two had long lived together. Legend has it that the headless Patishall and his dog can be seen today, wandering the island shores on moonlit nights.

The headless man and his dog were seen, according to local historian Harold W. Castner, by one of the workmen building the first Coast Guard station on Damariscove a hundred years ago. The petrified man rushed back into camp, trembling, ashen white, and dripping with perspiration, and spewed out his tale of terror to his workmates. Next morning the entire work crew hurriedly left the island. Months passed before other men could be persuaded to go back. Later, a highly respected fisherman, Captain Chase, saw the headless man and his dog. Chase refused to set foot on Damariscove again. "Now, living men," says Castner, "tell tales of ghostly barking across the treeless island." Today, a visiting dog will suddenly stop, cock its ears in surprise, and excitedly return the barks which humans cannot hear.

Pirates and smugglers have had their fling here, too. Captain Kidd, that peripatetic pirate, is supposed to have sunk a cable across the harbor mouth and then buried treasure on its shores. The notorious Dixey Bull, who pillaged Pemaquid 350 years ago, is said to have buried treasure in the bottomless pond of Damariscove.

Sweet-smelling roses with an unusual flower bloom in profusion in a few sheltered spots beside the shore. The story is that the seeds were brought here from France by a French trader 365 years ago. On the freshwater pond, 200 yards from the head of the harbor, yellow cow lilies make a dazzling display. But all the trees of Damariscove, once used for ship repairs, for barrel staves, shelters, and firewood, are gone. The northern half of the island is still called Wood End; but there is barely a tree left where thousands once grew. Fires destroyed great stands of timber and herds of sheep chewed all vegetation down to the roots.

Certain of those early sheep served a traitorous cause, just before the Revolution. The British Captain Henry Mowatt, in October 1775, put into Damariscove and requisitioned sheep from a farmer there. That night, on the eve of battle, he served his men a great meal of roast mutton. The next day, Mowatt bombarded and burned Portland, or Falmouth as it was then called.

Damariscove enjoyed a touch of revenge some years later. In early September 1813, *Boxer*, a British brig of eighteen guns and 104 men, and the American brig *Enterprise*, with sixteen guns and 102 men, met and fought within sight of Damariscove. For thirty-five minutes the firing of their guns was incessant. Then *Boxer*, having lost her masts, her captain, and 46 of her crew, struck her colors. A spar from

Boxer washed ashore on Damariscove. The islanders promptly made it into their flagpole.

Island families farmed and fished on Damariscove from the 1600s into the 1930s. In 1918, a tutor was teaching fourteen young island children. In 1937, five families were still living year-round on the island, but at the bottom of the Great Depression the last of the year-round fisherman-farmers came ashore. The brothers, Isaac and Chester Poole, and their thirteen children packed up and sold out. Later, summer folk came to enjoy Damariscove. The last of them, the Kenneth L. Parkers of Cornwall Bridge, Connecticut, grew discouraged by repeated vandalism. In 1966 they gave the island to The Nature Conservancy, which holds Damariscove in trust today.

The greatest single-handed sailor in the world went aground coming into Damariscove. Joshua Slocum and his fifteen-year-old son, in the famous boat *Spray*, in which Slocum circumnavigated the world alone, got off the ledge on a rising tide.

On one large rock is a strange carving, very faint today, after untold years of salt and sea and wind. Some think it may have been drawn by Phoenician voyagers ten thousand years ago. That is wholly unsubstantiated, but it is certain that almost four hundred years ago, long before white men settled in the now famous places of Plymouth, Popham, and Jamestown, this 300-acre island of Damariscove was home and haven to hundreds of English and European seamen and fishermen. Some of those hardy men were the first white men to inhabit North America.

13

Monhegan
Shaped Like a Whale

Fog swirls in on the night wind. Its wet white blanket blots out brilliant stars that, an hour ago, canopied the sky, helping to light the narrow dirt road from Deadman's Cove, past the creaking pines of Cathedral Woods. We walk past Dr. Alta Ashley's house, called The Pill Box, past the little white school, past Don Cundy's big gray home and its swimming pool, past the summertime store, Island Spa, down to the island wharf.

The beam of Monhegan Light flashes yellow in the fog. A light from Monhegan has been warning men at sea on nights like this since 1824. Across the harbor, where the fog horn now wails on Manana, a giant bell stood, cast in Boston in 1832, and a man stood by it on foggy nights, sounding its clapper by hand to warn ships off the death-trap rocks below.

Monhegan is historic ground. Some believe the runes near today's Coast Guard station on Manana were carved into the rock there by Viking sailors about 1000 A.D. Six hundred years after the Vikings, English fishermen salted shiploads of cod on these shores. Hundreds of years ago, men and ships perished here, not far from the Washerwoman Ledge. These Monhegan shores are where Captain John Smith of Pocahontas fame came ashore in May of 1614 and where, for centuries before him, Indians encamped and harvested the sea.

Now, some four hundred years later, on this stormy night in January, seventy-five or so people sleep on Monhegan.

This island, 11 miles out to sea, high, rocky, unprotected, alone and beautiful, is a unique and almost foreign land.

For example, here are a few everyday matters on Monhegan that are perhaps unique to the wonderful island.

Monhegan may have had the only doctor in the United States who was the town clerk, director of civil defense, collector of taxes, registrar of voters, school physician, and newspaper correspondent. Dr. Alta Ashley was proud to be the oldest winter resident on Monhegan. She was the medical examiner, island historian, and local correspondent for Maine newspapers.

Monhegan may have had the only road worker, David Boynton, who was a nuclear scientist at MIT, and the only two Maine lobstermen, Bill and Duggie Boynton, who graduated from Wesleyan University, in political science, and from Trinity College, in Chinese studies.

Monhegan children attend a one-room schoolhouse, but the island had its own truant officer, Alfred Stanley, highliner, lobsterman, and third-generation islander.

The crime rate on Monhegan is a marvel to gladden most hearts. The big crime of summer was when a young man was caught putting slugs instead of coins into the pay phones. He caught the next boat back to the mainland.

There is no town water on Monhegan in the winter. When you want water, you go to the kitchen and pump it, and when you want light you use a kerosene lamp. If you must have electricity, to watch television for example, you go out and start up your own generator. There is no central source of power on Monhegan. A few homes use solar power.

Just getting out to Monhegan in winter is not easy. The only public transport is by the mail boat *Laura B.*, which runs out of Port Clyde on Monday, Wednesday, and Friday. The trip takes just over an hour and the necessities of life on Monhegan, from milk to stovepipes, travel with you as deck cargo.

In summer, when up to eight hundred people instead of fewer than a hundred may inhabit Monhegan, the *Laura B.* makes two round-trips a day, and excursion boats make daily trips from Boothbay Harbor and weekend trips from New Harbor.

It is winter on Monhegan Island, a special kingdom.

In the schoolhouse on the hill, four big days of Monhegan's winter are written on the blackboard—Thanksgiving, Christmas, New Year—and Trap Day.

Trap Day is unique to this island, the December day Monhegan lobstermen set out their traps. Lobstermen of Monhegan long ago made their own rules, rules that are rigid and excellent, but which no other lobstermen in Maine have been able to establish.

Maine law now prohibits catching of lobsters within two miles in any direction of Monhegan shores from sundown on the 25th of June till dawn of the 1st of December. Monhegan is the only spot in Maine with a closed season on lobstering. The men out here go lobstering in the coldest, roughest winter weather. When other lobstermen on the mainland quit, the Monhegan men begin.

Sherman Stanley, whose family has lived on Monhegan and fished these waters for three generations, explained how Trap Day began.

"Back about 1907, Monhegan lobstermen made their own closed season. No lobstering between late June and New Year. Then two years later they petitioned the State Legislature and got the rules made into law in 1909. My father spearheaded that effort."

Monhegan Island and the ocean around it are special territory. No fisherman from the mainland or other islands in the bay is fool enough to set traps within Monhegan waters, winter or summer. The outsider may be deterred more by Monhegan lobstermen than by the Maine law. The ocean within two miles of Monhegan is off-limits for fishing to all outsiders, and wise outsiders stay away when it comes to setting traps.

Not many men choose to go lobstering in winter out here, living on this high, windswept, high-cliffed island that measures 1¾ miles long and ¾ mile across. Seventeen lobster boats fish from here in the winter Atlantic. But precisely because the Monhegan tradition for seventy-four years has been to let the lobsters breed and live in peace from July till December, the lobsters they get are likely to be fat, plentiful, and fetch high prices in the winter, when other lobsters are scarce on the market. The lobsters are kept alive and fresh in storage cars, securely anchored in the cold harbor.

On a day of good hauling in January or February, a Monhegan lobster boat may bring in several hundred dollars worth of lobsters. When the season ends June 25, the bank accounts are often fat. Winter lobstering in these far offshore waters is not for many men, yet, in recent years, there has been a fine resurgence of new young blood into the island's year-round community. Sometimes men from distant places get bitten by the love of Monhegan, through Coast Guard duty here or through a summer job in an island hotel, and come back here to live and work year-round.

"Can a new fisherman move onto Monhegan and be welcome?" I asked Sherman Stanley, Sr., an island power.

I was a bit surprised when he answered: "We'd welcome a new fisherman—provided he showed good intent to live here year-round, and proved himself to be an honest individual. He'd be welcomed more than hindered by us; but it would be a different story if a fellow tried to move onto Monhegan, fish our six months, and then move off—or if he couldn't keep to our Monhegan standards of honesty and fair play."

I asked Stanley what he meant by "Monhegan honesty." He said; "If I go off on vacation or get sick and can't get out hauling traps, on Monhegan I know for sure that no one will touch my gear or my traps or my house. That's Monhegan honesty." I didn't need to ask him what "Monhegan fair play" meant. I had seen "Monhegan fair play" in action one night at the island store in a fisherman's meeting.

Late fall each year, the fishermen get together to talk, vote, and then decide the date for Trap Day, usually close to December 1. The men swap news, then slowly creep up on the subject of Trap Day. This time they voted to put off Trap Day for a week or so.

That meant they'd all miss some $500 days. Why did they vote to postpone? Because one man's engine was out; another was on shore visiting a mother near death. So all the other fishermen voted to put off Trap Day until the engine was fixed and the man with a sick mother was back. That way, they said, everyone got an equal chance.

Monhegan is one community where the dollar is not king, and where "dog eat dog and the devil take the hindmost" is not the business code. Instead they live by Monhegan fair play.

Just before Trap Day, the wharf gets piled high with traps ready to go. To get to the boats, you walk through a forest of traps, higher than a man's head, piled on all sides. When first light of Trap Day dawns, wives, friends, and helpers load the boats high with traps, the engines roar, and the fleet is off, each boat racing out to set traps where the skipper thinks the most lobsters will be. After setting one load, the boats race back to harbor for the next. Wives send down re-plenishments of food. It takes each boat two or three days of work to set out up to eight hundred traps each.

From December till June 25, the men lobster, often in high seas and sub-zero weather. Boats that work in this water are built big and strong, and men seldom go out single-handed. For safety, and to share the work and the money, there is almost always a helper aboard every boat. In fine weather or foul, the younger wives are often out with their husbands. In 1981, three husband-and-wife teams were lobstering, and on Don Cundy's boat a father-daughter-son team was seen fishing.

On the island, weather dominates everyone's mind around the clock. Storms at night can damage boats or the precious lobster car full of the island wealth; or drag away traps by the hundreds from the ocean bottom. In lost traps alone, a storm can cost thousands of dollars because each trap costs $30 or more. Storms sometimes isolate the island by knocking out Monhegan's tenuous telephone link to the mainland. Storms prevent the *Laura B.*, the supply boat in Port Clyde, from delivering essential bottled gas or food, spare parts for boats, or mail.

One year, when I was on Monhegan for Trap Day, I stayed with June and Henley Day. That year, Henley, at sixty-five, was the oldest working fisherman there. June Day is an island-born girl. "My great grandfather came out here and my family, the Bracketts, have been on the island ever since." June's mother owned the Monhegan House, a hotel that housed sixty-five guests in summer. Henley used to be the postmaster, the lighthouse keeper, and for a while lived in the fogsignal keeper's house across the harbor on Manana.

Soon after dark in winter, the anxious eyes of women begin to look out the windows to scan the harbor, checking which boats are back in. The women light the lamps, begin supper, and wait. June Day, while she was still wintering on the island, could look out her windows and, in a flash-glance at the moorings, she'd know which boats were back. "Unless the weather is real bad, I didn't worry. But no matter how good the weather, I felt better when I looked out and saw everyone back in on their mooring." By the light of kerosene or gas lamps, June knitted bait bags. "Having extra bait bags filled and ready saves time when a man is out hauling."

That winter, Doug and Harry Odom, inseparable bachelor brothers, were still keeping the only store on the island. In winter, the brothers would go fishing for six or eight hours in the morning, then, at two in the afternoon, Odom's store would open and stay open till six at night to serve the needs of the few people on the island that winter. In summer, of course, when eight hundred people are on the island, the store does a roaring business all day long.

Doug and Harry Odom sold out to Bud and Sally Murdock in 1979, after keeping the island store for forty-nine years.

Come October and November, the summer people have gone. The island men overhaul their boats, traps, and gear, getting ready for Trap Day. In the fall, Doug and Harry, like many islanders, take a holiday. The brothers may spend it luxuriating on Barbados, with a stopover in New York City, where their friend, Zero Mostel, who lived, loved, and painted here, used to get them good theater seats and throw a party in their honor. Sometimes they'd go to Chadd's

Ford to visit their friend Jamie Wyeth, another Monhegan neighbor. (A painting by Jamie Wyeth hangs in the Odom's living room, above the stove—young Wyeth's birthday present to Harry one year).

The Manana hermit, Ray Phillips, was alive that winter and came into the store. He'd row his skiff over from Manana, where he had lived alone with his sheep on the hillside in a ramshackle set of shanties for forty years. His brown eyes were merry and his long beard and hair were, to say the least, off-white. He wore an incongruous, bright, hand-knit beanie, made for him by Pat Ellis, one of the young Monhegan summer girls. He wore two pairs of baggy wool pants and two belts. He bought a pound of sugar, a bottle of red wine, and three packs of tobacco, then pulled over an empty crate and sat down.

Ray Phillips sailed his sloop into Monhegan harbor about 1930. He originally came from Newport, near Bangor, but once here, he never left. In time, he became famous as the Hermit of Manana and the most photographed man out here, but was not above taking a dollar or two from summer tourists when he posed for their cameras. Over the years, he posed for thousands of pictures.

Ray was a beguiling, wise, and college-educated man, despite his awful-smelling clothes and the hovel he shared with his sheep. "I laughed at the income-tax man," he told me. "He came all the way out here to question me. Said he knew I had about thirty sheep and knew I sheared 'em. And got nosey because I had not reported income from selling my wool. Never struck him that I might have sheared the sheep but never sold the wool. I told him I couldn't get the right bags to ship the wool in. Off he went on the next boat, with a funny look in his eye."

Pretty Pat Ellis stopped in for her groceries that day and greeted her friend Ray gaily. "He is a very, very nice man indeed," she told me. Pat offered to wash Ray's long-worn longjohns. He turned the offer down, saying she didn't have any soap strong enough.

Toward six o'clock, the young fishermen, home from hauling, came by the store to pick up their cartons of groceries. Almost all business was done on the cuff—except for wine sales, for which cash had to be paid. Most of the wine sold was from California, but a few very fine French wines were left on the shelves, some with price tags as high as $60 a bottle. They were left over from the summer trade and it was odd to see them in December on Monhegan.

In summer, Monhegan is a vastly different world. Fewer than a hundred winter residents multiply to six or eight hundred. Summer houses fill with families and friends who've been coming here for years, often for generations. The two or three hotels are filled. Tourist boats from Boothbay, Port Clyde, and New Harbor disgorge visitors by the hundreds on day excursions. Visiting yachts try, often in vain, to find a sheltered anchorage. The winter lobstermen either turn to building work on the island or go off dragging on other boats in other waters. But, despite the summertime invasion, Monhegan's rugged character cannot be changed. It remains a remote and enchanting place.

Artists have always found joy working here. Robert Henri came here to paint as early as 1903. He told his young pupil, Rockwell Kent, about the island and, in 1905, Rockwell Kent, just turned twenty-three, came, loved it, and stayed. He was broke, of course, and turned to house-building, at first for others and then for himself. He was a strong, able man and a daring and experienced sailor. He worked as stern man on lobster boats and became accepted by the islanders as much as the stormy, womanizing, rebellious Kent was ever accepted anywhere. He spent several winters here. Some of the best paintings ever done of the island were done by Kent. His clarity, his concentration on the stark forms of the island cliffs, his relish of the great expanses of wild sea and northern sky all fused together to make Kent's paintings on Monhegan among his most moving work.

Henri sent another pupil to Monhegan, the brilliant and prolific George Bellows, who worked here in 1911, 1913, and 1914. His major work, *Fisherman's Family*, first done in small scale while on Monhegan, was redone and enlarged ten years later, in 1923, as a tribute to his happy life with his wife and first child during their Monhegan summer of 1913.

Jay Connaway and Andrew Winter lived and painted on Monhegan, winter and summer. They were followed by Ernest Fiene, Joseph de Martini, Leo Meissner, and Ernest Hekking. They, in turn, have been followed by Reuben Tam, with his original interpretations of the breaking sea; and, of course, by Jamie Wyeth, whose recent work on Monhegan is a fine culmination of almost eighty years of continuous great paintings on Monhegan by many artists.

Brilliant flowers are a special, surprisingly gentle hallmark of Monhegan. Most homes have flower gardens. Botanists say there are more than six hundred varieties of wildflowers on thousand-acre Monhegan. Bird watchers have logged more than two hundred bird species here. On the stormy eastern side of the island, where the surf boils and the waves never cease to pound and fume, stand the dangerous cliffs of Burnt Head, Black Head, and White Head. They rise 80 to 165 feet straight from the tormented sea at their base. Several lives have been lost here, usually the lives of visitors who climb on rocks too close to the sea. Once a wave snatches a body wandering too far on a ledge, there is no way to render help. The Monhegan Library is a memorial to Jacqueline Stewart Barstow, ten years old, and Edward Winslow Vaughn, fourteen, who were swept off the rocks to their early deaths on August 10, 1926. The book plates in each juvenile book reads "Jackie and Edward's library to the children of Monhegan."

Cathedral Woods is the gentlest, quietest part of this wonderful island. High, quiet as a church, the trees gentle the sound of wind and sea. Birds sing, hidden in the branches, and the air is aromatic with a heady mixture of balsam and sea. In here, you feel remote and safe from storm, but, even as you stand deep in the woods, you can feel the rote of the pull and the booming strength of the ocean, out of view; and you can begin to feel that special island bond that links you closely to all those who stood centuries ago on this same island.

Magnet that Monhegan is and will always be to island lovers, much future growth in homes or hotels is unlikely here. First, the water supply is limited. The Plantation of Monhegan has set limits on the number of people who can be served by the available fresh water and those limits are close to being filled. Building permits, therefore, are hard to get. Second, in 1956, a group of people on the island, spearheaded by the Edison family of inventor Thomas Edison, formed a trust called Monhegan Associates, Inc. and together they bought or were given most of the eastern part of the island. The Association wisely wrote restrictions into the deed that, in effect, prohibit building and development on the island.

Monhegan is the boldest outpost of the New World. For a thousand years, Monhegan has been a landfall for seamen from the Old World. To understand why, it is necessary to see Monhegan by approaching it from far at sea, rather than from the Maine coast. From 40 miles—some say 60 miles—out in the Atlantic, it is possible to see the outline of tree-crested Monhegan rising more than 200 feet from the sea. Add to this the fact that the coast of Maine is 30 miles closer to Europe than any other part of the United States, and it becomes easier to realize why the great whale shape of Monhegan has been such a vital landfall to sailors exploring the New World.

Who came here first?

There is a legend that, about 565 A.D., Brendan, an Irish monk, came to Monhegan. The story is that Brendan heard of an Isle of Saints across the ocean and, with a band of seventeen followers, set sail in a reed boat covered with well-greased, tanned hides. In forty days, Brendan came to an island with steep cliffs. Carried by winds and tides, the monks came next to an island with countless sheep. They took a lamb and went to a nearby barren island rock to set up an altar and celebrate Easter. On this barren rock, they started a fire to roast the lamb. Then, to their consternation, the island began to move. They leaped back into their boat and watched the island slowly swim away. They realized then that they had set up their altar and begun to roast their lamb on the back of a giant whale ("Jasconius is his name"). Thereafter, for six years, St. Brendan and his band sailed among the islands, searching for the Isle of Saints. Finally, an angel appeared to Brendan and told him to take his monks back to their own country.

Some think that the Vikings were the first white men to come to Monhegan. They contend that, about the year 1000 A.D., Leif and Thorwold, sons of Eric the Red, sailed this coast on a trip from Iceland and put ashore on Monhegan and Manana to cut long timber. Advocates of this story point to the strange inscriptions found on rocks on Manana Island and say they are old Norse writings.

John Cabot, in his explorations of 1494, made his first landfall at Monhegan, according to some, but others deny this and say Cabot's landfall was Newfoundland.

The evidence is strong, however, that Verrazano, in 1524, inspected Monhegan. The records of his ship *La Dauphine* (told in Chapter 3) describe Monhegan and position these midcoast islands accurately.

The first recorded English description of Monhegan came from David Ingram, who said he saw the island in 1569. Ingram is that remarkable sailor (described also in Chapter 3) who was marooned on the Gulf of Mexico while he was a crew member of Captain John Hawkins' famous expedition. Ingram told the world he walked from the Gulf of Mexico to Canada. When Ingram finally got home to England, part of the testimony he gave before a law court contained this description of Monhegan, which has lasted four hundred years:

> Taking me into his canoe, the Indian paddled from the place he called Sabino to a peninsula he called Pemcuit (Pemaquid), where we rested over that night. When the morning broke, I saw not far to seaward, a great island that was backed like a whale ... The Sagamo said it was an island, and that the people who lived on it were the subjects of

Bashaba. (Bashaba was the Indian chief of this region and his title crops up often in the writings of Sir Ferdinando Gorges and Captain John Smith).

Martin Pring, with his two ships *Discovery* and *Speedwell*, dropped anchor in Monhegan harbor in 1603. His log describes the island and plots its exact latitude, 43½ degrees north.

But it was the irrepressible Captain John Smith who put Monhegan truly on the map. Here is Smith's description:

> In the moneth of Aprill, 1614, with two ships from London, I chanced to arive in New Englande, a parte of Ameryca, at the Ile of Monahigan in the 43½ of Northerly latitude; our plot was there to take Whales and make tryalls of a Myne of Gold and Copper ... We found this Whale-fishing a costly conclusion; we saw many, and spent much time in chasing them, but could not kill any ... For our Golde, it was more the Master's device to get a voyage that projected it, than any knowledge he had at all of any such matter. Fish and Furres are now our gold ... Of dry fish we made! about 4000. Of cor fish about 7000. Whilst our sailors fished, myselfe with nine others ranging the coast in a small boat, got for trifles neer 1100 Beaver skinnes, 100 Martine and near as many Otters ... With these furres and the cor fish I returned to England in the Bark; where within six months of our departure we arrived safe back. The best of the fishe was solde for five pounds the hundredth, the rest, by ill visage betwixt three and four pounds. The other ship staied to fit herselfe for Spaine with the dry fish."

That other ship was captained by Thomas Hunt, who kidnapped twenty-seven Indians at Cape Cod, put them in the hold, and carried them to Spain, where he tried to sell them as slaves.

Smith's enthusiasm for Monhegan led quickly to the island becoming the first port of call and a fishing center. In March of the next year, 1615, three more London ships sailed into Monhegan and fished there. In 1616, the Plymouth company sent out four ships and London sent out two more; and "eight voluntaire" ships also showed up in Monhegan harbor that year. By 1618, Monhegan had a year-round settlement.

The prosperity attracted a new investor. Ownership of the island changed from Gorges to Abraham Jennens or Jennings. Jennens, a merchant who owned many fishing vessels, was a member of the North Virginia colony headed by Gorges. Jennens expanded Monhegan's trade in furs and fish and attracted more settlers. Governor Bradford of the Plymouth colony reports buying supplies worth four hundred pounds sterling from Monhegan in 1626. Then the Jennens sold Monhegan to two merchants of Bristol, England, named

Abraham Aldworth and Gyles Elbridge. The price was fifty pounds and the new owners sent over their trusted agent, Abraham Shurt, to negotiate the sale.

Soon after, turbulent changes in England led to troubled times on Monhegan. In England, King James died suddenly in March 1625, and Charles I came to the throne. Charles, as prince, had been forced by his father to become engaged to marry Maria, sister of the King of Spain. But once Charles became king, he dumped Maria of Spain for Princess Henrietta of France. The repercussions were felt along the Maine coast. England and France, so long at war in the New World, now became friendly. England gave back to France the contested title to lands in Acadia and Nova Scotia. The French immediately expanded their land and trading ambitions there and began to ravage English trading outposts along the Maine coast, including Monhegan. Shurt had to evacuate the settlers on his Monhegan Island and move them to greater safety in the fort at Pemaquid, on the mainland.

By 1635, no one lived on Monhegan. During the next twenty years, Monhegan was used only as a summertime fishing post. Meanwhile, in England, Charles I was beheaded, the crown was deposed, and Cromwell took over the country, establishing a short-lived republic.

By 1657, Monhegan changed hands again. The new owner was Nicholas Davidson, merchant, of Charlestown, Massachusetts. Davidson and his heirs owned the island till 1747. During the next ninety years, Monhegan grew, was ravaged, and finally resettled again.

Soon after Davidson became the owner, settlers moved back onto the island and the records of the time reveal human weaknesses went with them, weaknesses often blamed on sailors from visiting boats. For instance, the first murder case from Monhegan to come before the Massachusetts Court.

A fishing boat from Boston, skippered by a Mathew Keninge, came to Monhegan for a season's fishing. In the young five-man crew was one Gregory Castle, a hard-drinking fellow, quarrelsome in his cups—according to the records—who picked fights with his captain. One day, as Captain Keninge sat outside his Monhegan home, mending a pair of shoes, sailor Castle came staggering along. Bitter words were exchanged and Castle picked up the hammer the captain was using to mend his shoes, and whacked him on the head, inflicting injuries from which Captain Keninge died. Castle was arrested and hauled off to Boston to stand trial.

Then there was a lawsuit filed by Francis Johnson of Marblehead against Richard Bedford in 1672 for "damage done on a fishing voyage at Monhegan." Johnson charged that Bedford was so drunk he "caused injury to the fish to the extent of 30 English pounds." The evidence given in court says "Bedford would make himself drunk … would lie under flakes upon which fish were drying, or in one house or another, and let the fish rot in the sun until spoiled." He would also get others in the crew to drink with him "from the bottle hidden in the knee of his breeches."

The Monhegan settlers, and other settlers on the mainland, were having a hard time with "vagabonds," drunken sailors, and "riff-raff from shippes." In desperation, six settlements joined together and sent a petition to the Governor and Deputies of the Massachusetts General Court, asking "that you please take us under your government and protection that we may have benefit of laws." The document contained twenty-one signatures from Kennebec, fifteen from Sheepscot, sixteen from Cape Newagen, eleven from Pemaquid, fifteen from Damariscove, and twenty from Monhegan Island. The number of   signatures from Monhegan indicates it was close to the largest settlement in the area.

The petition was granted and each town was taxed for the new protection. Monhegan was assessed 5 pounds, 10 shillings—more by far than any other settlement, indicating it was the most prosperous.

Law and civic officers were appointed. Among the senior officers for the County Court of "Devon," held at Pemaquid July 22, 1674, were various Monhegan men, among them Richard Olliver, named "Clarke of Writs"; John Palmer, named as magistrate, who could also perform marriages; and John Dolling as constable; while George Bickford and Reynold Kelly were named "grand jurymen." One Monhegan man held an interesting combination of offices. Constable John Dolling was also "licensed to keep a house of public entertainment and was given a license to retail beer, wine and liquor" on the island.

Far worse trouble lay ahead—war with the French and Indians. Again, the major cause lay in political turbulence in faraway England. There, in 1688, another revolution had taken place. King James II was forced to abdicate and flee for his life to France. The Protestant William of Orange sat on the English throne and ruled with his Queen as the William and Mary team till 1702. The news shook Boston. The populace there grabbed the chance to seize the hated Governor Andros, appointed by King James, and threw him and his top men into the Boston jail. The deposed and exiled King James took his revenge by stirring up the French, who had given him refuge, urging them to make war on the English colonies in North America. This was all the encouragement needed by the French Baron Castine. He emerged from his fort at Castine and his first target was Pemaquid. Baron Castine had a special score to settle with Pemaquid and Monhegan, for John Palmer had seized a ship there with a cargo of wine belonging to the Baron. The cargo consisted of seventy pipes of Malaga, one of brandy, two of oil, plus seventeen barrels of fruit. (A "pipe" of wine equals 126 gallons, so Baron Castine had lost a lot of precious liquor.)

Baron Castine used the Indians to do most of his dirty work. He had special influence with the Indians because he had married an Indian princess and fathered a family of half-breed children. He sent a frigate plus a land force of Indians to attack the fort at Pemaquid on August 5, 1689, and then to go on to destroy the flourishing settlement at Monhegan Island, stronghold of the fishing fleet. The destruction of Monhegan took place that October.

The islanders, forewarned by the attack on Pemaquid, fled to save their lives before the attack came, and the Indians destroyed the island by fire. No records of the attack, written from Monhegan, exist; but records from Charlestown show the arrival there of island families who fled from Monhegan.

The ruination of the island is a sad chapter in the nation's early history. The sadness was well expressed by Ida Sedgwick Proper in her fine, detailed book, *Monhegan, Cradle of New England*, published in 1930. In it she wrote:

> "There is immeasurable pathos in the destruction of this island, the oldest English settlement … which had sheltered fishing boats for more than 200 years. Many of the inhabitants may well have been descendants of the men sent over by Gorges, when he planted the Island in 1608 or 1609. All the labor that they so joyously expended on building their homes and clearing out fields was wasted. The stone fences and cellars, are all that remain of their heroic efforts to establish themselves in the new and free world. An occasional spoon, button, bricks, pieces of broken clay pipes, an axe head … are mute evidences of their occupations and habits."

Indian attacks and devastation could not change the strategic geography of Monhegan or deplete the rich fishing grounds. Though settlers were scared to return, the Royal Navy began using strategic Monhegan as a rendezvous point in the wars against the French; and fishermen from the mainland still ventured out to fish from the island in summer, though they never lived there during those perilous years.

In the face of all these troubles, the heirs of the Davidson family of Boston, who had owned Monhegan for ninety years, decided to sell out. In 1749, Shem Drowne, a Boston tinsmith, bought the splendid island for a mere ten pounds, thirteen shillings. Tinsmith Drowne was the artist who made the grasshopper weathervane still to be seen atop Faneuil Hall in Boston, and he made the gilt-bronze figure of an Indian with drawn bow and arrow atop the Province House of Boston.

Drowne's son, Thomas, sold the island at a handsome profit to the Bickford family of Salem and Beverly, Massachusetts, in 1770 for 160 pounds. But the Bickfords, too, sold at almost a 100 percent profit seven years later, to Henry Trefethren, a cabinetmaker from Kittery. Trefethren paid three hundred pounds for Monhegan. He never came to the island. But his son, Henry Trefethren, and his married daughters, Mary Starling and Sarah Horn, moved to Monhegan. They had to buy the island all over again in 1823. The cause of this double purchase was the fact that, when Maine separated in 1820 from Massachusetts, the government of Massachusetts chose to keep Monhegan. But when offered two hundred pounds, they sold it back again.

The population was far smaller than it had been a hundred years earlier. Records show that in 1810 there were forty-three inhabitants and by 1820 the number was up to only sixty-eight. But the importance of the island as a landfall was reaffirmed by the building of the Monhegan Lighthouse in 1824, four years after Maine won statehood.

That light is still a landfall for ships at sea. Monhegan, so highly praised by Captain John Smith in the early 1600s, is still praised as perhaps the most beautiful of Maine islands.

Monhegan, the island where the first fishing fleets gathered hundreds of years ago, is still the gathering place for thousands of visitors each summer. Its magnetism and its majesty are as strong as ever.

14

The Fox Islands
North Haven and Vinalhaven

There is probably more blue blood and old money along the Fox Islands Thorofare than can be found along any other short stretch of salt water in the United States. On North Haven and Vinalhaven both are subdued instead of flaunted.

Here, a dozen miles out to sea from Rockland, are clans of Cabots, tribes of Lamonts and Saltonstalls, roomfuls of Rockefellers, Reynolds, and Rhinelanders, a punch card of IBM Watsons, a rich strike of Standard Oil Jennings, coveys of college presidents, judges and lawyers enough to pack a Supreme Court, surgeons enough to staff the most prestigious hospital, and a battery of bishops big enough to talk all Maine past St. Peter's Gate.

But seldom does one hear the crass clink of money or see the muscle of power on these islands. Yet here, from July to September, U.S. senators in tattered shorts sail North Haven dinghies their grandfathers sailed and ambassadors in sweatshirts barbecue hamburgers at cookouts. Here Supreme Court Justices patiently lick ice cream cones while their wives buy groceries at Waterman's or Carver's store. Here college presidents in filthy sneakers clean fish their grandchildren just caught. Bankers from Wall Street and Back Bay borrow dimes to buy licorice shoelaces. Dowagers with diamonds shining on wrinkled fingers go raspberrying, and Episcopalian bishops cuss like stevedores at outboards that won't start.

For a hundred years, the islands of North Haven and Vinalhaven have been summer havens for blood that is very blue and money that is very old, very quiet, and very plentiful.

These "first families" of America do not impress the island people. One reason is that the islanders are wholly competent in island living, in self-sufficiency, and the summer folk are not. Another reason is that the island people are, very often, the true First Families. For instance, when I pulled into Calderwood's dock at Carver's Harbor, Vinalhaven, for the first time in 1968, the man who gassed my boat was James Calderwood. Back in 1785, another James Calderwood, and his brother John, were already important men on Vinalhaven. Those Calderwoods signed a petition from the eight hundred Fox Islanders living here then to the General Court of Massachusetts. The petition asked that their land titles, issued by the English before the American Revolution, be reconfirmed. The Court granted new legal titles to all who had settled land on the islands prior to 1784, provided the islanders agreed to set aside 200 acres to supply funds for a minister and church and another 200 acres to fund a grammar school, and that the islanders agree to pay the cost of surveying their 10,000 acres.

The same day Calderwood gassed my boat, I walked from the dock to the Town Hall and met First Selectman Wyman Philbrook, and found that his ancestor, Joel Philbrook, had also signed that 1785 petition. In the store, I drank a soda with John Carver and found that he was part of the family Thaddeus Carver started here before the Revolution and for whom the harbor was named. On this close-knit island, almost everyone's roots run long and deep into the beginnings of this nation.

The first white man to name these islands was Martin Pring, from Bristol, England. He sailed down this Thorofare in 1603, long before any colonist landed at Jamestown. Pring, in his 50-ton vessel *Speedwell*, with a crew of thirty men and boys, and accompanied by the smaller vessel *Discoverer*, 26 tons with thirteen men and one boy aboard, anchored here. Pring admired the high, sheltering shores full of good woods and the excellent fish his crew caught. He was especially impressed by the sight of many handsome silver-gray foxes and gave the name "Fox Islands" to what we now call North Haven and Vinalhaven.

How did Pring's Fox Islands get their names changed to Vinalhaven and North Haven? The answer is by the persuasion of a lobbyist—one of the first political lobbyists, John Vinal, of Boston. Soon after Calderwood, Philbrook, Carver, and others signed that land-title petition mentioned above, the islanders spent the rather large sum of thirty-six pounds to hire John Vinal as their lobbyist at the Massachusetts legislature in Boston. He did the job they wanted and the islanders acknowledged this by marking their payment to him with the words "for obtaining legislation in our favor." But Vinal did himself a lasting favor, too. The law he lobbied through the Massachusetts legislature on June 25, 1789, incorporates the islands commonly called the North and South Fox Islands in the County of Lincoln, into the town by the name of Vinal Haven." Later, his son William Vinal came to settle on the island bearing his name. Soon Arthur Vinal was appointed assessor. The next move of the newly incorporated town of Vinalhaven was to build roads. At the first town meeting, it was voted that "for labor on the roads, men should be paid three shillings a day, plus one shilling and six-pence for oxen and the roads should be 18 feet wide."

The new town grew rapidly and prospered. By 1790 the population was 855. By 1880, when granite quarrying on Vinalhaven was at its peak, there were 3,380 residents; and today the year-round population of Vinalhaven is just over a thousand and North Haven numbers about 350.

Carver's Harbor at Vinalhaven became the hub for business and pleasure for sixty islands in Penobscot Bay. Matinicus Island paid taxes to the Fox Islands till 1801. Hurricane Island was part of the township till 1878, when, at the height of the granite-quarrying boom, it was set off. Located at Indian Creek, Arey's Harbor, Coomb's Neck, Bartlett's Harbor, Crockett's Cove, Leadbetter's Island, and Lane's Island, sawmills, gristmills, and plants for salting abounded. The islanders made their own salt—a tedious process that required boiling 400 gallons of sea water to get one bushel of salt.

Lobstering was very big business. Firms from Boston and New York ran canning plants at Carver's Harbor from 1846 until the Civil War temporarily hindered the operation. Another big canning plant in The Reach operated till 1900. In 1884, a Boston firm, Johnson and Young, set up a massive fresh-lobster pound in The Basin, a rock-bound saltwater lake in which they kept up to 150,000 live lobsters. They made a handsome profit by shipping them to Boston when the price there for fresh Maine lobster reached a dime a pound!

Thaddeus Carver, for whom Carver's Harbor is named, was fifteen years old when he set foot on the Fox Islands, brought here by his father from Marshfield, Massachusetts. When Thaddeus Carver died in 1832, he was a wealthy patriarch of eighty-one years, living in his big house on the hill overlooking Carver's Harbor.

Young Thaddeus Carver got his first job in the sawmill owned by Francis Coggswell. In short order, Carver bought the sawmill and 700 acres of land from Coggswell and married an island girl—Hannah

Hall, of Matinicus Island, daughter of Ebenezer Hall, first settler on Matinicus, who was slain by Indians. Thaddeus and Hannah began married life in a rough log house he built, but they prospered and raised ten children. Thaddeus endured raids from the British at Castine, lived through the American Revolution, got new titles to his land as the result of that 1785 petition he signed, lived to see Maine win independence from Massachusetts in 1820, and to see his Carver's Harbor grow into an important fishing port.

By 1826, his son, Reuben Carver, was building the first vessels for the new granite trade. His first boat, *Plymouth Rock*, hauled granite quarried on Vinalhaven to build a prison in Massachusetts. Reuben went on to build eleven more boats for the growing granite trade.

The Carvers were an inventive, industrious clan. At the other end of Carver's Harbor, John Carver launched a new kind of enterprise in 1852—the business of knitting horse nets, which seems a strange trade on an island 16 miles to sea from Rockland. But the nation had millions of horses then and each horse was plagued by flies in summer. And so the horse-net business thrived at Carver's Harbor. John Carver passed the horse-net business on to his son and daughter, Thaddeus and Josephine, who enlarged it. By 1900, they passed it along to Edwin R. Roberts, a modern merchant who mechanized the business and eventually had a thousand people making horse nets for him, not only on Vinalhaven, but at Port Clyde and on Deer Isle, too. They produced horse nets in 140 different designs. As cars came in, the demand for horse nets dropped and the business begun by the Carvers passed into oblivion.

But the memory lives; the rise at the east end of Main Street is still called Net Factory Hill.

Carver's Harbor boomed. By 1878, the islands were curing 22 million pounds of fish a year. The Vinalhaven Fish Company by 1899 had a 50,000-square-foot factory, a 350-foot-long granite wharf, and five big vessels, each carrying 145,000 pounds of fish.

Many of the old island families who were here before the American Revolution are here still. Their homes are mostly clustered near Carver's Harbor. The softer folk, the families of the summer estates, live on the ocean rims of the island. That oceanfront once sold cheaply. Take the choice area called Arey's Harbor. Isaac Arey, a native of Cape Cod, saw it and loved it in 1770, while sailing to Mount Desert with his wife and child. He liked the harbor so well, he bought 700 acres of land around it; paid the sum of thirty pounds to a man named Wheeler for it. Isaac Arey met a tragic end. He drowned while crossing in a small boat to Isle au Haut, where his wife, a skilled midwife, had gone to deliver a baby. Today, a dozen Arey families are listed on the Vinalhaven tax rolls. Back in Isaac Arey's day, taxes were modest. In 1785, when forty-two taxpayers lived on Vinalhaven's 10,000 acres, the total town tax amounted to thirty-two pounds and two pence. Today, shorefront property costs well over a hunded dollars a front foot, and the town taxes are in the millions of dollars. A new fish-freezing and packing plant on the harbor began operation in 1981.

Walk five fascinating minutes up the hill from Carver's Harbor and you come to an extraordinary story of island sickness and health—The Vinalhaven Community Clinic, the only diagnostic and treatment center built in Maine under the Hill-Burton Act. It was opened in 1962, paid for with $60,000 raised on Vinalhaven and $60,000 from the federal government.

Inside, I met an amazing man and a wonderful doctor, Dr. Ralph Earle. Dr. Earle is dead now, but he will not and should not ever be forgotten. When I first met him in 1971 and spent an afternoon and night talking with him in his remarkable clinic, he had already been the island doctor for thirty-five years. The name of Ralph Earle, M.D. is on the birth certificate of every child born on this island from the mid-1930s to the mid-1970s, except those who snuck into the world while Dr. Earle was away in the military during World War II.

Ralph Earle came to Vinalhaven as a boy, on vacation with his father. After graduating from medical school, he returned to the island as its only active physician, although in the 1890s three doctors had made a living here, caring for the islanders with 50-cent office visits and 75-cent house calls.

"When I arrived in 1937," Dr. Earle told me, "it was the Depression. Almost all island men were on WPA at $11 a week. They ate off the land and sea; grew potatoes, dug clams, jigged mackerel, cut spruce for fuel. No one had cash to spare for a doctor."

Strangely, out of this came some of the finest preventive medicine in Maine, a doctor the islanders loved, and an amazing probe into hereditary diabetes.

Here is that story. It began, almost by accident, in 1965.

After being the island doctor for twenty-eight years, Dr. Earle became concerned about a major gap in his work with his island patients. "I knew too little about the adult males, medically. We had 138 men on the island, aged between forty and sixty, and most every one of them shied away from the annual physical checkups which I

had persuaded the island women and children to get. So I wrote letters to all 138 men. I spoke to every fishermen's group, firemen's
group, and civic group about how checkups and preventive medicine
could keep them healthy. The result was that 40 percent, 53 out of
the 138 men, volunteered to take part in a medical survey. For $15,
every man got a three-hour checkup, a careful review of his own and
his family's medical history, an electrocardiogram, a chest X-ray, a battery of lab tests, including blood, urine, and stool examinations, as
well as a glucose tolerance test."

Then Dr. Earle made his discovery. Out of 53 adult males examined, seventeen tested positive for diabetes and four more were
questionable.

Islanders showed a diabetes rate twenty times higher than the
general population of the U.S. On a national basis, about two percent
of all Americans have diabetes and half of them do not know it. But
tests on Vinalhaven indicated that 50 percent of the adult-male population might have diabetes.

Dr. Earle asked, "Why?"

Since heredity can play a part in diabetes, Earle began digging
into all available marriage, birth, and death records on the island.
Marriage records had been kept since 1790, but, because Maine did
not require birth and death certificates until 1892, Dr. Earle had to
find another way to discover what had happened in those hundred
years between 1790 and 1892 among Vinalhaven families. He spent
hours with the town clerk, an expert local genealogist. He scoured
records in the state archives at Augusta, the capital. Finally, he turned
to the family Bible, where rural America has kept the best family
records. The Bible proved fruitful ground.

"Vinalhaven is a stable, close-knit island community," Earle
explained, showing his charts. "Some 450 of the islanders—about
40 percent—trace their families back on both the mother's and the
father's side to the early settlers who landed here before the American
Revolution. Most of the other 60 percent trace their ancestry back
two hundred years through one line of descent, mother or father."

In such ways, Earle was able to trace back 21 suspect cases of
diabetes. He found, in almost every case, hereditary diabetes could
have been expected.

The doctor then drew detailed family charts with small circles,
some red, some white, the marks representing male and female,
children and grandchildren, diabetic and nondiabetic. He found one
woman who had no diabetes, yet gave birth to a diabetic daughter

who, in turn, gave birth to a diabetic son, whose wife, in turn, gave birth to a diabetic daughter. He found a diabetic grandmother who had five grandchildren—four of whom were diabetics. Finally, he found that he could predict with a high degree of accuracy the chances for diabetes in any native of Vinalhaven.

On the day I was with him, Dr. Earle was studying the records of an island girl married to an Air Force man serving in Spain. He estimated she had an 80 percent chance of being diabetic. He knew she was far advanced in pregnancy. He telephoned the obstetrician at the air base in Spain, suggesting tests be made. They were. Result—a confirmed case of preclinical diabetes, discovered in a patient in Spain on the information provided from Dr. Earle on Vinalhaven.

Earle won financial support for wider diagnostic tests among islanders, and for treatment. He then went house to house, lodge meeting to lodge meeting, urging all islanders to come to the clinic for tests. As a result, five hundred more islanders came to the clinic. Exactly 50 percent of the first 180 tested had indications of diabetes. The National Center for Chronic Disease Control, presented with the facts, said the island population "has one of the highest concentrations of diabetes known."

In following years, Earle's work in treatment, research, early diagnosis, and prediction progressed. In 1970, the islanders made more than three thousand visits to the clinic. Dr. Earle made 510 house calls that year.

Before his work was finished to his satisfaction, Earle, the remarkable island doctor, died.

Summer people blend well with island people on North Haven and Vinalhaven, though their lives and backgrounds are poles apart. Of course, each side has had a hundred years of experience since Dr. Weld started the summer colony.

The credit must go largely to the summer people. They bend to the island ways. They have to, for the island ways won't bend. Here, island ways are better than the ways brought in from Boston, New York, Washington, Pittsburgh, Cleveland, or Los Angeles, and the wise off-islander knows it.

Summer people get more satisfaction when an islander calls them by their first names than they do when their broker phones to say their stock has jumped ten points or their lawyer calls to say a corporate merger has been consummated. Local acceptance hinges wholly on personal qualities, not on bank accounts or family names. Not all summer residents get it, by a long shot.

Actor Robert Montgomery, liked as a North Haven neighbor, but almost ignored as a celebrity, lived for many summers in his lovely white farmhouse on Little Fox Thorofare. Then, in July 1970, Montgomery made it big. He was invited to be guest speaker at the alumni banquet of North Haven School. Those alumni are a select group. The year Montgomery spoke, there were two students in the graduating class.

The field where Charles Lindbergh used to land his plane at the Morrow estate—he married Anne Morrow—is an overgrown, unmarked meadow now. In North Haven, no one would dream of erecting a plaque. The lonely, lovely farmhouse where Ambassador Chester Bowles lived, became the retreat where Washington Judge Gerhard Gessel came to recharge his batteries while he was ruling in favor of the *Washington Post* on the publication of the Pentagon Papers.

Behind Pulpit Rock, where ospreys nested for three hundred years, the Cabots have a compound of cottages. There is a small sign on the drive that reads "No Lowells Allowed."

By the ferry slip on the Thorofare is Waterman's store, hub of North Haven life for generations. Irma Peters presided there. This brown-eyed cashier knew everyone, their parents, and their children. Irma was the first selectwoman elected in more than two hundred years of town government on the island. Her husband, Gordon, who kept the books in a cubbyhole office upstairs, taught cement production in Indonesia and Yugoslavia till stricken with polio. Their North Haven children went to Chinese schools. Irma and her husband supplied the needs of the plain white house by the mill stream, owned by John D. Rockefeller III, and meat and groceries to the big yellow house on the cliff where Mrs. Thomas Lamont, widow of J. P. Morgan's partner, looked out to the Camden Hills at sunset. Watermen's store supplied the long white farm where Thomas Watson of IBM kept a mile-long airstrip for his private jet planes and where he entertained the Kennedys and that horn-playing jazz musician, the King of Thailand and his beautiful queen.

Jim Brown, thin, spectacled, slow talking, built boats and tended the wharf that his grandfather, J. O. Brown, started in the summer of 1880. Jim and his sons built the same North Haven sailing dinghies his grandfather built for Dr. Weld of Boston 120 years ago, when Dr. Weld began the summer colony on the Fox Thorofare.

Dr. Weld and his sailing friends from Boston dropped anchor here one night in 1880. They rowed ashore and were so captivated by the island, they promptly bought land. They gave up their cruise and spent the rest of their vacation on the Thorofare, drawing plans for the summer cottages they wanted. Before they headed back to Boston, Dr. Weld and his friends had made arrangements with local craftsmen to build them by the following summer. The summer colony had begun on North Haven.

Dr. Weld's imprint is still strong on the Thorofare. His daughter, Mrs. Mary Pingree, lived in the big house at Iron Point, commanding the midpoint of the Thorofare. Duplicates of the 15-foot, 4-inch North Haven sailing dinghy first built for Dr. Weld by J. O. Brown, still crowd the Thorofare on race days. Some youngsters proudly sail the same dinghy in which their grandfathers learned to sail.

The most unusual home, architecturally, is the Norwegian Cottage, built for Ambassador Strong after he'd served as U. S. Ambassador to Norway in World War II. The roof, in Norwegian tradition, is of sod a half-foot thick with green grass and wildflowers growing out of it. Sometimes a goat was tethered up on the roof there, mowing the grass by eating it. A Norwegian sauna bathhouse stands nearby, complete with a huge bell atop it for summoning people from outside if anyone is parboiling inside.

The Vinalhaven side of the Fox Thorofare is another Gold Coast of large summer cottages, mostly belonging to the Rhinelanders, the Reynolds, the Saltonstalls, the Lewises, and the Brewster Jennings of Standard Oil.

The Saltonstalls were among the early summer people from Massachusetts who came here seventy-five years ago. (An earlier Saltonstall, Dudley, had lost most of the American Navy under his command when he got scared off and then defeated by the British at Castine in 1779. His artillery commander, Paul Revere, had to walk home to Boston in a towering rage.)

Today, Saltonstalls have summer places all along the Thorofare in a kind of protective family association. There was the mother's place, Richard's place, and Leverett's place. Then a Saltonstall married a Lewis, and now there are newer Lewis places.

Today, off-islanders own most of the shorefront and about 75 percent of all North Haven land. The native-born islanders have the remaining 25 percent. But there is a sweet irony to all this blue blood, quiet money property.

During the Depression, more than 1500 acres of the prime land came into the hands of a wonderful junk dealer in Rockland, named Isidor Gordon. "They couldn't give away island property in the 1930s and '40s," he told me. "I didn't pay much for the 1500 acres I bought and I couldn't get much when I sold them. Back in 1929, they wanted to sell me a beautiful waterfront estate with a fine house and 45 acres. I didn't want it at any price. But finally they got me out to take a look. I said I'd buy it for last year's taxes. So I got the house and estate for $700."

The price today would be well over $400,000. Even small houses in the village have rocketed in value. One small village house sold for $600 in 1945. It has changed hands six times since then, with the last price topping $60,000.

These Fox Islands are a second home for our boat from May to November. Every year, we spend happy days and mystical nights in a dozen different coves and harbors here. Our boat's log is filled each year with pages of notes about friends, newly made, and rediscovered island shores we've walked. Here is one entry:

> We are anchored 16 miles out to sea from the mainland, tucked in the shelter of two small islands along the Reach of Hurricane Sound. Just before dawn I climb out of the bunk and go topside, to be there, waiting and looking, when the new day's sun wakens North America. The first rays of the new day strike here first. The deck is wet from the night, drenched in dew, so I coil a mooring line into a circle the size of my bottom, sit on it, sip the first cup of coffee and wait alone in a cone of lovely silence for the new day's sun to rise up out of the Atlantic.
>
> The sea is dead calm, leaden, at this hour. No birds sing yet. No gulls fly yet. No breeze stirs yet. The whole world is quiet. At this pre-dawn hour the night animals are back in their homes, finished their prowling hunts.
>
> On shore thin grey light emerges from the night. I can see wet green meadows now, sloping slowly down to the rocky shore, and the shore becomes ledge, and the ledge becomes sea. On the high ground the roof of a house becomes outlined by the dawn. The first sun rays reach and glisten on the dew-wet roof.
>
> Sitting alone on the coiled rope, watching the day be born, time barriers of the 20th-century vanish. A man senses a close, strange unison with that old jetty, that wet granite ledge, that meadow where oxen once plowed, that gaunt old farmhouse. A man feels a link that reaches back 377 years to the first sailors who anchored here, to the first settlers and their successive generations who saw sunrises from this cove.
>
> Were they friends or enemies of the Indians here? When those early settlers watched the sun rising up out of the Atlantic, did their homesick thoughts leap three thousand miles across the ocean to their roots in coastal England, where the sun was shining at high noon? Did they hope or did they fear that another small boat might

be setting sail from Plymouth or Bristol with new settlers who might wind up as neighbors to them on these Fox Islands which Martin Pring had praised in his ship's log of 1603, the year Elizabeth was a dying queen?

Did their offspring, fishing these waters, farming that meadow, stand up at the town meeting of 1811 when it was voted to increase the pay for the road builders on this island "to 12 cents an hour for men, 12 cents for oxen and six cents for carts"; and how did they vote on the warrant which decided these islanders would "not raise any money for support of the gospel" and the warrant which decided "that William Vinal, Esq. be chosen Representative"; and the warrant which decided "that $400 be allocated to schools?"

Was there a man in the farmhouse near our cove who hid with other fishermen through that night of 1813 so they could surprise and capture the British privateer *Fly* when she dared anchor off Vinalhaven and fly false American colors from her mast? Was he one of those islanders who recaptured the three American vessels and crews which *Fly* had seized?

Were great-grandchildren of the first settlers on that farm working in the Vinalhaven granite quarry that memorable week of August 20–27, 1899, when they cut the unforgettable granite shaft that was 64 feet long and weighed 310 tons, and was bound for New York City, where it would become a spire on the Cathedral of St. John the Divine? Did they sail their boat from here over to Carver's Harbor to watch the first telephone message go out from Vinalhaven to Rockland at eight o'clock Monday morning, January 10, 1898?

Now the sun bursts out in full dawn and climbs fast. Birds wake, sing, and fly; gulls cry and swoop on their morning breakfast mission. The roars of lobster boats sound across The Reach as they start up and head out to haul traps. The new day is born. The 20th century is back. Aboard *Steer Clear* it is time to up anchor and head across the bay to Stonington and all the blessed islands that stretch out from Deer Isle to Isle au Haut.

15

Granite

How the Islands Built the Cities

Cruise among the lovely, peaceful islands of Penobscot Bay today and it is hard to realize that these islands were once the hub of Maine's heaviest, noisiest industry … granite.

A hundred years ago, these quiet Edens were exploding with the violence and noise of thousands of quarry workers and their vast machines, dynamiting and hammering millions of tons of granite out of the bowels of these islands. Men from Maine, Ireland, Spain, Italy, Scandinavia, using oxen and high-wheeled galamanders, performed an engineering miracle in moving granite slabs weighing far more than 100 tons from quarries to vessels at the wharves. On Vinalhaven in 1878, for example, they moved the largest granite shaft ever quarried until then. It was 60 feet long, weighed 185 tons, and was made into the General Wool Monument in Troy, New York. This shaft and its seven foundation stones weighed 650 tons when loaded aboard the barge *Jemima Leonard* on August 16, 1879.

Bright blue galamanders, with wheels high as a man, pulled by teams of oxen and horses, hauled these immense loads over rough and steep Vinalhaven roads. Tremendous brakes were needed to control the massive weight. One weird-looking galamander stands as a monument on the Vinalhaven village green.

Granite from Vinalhaven, Hurricane, Crotch, Deer Isle, Swan's Island, Dix, and High islands, off the Muscle Ridge Channel, stands today in distant cities, still performing tasks that seem incompatible with these remote, quiet, and lovely islands.

Here are a few buildings and monuments from the astonishing list made from Maine granite: The gravesite of President John F. Kennedy in Arlington National Cemetery (Kennedy sailed among these islands of Penobscot Bay, loved them well, and when you walk to his grave site, you walk on pink granite from Penobscot Bay, specially ordered by his family;) the Pennsylvania Railroad Station and the Girard Building in Philadelphia; the Board of Trade and the Auditorium in Chicago; the old Waldorf Astoria in New York; Jordan Marsh in Boston; the House of Representatives, the Library of Congress and the Executive Office Building, next to the White House, in Washington, D. C.; the New York Stock Exchange; the Triborough, Brooklyn, and George Washington bridges in New York City; Grant's Tomb; the Tomb of the Unknown Soldier; the U. S. Mint; the U. S. Naval Academy; the New York State Capitol in Albany and the State Capitol in Indianapolis; the St. Louis Bridge; the first block of the Washington Monument; the Arlington Memorial Bridge; the Cathedral of St. John the Divine in New York; the drydocks at Norfolk, Virginia; the Hibernia Bank of San Francisco; the Hartford Insurance Company in Connecticut; the New York City Post Office; the Washington Post Office; the St. Louis Post Office; the Cleveland Trust; the Andrew Mellon Foundation; the old *New York World* and *New York Herald Tribune* buildings; the Pilgrim's Monument in Plymouth; the Frick Building in Pittsburgh, and many more.

Besides granite for huge buildings, between fifty and a hundred million paving blocks a year left these Maine islands to be made into the busiest streets of dozens of our biggest cities.

The largest granite shaft in America was cut at Wharff's quarry on Vinalhaven in August 1899. It was 4 feet longer and many tons heavier than the shaft for the General Wool Monument. But tragedy befell it.

The Bodwell Company of Vinalhaven had been commissioned to quarry and lathe-turn eight immense granite columns for the Cathedral of St. John the Divine in New York City. These soaring columns were to be twice as high as those of the Parthenon in Athens, bigger than any in the world except those of St. Isaac's in Petrograd. The huge shaft, 64 feet long and weighing 310 tons in the rough, was cut at Wharff's quarry in a tense week's work in August 1899. To turn this mammoth piece of granite into soaring, graceful columns, E.R. Cheny of Boston designed and built the largest lathe in the world and installed it on Vinalhaven, but the first two monoliths broke on the lathe. Their vast weight, turning on the centers, could not endure the vibration and pressure without cracking. Maurice Calderwood, the Vinalhaven-born superintendent of the project, finally made the columns in two sections, one 90 tons, the other 40 tons. It took three years of work to complete the entire contract. One huge monolith, flawed and never used, lies beside the old Sands Road on Vinalhaven today.

Granite quarrying began here in 1826, when a man named Tuck, from New Hampshire, quarried stone to build a prison in Massachusetts. By 1852, Moses Webster, a granite cutter from Pelham, New Hampshire, came to Vinalhaven, and in partnership with George Bodwell of Maine, began the first East Boston quarry on Vinalhaven. Twenty years later, it had become the Bodwell Company and was employing fifteen hundred men. Other quarries started on Hurricane, operated by General Tillson, Garrett Coughlin, John Hogan, and Patrick McNamara. Close to a thousand men worked on that island where, today, only the Outward Bound School operates. On Crotch Island, across from Stonington, was another immense quarry. At Webb Cove on Deer Isle, the old granite wharf and the giant cranes still stand, dilapidated and rusted. In the Muscle Ridge Channel, on Dix and High islands, you can still see huge machinery, rusted hawsers, giant wharves, and cellar holes of the hotels and boarding houses where another one thousand quarrymen lived and labored a hundred years ago. The islands are silent and empty now; but the ghosts are there.

One summer night we slept aboard *Steer Clear*, anchored between Dix and High Islands, a little boat on a deserted sea. We had spent the hot summer day ashore, exploring Dix and High. We had clambered along overgrown traces of road beds where once hundreds of quarrymen walked, where horse and oxen teams had strained to pull tons of granite. Through wild grass and brambles, through thickets of brush, we climbed to abandoned quarry sites. Atop High Island, we came suddenly upon the precipitous cliff walls of an enormous old quarry. A strange, loud, eerie whirring noise frightened us. Then we saw hundreds of Canada geese rising in wing-beating panic as they heard us. They stop on their long journey to rest and feast on algae-green ponds that lie now in the bottom of the vast quarries. When the geese had flown, silence ebbed back. We looked in awe at the enormous slabs of perfectly cut granite, each weighing many tons, waiting for shipment. Mountains of paving blocks, perfectly trimmed, are piled, ready to pave the streets of distant cities. Machines, cranes, cables, left to rot where they stood, creaked in the sea breeze. Work seemed to have suddenly stopped, as if pestilence had struck and the men had fled.

On nearby Dix Island, we searched for the cellar holes of Shamrock and Aberdeen. These were the names of the vast hotel-barracks that housed a thousand quarry workers, from Ireland and Scotland. In all, 150 buildings, wharves, and stonesheds once crowded this little island.

The empty islands were once a hub of labor unions, strikes, politics, money-making, brawls, murders, and ghastly accidents. A great meeting hall to seat five hundred men was built on Dix. Music-hall singers and dancers entertained packed houses of granite workers. Politicians harangued for election. Union leaders took strike votes.

From the quarries on Dix came the granite for the Treasury Building in Washington, the New York and Philadelphia post offices. Now only birds sing and wildflowers bloom here.

That summer afternoon, we searched on the northwest high point of Dix Island for remnants of the 26-room mansion where Horace Beals of New York brought his beauteous wife in the 1870s. Despite the sumptuous rooms and marble fireplaces he built for her, the lady hated Dix; and later left the island, and her husband, and became the Duchess of Tomajo. The vivacious beauty married four times. Beals, who had reluctantly taken Dix as payment for a bad debt in 1850, became an even wealthier millionaire. He plowed some of his Dix Island profits into a huge hotel on the bank of the Kennebec River, hoping to create another Saratoga Spa. It flopped and was turned into a national soldiers' home after the Civil War, called Togus. Today, it is a big veterans' hospital.

The ghosts came that night as we slept aboard *Steer Clear*. Dreams were loud with the sound of dynamite exploding in the old quarries, with the noise of three 100-foot schooners loading granite at the abandoned wharves, with the singing of quarrymen arriving back in the wee hours from spending like princes in a night of women and drink in Rockland; with visions of the beauteous Mrs. Beals hating her island life inside her ornate 26-room mansion on the bluff.

Early in the 1900s, the great granite boom burst, pricked by the coming of concrete. One by one, the quarries were abandoned. From time to time, a few contracts trickled in and a spurt of the old activity would invigorate the dead quarries. As recently as 1972, Vinalhaven's quiet was shattered by the roar of jet torches 500-degrees hot, burning channels into the granite rock. Maine island granite was needed for the new Dupont headquarters in Brandywine, Delaware, and the new Michigan Telephone Building in Detroit. Between March and October of 1972, they cut five hundred massive slabs of Vinalhaven granite, each weighing up to 24 tons. The operation was puny compared to the operations of the old Bodwell Granite Company: a dozen men, where fifteen hundred once worked. Instead of seventy-two huge oxen, an $80,000 crane hoisted the slabs. The slabs went onto trucks instead of high-wheeled galamanders. Instead of loading onto stone sloops from Chebeague, the granite went ashore on the Rockland ferry (paying $20,000 in fares) and then was transferred onto multiple-axle trucks. But, for the most part, Maine island granite today is too hard, too heavy, too durable, too expensive to quarry and move. However, a hundred years ago, granite put more money and more jobs and trade into these quiet islands than they've seen before or since.

Fritz Johnson was close to eighty when he talked to me on Swan's Island one afternoon about his memories as a quarryman there.

"I was born in Sweden in 1900," he said with just a trace of Swedish accent still. "I came to America as a boy in 1915. My trade was stone cutter. And within a few years I came to work in the quarries here. I was the fastest stone cutter in the world in those days, when we cut stone by hand with a 32-pound hammer and chisel. My record still stands. I cut 786 paving blocks for New York City streets in seven hours. Each block was 4½ inches deep and 12 inches long, and I cut 'em absolutely straight on all sides."

Fritz went into his house and brought out a lighter hammer, a mere 3-pounder, and demonstrated the stonecutter's version of Russian roulette. He swung and twisted the hammer with lightning speed, in a dazzling array of arcs, around his head until it brushed his lips and he kissed it. "Lotta men lost a lotta teeth trying to do that trick," he grinned.

Fritz Johnson came to Swan's Island when he was a strapping twenty-one, in 1921. "I worked in the quarry till it closed in 1928. Usually there were forty of us top stone cutters here; but in busy times the crew went up to seventy-five. We lived in John McGuthrie's boarding house. Cost us $8 a week, room and board. We got paid about $50 a week, good wage back in the 1920s. I still remember the amount of rum we drank. The gambling and the fights were wild in that McGuthrie's boarding house back then."

Rockland was a boom town, Barbary Coast style, in those days of the quarry boom. Special boats ran out to the quarry workers on Hurricane, Swan's, Vinalhaven, Crotch, Dix, and High islands to bring the big spenders into town for Saturday night. Several hundreds of lonely men, with lots of money for a fling, descended on Rockland's waterfront. It was a blazing place. More than thirty steamships and hundreds of coasting vessels, plus the ships of Rockland's huge lime trade, crowded the harbor. Bars, whorehouses, gambling joints, and dance halls catered to sailors and quarrymen. Fights blazed and jails filled. And the money poured in.

16

Isle au Haut

Penobscot Jewel

Italians have always had an eye for beauty and a tongue for compliments. When Giovanni da Verrazano sailed this coast in the early 1520s and first saw Isle au Haut, Mount Desert, and Monhegan, he was inspired by their beauty to name them "The Princesses of Navarre." The three teenage daughters of his patron, King Henry of Navarre, were the most beautiful princesses in all of Europe. The beauty of Isle au Haut is inspiring still.

One summer morning, I moored *Steer Clear* in Duck Harbor and climbed to the top of the storm-beaten magnificence of Western Head. Climbing the soft-moss trail in silence, a man can become intoxicated by ocean air spiced with bayberry, juniper, and spruce. At the peak, I stood on a granite ledge and looked out to the Atlantic and down to the brilliant lobster buoys bouncing below in the green-white surf and over to Roaring Bull Ledge, where crashing seas foamed.

I was alone and awestruck. Suddenly I felt the presence of another human nearby and turned. A lady sat motionless, watching the splendor. I walked toward her. She looked up, smiled, and said: "This is where I go to church. This is the spot where I am awed by the majesty of creation."

Isle au Haut, the "High Island," lies 6 miles to sea from Stonington, Deer Isle. It measures about 6 miles north to south and 2 miles east to west, and is thickly wooded, with a long mountainous spine. Its high point thrusts up to a height of 554 feet and bears the name of the French explorer: Mount Champlain. The island has not, I think, changed very much since his day. There are no hotels, no restaurants, no gift shops, no movie houses. On a fine sparkling day, Isle au Haut can be the most peaceful, heavenly spot in all of Maine; but in rage of storm or thick of fog, Isle au Haut, and the journey to or from it, can be hellish and terrifying. This is why, in most winters these days, only about two dozen people live here. But before boats had engines, hundreds lived here because the island was close to the best of fishing grounds. Then the island was almost bare of trees and a thousand sheep grazed here. But winter hardship and economic isolation gradually drove out most people and sheep. In summer, the cottages at Point Look-Out Club fill, boats from Stonington run often, and close to three hundred people are here. However, the island is protected from much growth because two-thirds of it is now part of Acadia National Park, thanks to the large gift of land in 1946 from the Bowditch family of Boston. Only about 250 of the island's 7,000 acres remain in the hands of the island's year-round residents.

Captain John Smith, in the log of his 1614 voyage along the Maine coast, called this island "Sorico," after the Indians he met here. Huge heaps of ancient clamshells are the memories of the feasts and revels the Indians enjoyed here centuries ago. Duck Harbor was a favorite hunting ground of theirs. The tribes drove sea ducks by the thousands into funnel-shaped Duck Harbor, snared them in nets stretched across the narrow head of the harbor, smoked them, and took them inland in the fall to eat during winter. In the 1930s and '40s, a few Indians still came to the island from their mainland reservations to gather sweetgrass for basket-making. But they come no more.

The first known white settler to come to Isle au Haut was Seth Webb, who arrived in 1772. His mother-in-law had been scalped by Indians. Seth got a land grant from the crown to Kimball's Island, just across the Thorofare. He made friends with the Indian chief, Orono, either because of or despite the fact his mother-in-law had been scalped. The Indian chief and the white settler hunted together. On such a hunting trip in 1785, the unfortunate Seth Webb was killed by his own musket while climbing ashore from his skiff onto Isle au Haut. His widow was unable to cope with life on Kimball's Island and the stronger Kimball family took possession.

By 1792, a man with a wondrous first name, Peletiah Barter, arrived from Boothbay with his brothers, William and Henry. Peletiah fathered ten children here and died about 1832. The old cellar hole of his log cabin can still be seen in Thorofare Village. Calvin Turner arrived in 1800 and set up a salt works, an indication there must have been a fair-sized population of fishing men and boats here to buy his salt. His son, Asa Turner, grazed four hundred sheep here. The Robinsons, Kimballs, Sawyers, Smiths, Kemptons, and Lelands soon joined the settlement. By 1801, fifty settlers petitioned the court of Massachusetts to sell and deed to them the land they had settled.

The families seemingly prospered, for, by 1820, two dozen men were listed as shipmasters. A survey map of 1824 shows thirty-six deeded lots of land, varying in size from 32 to 182 acres each. If the families averaged five persons, about 180 people were living year-round here then, compared to a few dozen or so year-rounders now.

But the "get-rich-quick" bug bit a few, according to a remarkable story from the 1840s. News of gold strikes in the Great California Gold Rush reached this remote Maine island with so much force that a group of islanders decided they, too, would strike it rich in California. They built their own boat in the Thorofare and sailed her around the Horn to San Francisco. There the islanders joined the "forty-niners" in their wild, frenetic hunt for gold. How they fared, the records fail to tell.

A more mundane business enterprise came to the Thorofare in 1860, when a lobster-canning factory was built by a Boston firm. More than twenty-four island women and children worked in it, shipping Isle au Haut canned lobster to Crosse and Blackwell in London. The cannery closed in 1880, but live lobsters were shipped regularly in the island's own fleet of "wet smacks." Each one would carry fifteen hundred lobsters to market in New York City and make the round trip in a week. By 1880, the island population was up to 274.

Then the first of the summer people arrived. Soon they were to form Isle au Haut into a masculine outpost of proper Bostonians—the Point Look-Out Club. Finally, club members gave 4,000 acres of land to be preserved as a national park. That gift has made Isle au Haut among the least spoiled, best preserved islands on the entire coast.

The Point Look-Out Club began this way.

In 1879, Ernest Bowditch, a young landscape artist from Boston, was coming back from Bar Harbor across Penobscot Bay on a small steamer. He recalled the day, thirty-seven years later: "I saw to the southward a bigger island standing up from the sea and asked how to get there. 'Don't know,' replied the pilot, 'but suppose you get off at the mainland and charter a small boat.'" It was a Friday afternoon and Bowditch had the weekend free, so he got off at Stonington and chartered a small boat to take him through the network of islands, out 6 miles to Isle au Haut. On the way out, Bowditch asked the skipper about a hotel and was told there were no hotels or boarding houses. The skipper told him to try Captain William Turner, dropped Bowditch off, and left.

Bowditch, years later, recalled what happened next:

> I reached the old lobster factory and found sitting around a stove three or four old fishermen who looked up at me as I were some strange marine animal. I inquired which might be Captain William Turner, at which one spoke up asking what I wanted. I asked if he could keep me over Sunday, which he answered so abruptly in the negative that my vanity was hurt. Then he added, "What's your name?"
>
> "Bowditch," I replied.
>
> "That's a funny name. Any relation to the fellow who wrote the 'Navigator'?"
>
> "He was my grandfather," I replied.
>
> "Your grandfather? Then you go right on over there to that house and tell the old woman you have come to make a visit."

When Bowditch got home to Boston, he told his bachelor friends about the beauties of Isle au Haut. They joined forces, bought land, and formed the Point Look-Out Club.

Bowditch, who was an old man when he dictated the above account, said his personal capital at the time amounted to only $3,500, so the original Point Look-Out members were paupers compared to the tycoons beginning to build summer "cottages" on nearby Mount Desert. But land was cheap. Soon Bowditch and his group owned 3,000 acres. By 1945–'46 the Bowditch family owned more than half the island and gave it all away to make a national park.

The club built eight cottages plus a clubhouse for communal eating, and laid down the three cardinal rules: No women, no dogs, no children. Before long, however, the founding bachelors got married. The women came and threw out rules excluding women, children, and dogs. The exclusive club grew. In lean years, the club even took in a few carefully selected paying guests. Four times the directors bent enough to place small advertisements in the *Junior League Magazine*; even stooped, in the interests of solvency, to running one advertisement in *Vogue*.

The number of club cottages increased to two dozen. Other summer people bought old homes in the village or out on the promontories. Among them was Chief Justice Harlan Stone, who often took his meals at the Turner boarding house. One evening, a lady at his table talked too long about how much she loved clams and how many she could eat at a sitting. Justice Stone leaned over and quietly told her, "That reminds me of the story of the woman who ate so many clams that her bosom rose and fell with the tide."

Isle au Haut seemed tough and masculine, but it was women more than men who ran the island the year I first put ashore for a few days to do research for some newspaper articles.

Isabel B. MacDonald was town clerk. Dorothea Dodge and Mabelle Chapin were two of the three town selectmen. They were also the tax assessor and overseer of the poor. Dorothy R. Barter was the tax collector. Town treasurer was Isabel MacDonald. On the school board, three of the five members were women: Donna Tully, Belvia MacDonald, and Virginia MacDonald. A lady, Mabelle Chapin, was civil defense chief and town registrar; Edna Alley and Virginia MacDonald were the two election clerks. The bus driver and school janitor was a woman, Dorothea Dodge. And the senior school teacher was Ann Haynes, helped by her husband, Pat.

But there was no question then, or for decades earlier, about who was the ranking Isle au Haut citizen. She was Miss Lizzie: Miss Elizabeth Rich, postmaster, then aged seventy-nine, born at Rich's Cove, on Isle au Haut in 1893, delivered by a midwife who charged three dollars.

"I started working in this post office when I was a 16-year-old girl," Miss Rich told me. "I was named postmaster in 1927. When I got to be seventy, I had to retire because the rules said no postmaster can be over seventy. So I quit being postmaster and instead became supervising clerk in charge, doing the same job for another ten years. I've been in this post office over sixty-three years now."

The post office consisted of one corner of her front room, three chairs, one for Miss Lizzie and two for her constant visitors, and a parakeet in a cage.

Miss Lizzie Rich broke both hips just after dark on a March afternoon, when she was seventy-eight years old and alone.

"They just plumb cracked. I fell to the floor. Inch by inch I crawled and pulled myself across the room till I could reach my walkie-talkie. I called Stanley Dodge. He and some helpers came right over, sat me into my rocker, then lifted me and the rocker into the back of his truck and drove me to the town landing, where a boat was waiting. They carried me in the rocker down the ramp to the boat and strapped me and the rocker tight in the cockpit. Off we went across 6 miles of open water to Stonington. I'd busted my hips at 5 p.m. By 8 p.m., I was all fixed up in my bed at Blue Hill Hospital ...

Now that's some service."

Miss Lizzie was soon back at her post office, getting around on two walkers. She managed well on the walkers. Each day she made two trips to the well out back, lugging in a pail of water, sometimes spilling half on the way. Each Sunday she used her walkers to get up the hill in back to the church she had attended over seventy-five years. "Now I take fifteen minutes to get there instead of two minutes. But I get there."

In a storm, Isle au Haut can be a fearsome place. Then the power of the enraged Atlantic bursts upon Boom Beach. The mad ocean foams furiously over the ledges off Eastern Ear, then crashes on Thunder Gulch. Seas of terrifying size smash and fume past Morris' Mistake to pound at the feet of the towering granite cliffs. Even a mile inland, out of sight and sound of the storming sea, the island ground trembles.

In fog, which can wrap the island for days on end, ghosts of ship-wrecked, sea-blanched sailors drowned centuries before seem to haunt the shore. In hard winters, the ocean freezes over. No boat can move. In the bitter winter of 1935, there were no telephone links to the mainland and Isle au Haut was cut off from the world for five days.

Coast Guard planes from Boston flew over, dropping messages to see if the islanders needed help or rescue. They dropped instructions on how to put a reply on a rope strung between a pole and a rake held aloft by two islanders. On the third flyover, the grappling hook from the plane snatched the reply. It read:

"Thank you very much. We have plenty of supplies so far. No one sick. Thank you so much. C. W. Turner."

In the winter of 1857, the bay froze solid for 20 miles out and stayed that way for eight weeks. In 1950, Frank Barton froze to death when he collapsed carrying groceries home. His body lay in the snow, undiscovered, for three days.

On the south side, exposed to the Atlantic, lies Head Harbor, once a flourishing fishing community. When I was there, I found only one herring dory and one blue-hulled sailboat at their moorings. The twelve houses stood empty, their summer occupants gone from September till June. There was a "For Sale" sign on the house by the beach. The owner, Gooden Grant, was giving up and grudgingly moving to the mainland. He had turned ninety-four years old. Stone walls which once fenced in cattle on the farms are tumbled down around the unplanted meadows, where only wildflowers bloom, songbirds sing, and bees gather nectar.

On an island like this, everyone is his brother's keeper, especially when fire breaks out, the terror of almost defenseless islands. In the 1870s, a huge fire started in the blueberry barrens and burned the entire island. Gooden Grant saw the fire of 1894 at Duck Harbor. He was a boy then, sailing home at night with his father. At age ninety-four, Gooden Grant could still remember the sight he saw seventy-eight years before—sights of burning trees flying into the night air like torches, setting more fires across his island home.

In 1940, a kerosene stove in the Turners' house exploded. Harold Turner was over at Dennis Eaton's house when he heard the church bell ringing the alarm. His wife, Elthea, had fled from the burning house, driven to town, and rung the bell. The house burned to the ground. The whole town pitched in to build the Turners a new home. In 1947, Russ Devereux, who runs the work scow in Penobscot Bay, flew over another forest fire on the island. "Most of Maine was burning that summer. It was the year of the great fire at nearby Mount Desert. When the fire broke out in the forest here, I flew, circling low above it, shouting instructions to firefighters on the ground on where it was spreading. The whole island turned out to fight that blaze and got it under control after only 15 acres had been devastated."

Isle au Haut has dwindled in population in the last 150 years, but the special ways of a special island persist. For example, there is one gas pump on the island, not far from the town landing. Island custom is to drive up, fill your tank, and then leave the money on the honor system in a box nearby. It works.

But how long will such things last?

I asked a long-time islander and she pointed to a prayer tacked on her kitchen door.

"Lord, we thank thee that thy Grace
    Has brought us to this pleasant place,
And most earnestly we pray
That other folks will stay away."

17

Lobstering

Weird Wealth of Maine

Lobsters, plentiful and cheap in colonial days, were fed twice a day to indentured workers. Weary of too much lobster, they complained so loudly that a new clause in their contracts stated indentured workers should not be fed lobster more than four times a week.

Even a hundred years later, in the early 1800s, no boat and no traps were needed on the islands to catch lobster. Island children could go to the shore, turn over a rock, and catch lobsters for supper with their bare hands. They were so plentiful that island farmers spread lobsters on their fields and vegetable gardens as fertilizer. Nobody thought of selling lobsters.

Not until the 1840s did lobstering become a way of making a living, and it spread slowly west to east. In the autumn of 1850, the first lobster carrier, a "wet-smack" from Gloucester, with four men aboard, sailed into Swan's Island. They hired a few islanders to help them catch lobsters, paid cash, and left, their cargo hold swarming with live lobsters. The hold of a "wet-smack" has holes in it, allowing fresh seawater to run in and out, thus keeping live lobsters in prime condition for market. This is the way commercial lobstering began, with dealers sailing into the islands and teaching the islanders how to catch lobsters in quantity with traps and how to keep them alive until a wet smack arrived to buy them. The dealers, of course, were businessmen interested in building up their sources of supply.

But the dealers didn't pay much. In the 1850s, they paid two, sometimes three, cents a lobster. Not per pound, but per lobster; and the lobsters were very big as well as plentiful. Stories can be heard on the islands today about lobsters weighing 20 and 25 pounds. One giant creature of 43 pounds was caught at Friendship Long Island.

At the start, lobstering was the job of men too old to go on long, hard trips out to the fishing grounds. The older men, with young grandsons along as helpers, went out in a rowing dory or small sailboat and set only thirty to sixty traps close inshore; but they'd catch 200 pounds of lobsters or more. Today, young fishermen in big and powerful boats fish up to eight hundred traps off the islands and sometimes come home with less than 200 pounds.

The traps a hundred years ago looked rather like bird cages. They were cumbersome affairs 4 feet long, 2 feet high, and 2 feet wide, with slats far enough apart "to afford the proposed victims a clear view of the baits." The baits were cod heads and cunners hung on a row of hooks, rather than the bait bags or redfish carcasses used today in smaller metal or wood traps. The traps' ends then were simply tarred rope netting, with a big opening in one end. Lobsters then, as now, would back into the trap through that opening to get at the tempting bait inside. Then, as now, it never occurred to the lobster to back out. Lobsters always try to get out head first and can't do it. The big claws on their forward end are too wide to permit escape.

Lobsters were so plentiful in the 1850s that these traps fished well. The average catch per trap was six or seven lobsters weighing 4–6 pounds each, for a total of about 25–30 pounds per trap. Today, a lobsterman often averages less than one lobster of keeping size per trap, and a keeping-size lobster weighs only about a pound. But today the price per pound runs from two to three dollars, compared to a fraction of a cent then.

Canning lobster soon became a big and widespread business. By the 1880s, there were canning factories on Swan's Island, Isle au Haut, Deer Isle, Vinalhaven, and all the way along the coast (close to a hundred in all), on islands and in mainland harbors. Each year on the islands, more and more men, including the younger men, went lobstering, though in midsummer many younger island fishermen would go off to sea for a few months so they could make more money mackerel seining.

The total Maine lobster catch in 1880 was 14 million pounds. Of this, almost 9 million pounds went into cans. The canning business opened new jobs for island women and children.

Island lobster-canning factories were on the wharf, open at the end so men could bring the catch straight off the boat, carrying loads of live lobsters on a stretcher and dumping them directly into huge copper cauldrons of boiling water. When they were cooked, the lobsters were spread on long tables where the women cut them into various parts. One would punch out the chunky meat from the tail. Another, called a "cracker," would cut off the claws with a cleaver, and still others would pick the meat. Other groups of women did the packing, filling each can with a selection of various parts. One girl weighed the packed cans, adding or subtracting lobster meat till it weighed the specified one or two pounds. The next girl on the assembly line forced the meat down with a special "stamper" made for that job. The next put on a tin cover, banging it down with a hammer made specifically for that job. A trayload of filled cans went next to the solderer, a man who sealed them, leaving a tiny hole in the lid. The load was then lowered into a cauldron of boiling water until all the air was expelled from each tin. Then the solderer sealed the tiny hole in the lid and the tins were cooked again.

In the packing room, the cans were cleaned with acid, painted to prevent rust, and pasted with a bright label showing a scarlet lobster against a blue sea and bearing the words "Maine Lobster" and the town or island where packed. Thousands of such cans were packed daily into pine boxes, which were collected by the canning company's freight vessel and shipped to Boston or New York, usually for export.

In a canning factory, men were paid reasonably well. Solderers got $12 to $15 a week. Other men received $7 to $10 a week; but the women got only $2 to $3 a week. Even that wage was sought after, because, at the time, women schoolteachers on the islands were paid even less—only $1 a week. Boys from ten to fourteen years old earned 25 cents a day, the same wage paid to boys working in the island granite quarries.

The lobster-canning season lasted from April to August. When it was over, the canning of other fish, or corn or vegetables, began.

Most canned Maine lobster was sold abroad by distributors in New York and Boston. Perhaps this was because fresh lobster was available in the east; perhaps because housewives were suspicious lest the canned lobster go bad.

There is little evidence of this. Maine indeed was an expert in canning. Eastport led the way. The first lobster cannery was started at Eastport in the 1840s. Eastport also perfected the mass canning of sardines. By 1898, there were sixty-one sardine canneries producing several million cases of sardines each year. Toward the end of the 1890s, the larger islands and most coastal towns had one or more factories canning lobsters, sardines, clams, cod, and mackerel.

Island lobstermen sold their smallest lobsters, "shorts" by today's standards, to the cannery and kept the big ones to sell live to the smack buyer, who came weekly in his wetsmack schooner. The island lobstermen would tow their "cars" or crates filled with the big live lobsters over to the smack. They'd agree on a price with the smack-buyer, who would dump the live lobsters out of their cars into the saltwater compartments on his little schooner.

There was more to the exchange than money. There was a visit. The smack-buyer brought news and gossip with him from other islands and the mainland. A good buyer also brought the essential stone jugs containing rum or whiskey. He knew island lobstermen could not pursue their hard trade fueled only by the spruce beer or dandelion wines made by island women. The island men relied on the smack-buyer to bring them a needed supply of stone jugs. The buyer who arrived at an island with only cash soon learned more was expected of him. "No rum brought, no lobsters sold" was the code of most islands.

On nights after the smack buyer had disbursed cash and stone jugs, islanders would put on a square dance in the canning factory.

Another welcome visitor was the "trader." The trader was essentially a small schooner fitted out as a floating store, which sailed from island to island. The sailor-storekeeper would sail his boat up the harbor and tie up at the lobster wharf or canning factory and do business for a few days. The inside of his boat was filled with shelves stocked with scented soaps for ladies, shaving mugs and razors for men, jackknives and toys for children. He carried shoes and boots, dry goods of all kinds, needles, threads, and laces. Below decks was the heavier merchandise: wash tubs, crockery, pots and pans, cans of kerosene, barrels of molasses and apples. The trader would sell his stock for cash or, if necessary, he'd barter. He'd swap his store goods for animal furs, sails, rope, dried fish. There was even a floating cobbler in a flat-bottomed scow who, in fair weather, would call at islands in Penobscot Bay. George S. Wasson, in his book *Sailing Days on the Penobscot*, described the odd-looking scow as being painted light blue and carrying the words, painted in yellow, "W. Cottle. Boots and Shoes Repaired on the Rolling Deep."

By 1900, lobster canning was on its way out. As a conservation measure, the Maine legislature passed a law forbidding the canning of lobsters. Lobsters too small for the wet-smack buyer were going to the canneries, no matter how small they were. As a result, lobsters were being caught before they had a chance to breed, and the lobster shortage was so serious in the 1880s that future stocks were threatened. The commissioners of all New England states met in Boston to establish conservation laws. A hundred years later, in the 1980s, the commissioners were still meeting, discussing the same topic. The trouble is that lobsters are slow developers. A lobster takes five years to reach one pound. It sheds old shells and grows new ones to fit larger bodies many times. It does not reproduce until it is at least five years old. So, as a conservation device, Maine has minimum and maximum size limits for legal lobsters.

As lobsters became more scarce, the price, of course, went up. Lobsters, which had fetched only two cents each in the 1850s, regardless of weight, were by 1900 bringing nine cents a pound. More islanders were going lobstering. On Swan's Island, for example, where only ten men were lobstering in 1855, more than 140 men were lobstering by 1900. Today, 6,800 licensed lobstermen all along the Maine coast catch well more than one hundred million dollars worth of lobster a year. The price they get is a hundred times greater than the price their forefathers got a hundred years ago. But because of enormous increases in the number of lobstermen and number of lobster traps, the amount of lobster they catch is barely more.

18

Swan's Island
King David to Rockefellers

Swan's Island is 10½ square miles of rather flat land halfway between Isle au Haut and Mount Desert. Almost every acre is rich with tales of fascinating people who've lived on it over the centuries.

But let's begin with the value of the island itself. Thomas Kench, the first white settler in 1776, paid nothing for it. He fled here as a deserter from the Revolutionary Army and, for fourteen years, existed here as a solitary recluse. More about Kench later. Then in 1791, fabled "King David" Smith landed, fathered twenty-four children, more than fifty grandchildren, bossed the island, and lived to be eighty. Spectacular and swashbuckler extraordinaire Colonel James Swan, Kench's old army commander, then bought Swan's Island and twenty-four nearby islands, over nine thousand acres in all. Swan paid two pounds an acre in 1786. The colorful Swan envisioned creating a feudal kingdom here, with himself as king. He gave the island his name, but he died in a Paris prison. More on him in a moment, too.

Now leap from early days of American independence to the 20th-century. In 1952, an oceanfront acre of Swan's still fetched only $15, but the price of a building lot on Mackerel Cove in the 1980s was $50,000. Lawsuits about this land have involved the Rockefellers, who own lots of it. The big change was due to a boat—the Maine State Ferry, which carries cars and makes six trips daily on a forty-minute run to the mainland. The ferry service, begun in 1960, sent population and the price of precious land zooming. So today, Swan's Island has an airfield, a huge campground, paved roads, summer colonies, a school, churches, and about 350 resident taxpayers.

But Swan's Islanders saw the dangers of speculative land development and quickly passed some of the best land-use ordinances in Maine. The result is that they have saved their island. Swan's is still a fascinating, lovely jewel in Penobscot Bay.

And now, back to the first white settler on Swan's Island. Thomas Kench, ex-soldier of the Revolution, hauled his small boat ashore here and turned hermit for fourteen years of solitary existence. Kench came from England to the colonies before the Revolution, perhaps a lonely adventurer from the start. He enlisted when Benedict Arnold led that ghastly march on Quebec in the autumn of 1775. Kench paddled up the Kennebec in one of those leaky bateaux built in a hurry from green wood at Pittston; portaged those damnable heavy boats across the Maine wilderness. Like all in that heroic company, Kench became sick, cold, desperately hungry, munching with joy when he ate the carcass of a dog. He survived, only to freeze in a tent during November and December on the Plains of Abraham. He survived a raging epidemic of smallpox that killed men around him. Kench came through it, strong enough to be among the first American soldiers to climb the cliffs, scale the walls and attack Quebec's Citadel. He survived again, one of the few to get back alive to American lines. In defeat, Kench survived that terrible winter of retreat, struggling and straggling back to Maine through the wilderness, hip deep in snow. He finally reached Boston. Even after that experience, Kench volunteered for more. In 1776, he became a gunner in the artillery company commanded by a very young captain named James Swan.

There something went badly wrong. Maybe Kench, the soldier who'd survived the Arnold march, rebelled against the spit-and-polish of an artillery company headed by a Boston dandy. Kench deserted and fled, heading to the lonely islands off Mount Desert. On a day late in 1776, Kench grounded out his boat on a tiny islet of Swan's Island. He arrived a desperate, angry man, but a survivor.

He was to live the next fourteen years alone there; then six more years with "King David" Smith for unwanted company. After twenty years on Swan's, Kench moved off, a changed man. He bought 100 acres of land at Brooksville, on Cape Rosier, took up farming, married, sired six children, and when he was past ninety, Kench died.

For fourteen years, Kench's only company on the island had been a cow and a few sheep. He kept apart from the fishermen from Mount Desert, 10 miles away, who would occasionally sail into the harbor. He kept apart from the Indians who came down in summer from Old

Town in canoes and went about their summer business; the braves hunting seals and fishing from their canoes, the squaws and children digging and drying clams for winter food, making baskets from the island's long sweetgrass. Kench kept his distance from them, too.

The one person Kench could not keep away from was David Smith. Smith and his family arrived fourteen years after Kench had found his solitude; and Smith intruded grossly by building a log cabin on the same islet in Burnt Coat Harbor. Smith, like Kench, was a wounded veteran of the Revolutionary War. After the Revolution, Smith had moved from New Hampshire to Deer Isle and married there. In 1791, Smith, his wife, and children left Deer Isle, sailed out to the island, and settled in close to the recluse, Kench. Perhaps it was this exposure to the Smith family, especially the children, that turned Kench around from a total "loner" into the new man, a man who, five years later, would move to the mainland, become a farmer, a husband, a father, and live to be a patriarch of ninety years.

This David Smith is revered today as the true father of Swan's Island. He married three times, fathered at least twenty-four children, farmed 240 acres, and saw his children's children grow and build homes on the island. He was known then, and is still known, as "King David," the man who dominated life on Swan's Island till he died at eighty years.

But the most colorful of Swan's early white men was Colonel James Swan, the officer from whom Kench deserted. Swan was a swashbuckling, ambitious, enthusiastic businessman, bon vivant, and dreamer. His name lives on in Swan's Island.

Swan, born a Scotsman, left Fifeshire at eleven years of age and landed in Boston. There he soon became a star among the young bloods. He worked as a teenager in banks, brokerage offices, and counting houses. A fellow clerk he liked and admired was Henry Knox, the man who became Secretary of War under George Washington, who built the palatial mansion, "Montpelier," at Thomaston, Maine, and who remained Swan's hero forever.

Swan was a free-thinking, fast-writing, liberal. By the time he was seventeen, he had published a fiery book titled *A Dissuasion of Great Britain from the Slave Trade*, which made him one of the youngest and first abolitionists. He became an early and ardent member of the Sons of Liberty and helped dump 342 chests of English tea into Boston Harbor. He fought at the Battle of Bunker Hill, was wounded twice, recovered, and came back to serve as an artillery captain in the siege

of Boston. The rising star, still in his twenties, became Secretary of
the Massachusetts Board of War, Adjutant-General of the Commonwealth, and a member of the legislature.

Swan also became rich early, and a friend of the famous and powerful. He was lucky enough to inherit an unexpected fortune from a
crusty Scotch uncle, a bachelor, who admired the guts of the young-
ster who had left Fifeshire at age eleven and done so well in the New
World. Swan soon parlayed this fortune into a bigger fortune. He
used the inherited money to buy confiscated Tory lands cheaply
around Boston and Dorchester. He also bought vast tracts of land in
Virginia, West Virginia, and Kentucky. He bought privateers and made
money fast on the cargoes and ships they captured. He speculated
wildly, sometimes losing heavily. He lived high on the hog. He kept a
grandiose home at the corner of West and Tremont streets in Boston.
There he and his wife entertained Lafayette, Rochambeau, and George
Washington. He drove the most ornate carriage in North America.

This was the man who, at thirty years of age, bought Swan's
Island (then called Burnt Coat Island) and twenty-four nearby islands
from the Commonwealth of Massachusetts in 1786. Young Swan and
his family began talking about their new holdings as their "island
empire." They planned to build a magnificent home on their island,
entertain in kingly style—and make money from the 9,000 acres.

Swan, the dreamer, saw lumber mills, flour mills, his own great
manor house, and many settlements of workers' and farmers' cottages; and himself as lord of all he surveyed in Penobscot Bay.

He offered free land, up to 100 acres, to settlers. Many came. He
began felling trees for sawmills and started trade with Boston. Above
all, he started building a grand manor for himself. Up went a huge
structure, complete with colonnades, balconies, porches, ballrooms; a
palatial home totally out of place on a rough, barely settled island. He
was doomed never to live in it.

Swan, ever a businessman, persuaded his political friends in
Massachusetts to exempt his twenty-five islands from all taxes for
twenty years, provided he got twenty-two Protestant families settled,
each in a home at least 22 feet square, and built a church and school.

But Swan, the high flyer, high liver, and gambler, hit a streak of
bad financial luck. He was suddenly on the verge of bankruptcy. To
escape his creditors, he fled incognito to France in 1788, only two
years after beginning his island empire. Swan even spoke of entering
a monastery and starting an entirely new life in France.

But the French Revolution killed that unlikely idea. Swan, the maker of deals, the friend of the great in France and America, the man who had dumped tea in Boston Harbor and been wounded at Bunker Hill, began an exciting new enterprise in Paris. He became the American agent of the revolutionary French government, the man who purchased needed goods for them in America and then got the goods smuggled through the British blockade. By 1795, Swan, who had fled to escape bankruptcy, was back in the United States, flying very high again. He successfully negotiated settlement of the American debt to France, thereby providing France with dollars to buy needed goods in America. But his creditors were soon on his tail and Swan fled back to France.

Swan's Island was by now far out of his mind. The great mansion, though still new, was on its way downhill. "King David" Smith, by now the father of a dozen or more children, moved into the abandoned manor and took squatter's possession. He renamed it "King David's Palace." But King David left it for his new 240-acre farm on the northern shore. By 1840, the big house had served as home to a dozen squatters and had become a hovel. Fire swept through it that year and reduced Swan's dream to ashes.

In Paris, the sky was falling on Swan. The French Republic stripped him of his monopoly as its American agent. He was accused of pocketing two million francs and thrown into jail in Paris. He absolutely refused to pay the two million francs, contending he was innocent. He chose to stay in a debtor's prison for twenty-two years. His wife, in Boston, supplied ample funds. Swan used the money to buy presents for his guards, rich furnishings for his jail quarters, and to pay off debts for other prisoners. He spent lavishly to establish an elegant household across the street from the jail. There, in absentia, he gave huge dinners for his friends. He kept boxes at the theater and opera and entertained friends there, again in absentia. Swan asked only one thing—that a chair be set for him at the head of the table, that a seat be kept for him in the boxes at the opera and theater.

In 1830, Louis Phillipe was restored to the throne of France. The king released all debtors, including Swan. Swan left the prison only to do one thing—to embrace his old friend, Lafayette. This he did, and then he returned voluntarily to prison. After twenty-two years in that prison, he felt at home only there; and there he died in 1830.

Swan's Island, meanwhile, was in a legal mess. Swan's agent, Joseph Price, torn between Swan, creditors, settlers, claims, and counterclaims, had given up and left. Daniel Webster was involved as a lawyer, trying to unravel Swan's mortgage complications.

The islanders took matters into their own hands. In 1834, the two hundred residents formed their own government as a plantation, drew up a tax list, built a school and a road, and changed Swan's Island from a mixed-up feudal proprietorship into an orderly, self-governing community of Maine. All that remained of Swan was his name. The island Champlain had christened Brule Cote (Burned Coat) Island in 1603 has now been called Swan's Island for more than two hundred years.

Fishing, not lumber, not flour mills, became the basis of Swan's Island prosperity. The island led all the New England coast in catching mackerel. In 1879, the Swan's Island fleet landed 15,000 barrels of mackerel, valued at five dollars each. The Swan's Island schooner, *Alice*, and her fabled skipper, Captain H. B. Joyce, ranked first in mackerel catching. The *Alice*, with forty men in her crew, netted 30,000 fish in one spring day off Block Island. In 1881, the *Alice* cured 5,000 barrels of fish, worth $28,000. Then, five years later, the mackerel vanished. The Swan's Island fleet fell apart. Even Captain Joyce had to sell his *Alice*. The male population of the island was thrown out of work, after years of being 100 percent employed in fishing or building fishing boats. Slowly the island turned, less successfully, to herring fishing. Later, lobstering became the fore-most occupation.

Almost a hundred years later, aboard *Steer Clear*, we crept through thick fog along the shore off Swan's Island, trying to find the entrance into Burnt Coat Harbor. This was the same approach Thomas Kench made in late 1776 when—on a clearer day, I hope— the first settler went ashore at Burnt Coat. But in this twentieth century we had the light and the fog signal on Hockamock Point to guide us. Trouble was we could not hear the fog signal or see the light. We cut the motors to listen hard, and lay wallowing in the slow swell, straining our ears. Not a sound from the big fog horn, though we should be abreast of it according to my dead reckoning. Then we heard the gong at the harbor entrance, its clappers clanging in the slow swell. With relief, I put the engines into gear and crept to that sound. Suddenly the fog horn blew so loudly it made us jump. It was only a hundred yards to port, but the breeze had been carrying the sound inland, over the island, and up the bay toward Blue Hill.

Later, we heard that fishermen from Burnt Coat Harbor had complained for years to the Coast Guard that they couldn't hear the horn coming in from the sea. They had asked for a noise reflector. They never got it. Now, there is no fog-signal keeper. The Coast Guard abandoned the lighthouse, despite protests from fishermen, and pulled out Coast Guardsman E-5 Philip Felch, who had kept the light, and his redhaired wife and three children. Today, there is only an automated beacon.

We crept into the harbor and anchored. Late that night, when the wind blew 50 miles an hour, it proved an uncomfortable, bouncy place. In the gale of wind, our anchor dragged. We had to reset it from a bouncing bow at 3 a.m.

Next day, we went ashore. First stop was the town office. It was one small room at the back of the fire station at Burnt Coat Harbor; two desks, three straight chairs, some filing cabinets, and a closet.

"Come Election Day, we clean out the closet, take off the door, hang up a red, white, and blue curtain, and the closet becomes the Swan's Island voting booth," said Myron Sprague, Jr., first selectman that year, at a salary of $2 a day. Swan's Island officials were mostly young. Sprague was 26 when he was first elected a selectman. The night we talked with him, he was 31, the oldest man on the board, and chairman. David Joyce, 30, and Dexter Lee, 28, were the other two selectmen of the island. The three-man school board was even younger. Gerry Smith was 29, Terence Staples was 27, and Sheldon Carlson, old man of the school board, was a World War II veteran. That summer of '72, Swan's Island had hired its first policeman, Tom Collins, only twenty-one. "We chose an off-islander so he couldn't be accused of playing favorites," said Myron Sprague, Jr. "Tom came from as far away as you'd want to go—Bridgton, Maine."

After dinner that first night, the wind picked up and the rain started, signs of a coming squall. We sat in the one-room town office with Sprague while he showed us old town reports. The names of the town officers had not changed much. In the 1952 report, his father, Myron Sprague, was moderator of town meetings, member of the school committee, the budget committee, and the planning committee. The Staples name was there, too. Herman W. Staples was town clerk, member of the school committee, budget committee, and the committee for health and sanitation. Loel Staples was a selectman; Milton Staples was road commissioner; Carroll Staples was constable; Norman Staples and Maynard Staples were on other town boards.

The continuity of the same family names in the governance of Swan's Island, generation after generation, holds true with the Joyces, the Burns, the Norwoods, the Holmes, and the Kents, as well as the Spragues and the Staples.

Families like these, rooted to the island's soil, have long been and still are the best guardians of Swan's future. Nowadays, the old island families reach out sometimes to draw on the special abilities of new-comers in the summer colony. Take the time in 1970, when rumors flew that developers planned to put 243 cottages on handkerchief-size lots. Eugene Norwood was a 54-year-old lobsterman at the time and head of the planning committee. He and his committee knew fast action was needed to protect the island. They knew that words like "zoning" might put up the hackles of island families, fearful that state bureaucrats would dictate what they could or could not do with their property. They knew, too, that whatever local ordinances the island might write, those ordinances might face court challenges by smart lawyers from the city.

"We worked like the deuce," Norwood told me, "and drafted a proposed ordinance regulating subdivision development of the island, but none of us on the planning board were lawyers. We were mostly lobstermen. So for expert help we went to a Boston lawyer and a New York lawyer who summered here. They soon put what we wanted on paper and we called a public meeting to explain to our neighbors what we had in mind and to scotch some crazy rumors flying around. The neighbors raised, and we answered, questions for hours. After that meeting, we waited a week so everyone had a fair chance to talk it over. Then we called a special town meeting on March 17, 1971, to vote on the proposed zoning ordinance."

The closet at the back of the fire station was emptied out to serve, as always, as the voting booth. The island people passed the ordinance by a vote of 49 to 12.

The ordinance was later seen by a Rockefeller lawyer, who wrote from New York to say it was about the finest ordinance of its kind enacted anywhere in the United States.

The ordinance required that every lot in a subdivision should have at least 2 acres and that lots which bordered on the shore or any road should have at least 200 feet of frontage; that no building could be closer than 30 feet to the boundary line of another lot, nor closer than 100 feet to any existing building on an adjacent lot, nor closer than 60 feet from the center of any road, nor closer than 30 feet to the high-tide line. Other provisions prohibited tents, campers, house trailers, and set strict standards for sewer systems, water systems, fire hydrants, and telephone and power lines. The island required that de-tails of all proposed development be first submitted for approval to the planning board, and that performance guarantees of substantial amounts be posted before the final plans would be considered.

The ordinance has prevented mass development; but it has also pushed land prices so high that only the well-to-do can now buy property on Swan's Island. Therein lies a predicament, voiced to me by a young fisherman. "I was born here and I'm twenty-two now and fishing on my own. I'm in a mood to get married and start my own family here. Of course, we want a place of our own, near the water, where I can get to my boat. But how am I going to get that building lot when someone from away is ready to pay so much more for it? Am I going to be frozen out now so I have to move off the island where I was born and where I fish, where I want to raise my new family?"

The same predicament faces many Maine islanders.

People from away now own more than two-thirds of Swan's Island, and they pay most of the taxes. This change in ownership is a direct result of the frequent car-ferry service to the mainland, which started in 1960. Within ten years of the start of the Maine State Ferry Service, most of the island was owned by people from away. Whoever owns the land and pays the taxes finally calls the tune.

But no ferry service and no amount of newcomers changed Clyde Torrey. Clyde Torrey was, for over thirty years after World War II, the most colorful, most eccentric, most loved character on Swan's Island, and surely the island's most photographed man. That fine book about Swan's Island, *Biography of an Island* by Perry D. Westbrook, was dedicated to Clyde Torrey and he enjoyed autographing copies. Clyde is dead now.

Clyde Torrey was past seventy-five when I last talked with him years back. He had an old, gray, dilapidated farmhouse on the east side of the island, with spectacular views across the open water to the islands of Placentia and Great Gott, on to Mount Desert and Cadillac Mountain. But Clyde seldom lived inside the farmhouse. He preferred to cook and sleep in the abandoned cars beside it, even in winter. Clyde Torrey looked weird and made that weirdness a point of personal pride. In summer he usually wore old blue overalls, over a series of longjohn undershirts. He rolled his pants leg up over his calf to let the salt air get to a place that pained him, and on his head he wore a wild-looking Scotch tam o' shanter, a gift from God knows whom. He was a lean man with bad teeth, a good smile, and a dirty stubble of beard, and he played endlessly on his accordion—ballads, bawdy songs, sea chanties, drinking songs, and square dances.

Clyde looked like a bum, but he was a well-educated, well-spoken man who simply preferred his odd and lonely lifestyle. He grew a few vegetables and potatoes, dug clams, and often shared talk and sometimes a bottle with summer campers on Mertic Morrison's nearby campgrounds.

"Way back, Clyde went to school with me," said a classmate with a long memory. "That was over sixty years ago, when 120 kids went to three schools in the island's three communities of Atlantic, Minturn, and Swan's Island. He drove us crazy, even then. Clyde would get straight A's without seeming to do a lick of work."

Clyde played his accordion and stomped out the beat for hundreds of country dances on the island. He played and called square dances for years down at the campgrounds in summer. When Myron Sprague, Jr. went off to the army, Clyde stuck posters on the island roads that read "Hootenanny for Sonny Sprague tonight, before he goes into the army. Dancing to the music of Clyde Torrey!"

During World War II, Torrey himself got a notice from the draft board on the mainland, saying that he was being called up. "Struck me as odd," he said, "because I was forty-five years old then. But I got into my skiff before daybreak and rowed clear over to the mainland. With currents and all I rowed better than 10 miles. When I got to the draft board I found it was a government snafu. They didn't want me at that age. So I got into my skiff and rowed back 10 miles. That was my army career."

Another Swan's Island eccentric, long before Clyde Torrey, grew the world's finest tuberous begonias here. He was an able, inventive man from Pennsylvania, who came to Swan's Island for his health after World War I and bought himself a house on Mackerel Cove. To shelter it from cold winds, he amazed islanders by encasing the entire wooden frame house with an outer wall of granite blocks, hewn from local quarries.

Then he installed an electricity plant and plumbing, and began growing his tuberous begonias. To fertilize the soil, he gathered huge amounts of rockweed washed up on the shore near his house. Then he sheltered his flower garden from the winds by planting evergreen hedges. When his beds were ready, he eventually planted more than twenty-five hundred begonias in each one. The flowers were so spectacular in their dazzling colors they drew worldwide attention. He hired an English gardener to work year-round on them, built a greenhouse and a potting shed. Millionaires in their yachts sailed over from Bar Harbor to see the begonia gardens on Swan's Island and bought plants to take home. Even Lady Astor took his plants home to

England. Between 1920 and 1945, this eccentric gardener sold up to forty thousand tuberous begonias a year, all across the nation and overseas. His secret was the heavy application of seaweed to the thin soil lying atop island granite.

The gardens and the begonias are long since gone. The greenhouse, the dwelling, the wharf have rotted away. Weeds are the only crop where tens of thousands of dazzling begonias, the finest in the world, once grew.

19

Mount Desert

From the French to the Fire

The feet of three and a half million visitors a year are wearing away the topsoil and even the granite of ancient Acadia. Mount Desert is the mecca for millions who come to feast their eyes on its bold beauty and stirring seascapes.

As they stand atop Cadillac Mountain and look to islands off-shore and the Atlantic beyond, their feet rest on pink granite 400 million years old. This granite forced its way up through volcanic turbulence as magma, the molten mass of the earth's inner crust. As it cooled, it fell back into the tortured gaping holes and hardened to become the massive granite of Mount Desert. Out of it came Cadillac Mountain, towering 1,532 feet over the sea, highest mountain on the Atlantic coast; and the seventeen other mountains beside Cadillac that form the spectacular spine of Mount Desert.

Today, a handsome road with hairpin bends and magnificent lookouts for sightseers in cars and buses has opened the beauties of Cadillac to millions.

Europeans came to Mt. Desert four hundred years ago; Indians were here four thousand years before Christ. Archaeologists have discovered artifacts that, by the carbon-14 method of dating, were left here about 4000 B.C. They are much like "finds" from the ancient Indian grounds in New Mexico.

Three thousand years later, around 1000 A.D., came another Indian civilization called the Red Paint people, because of the red ocher found in their grave sites. Where they came from or where they vanished to is not known. Long after them came the Abnaki Indians, about whom we know quite a lot. They did not live year-round on Mount Desert, but only summered here.

They came down streams and rivers and across carry points in birch-bark canoes from May to October to fish, plant corn, and paddle to the nearby islands. After the settlers arrived, the Indians slowly ceased even their summer visits.

The beauty remains. Some believe this island, 16 miles long and 12 miles wide, is the most dramatically beautiful island in the world.

Mount Desert is the boundary line, in terms of birds and of plants, between the sub-arctic and the temperate zones. Here, birds and plants from both climates meet and abound together. Two of America's great naturalists, James Audubon and Louis Agassiz, were so enthralled by Mount Desert that they did much of their great work here.

A Portugese, Esteban Gomez (Stephen Smith), was probably the first European to sail here, in 1525, and he ventured up river as far as Bangor. What we call the Penobscot River Gomez christened on his map "Rio de las Gamas"—River of the Deer.

Next came a Frenchman. In 1604, Samuel de Champlain, navigator for Sieurs de Monts, sailed to this island and called the region La Cadie; which became L'Acadie, which became today's Acadia National Park. Champlain left the main French camp on St. Croix Island in a 17-ton ketch. With twelve sailors and two Indian guides, he came one September day in 1604 on an exploring trip and discovered Mount Desert.

"This island," he wrote four hundred years ago, "is very high, and cleft into seven or eight mountains all in a line:. The summits are bare and deserted. Nothing but rock. I named it Isle des Monts-deserts."

Champlain made that one short stopover here, then sailed off to explore the rest of the Maine coast, naming Isle au Haut on the way. On his map, Champlain drew Mount Desert and the Cranberry Isles with remarkable accuracy. He then left Maine's coast to become the founding father of Quebec.

A French lady, Antoinette de Pons, the beautiful but virtuous Marquise de Guerchville, who refused to become mistress of King Henry of Navarre, now enters the Mount Desert story. In 1613, this lady of extreme virtue got the land deed formerly held by Sieurs de Monts. The deed, given her by King Louis XIII, was enlarged to cover all of North America south to the Gulf of Mexico.

Antoinette financed a Jesuit expedition to make Catholic converts of the Indians. The expedition commander was Sieur de la Sausseye. The religious leader on Mount Desert was a Jesuit priest, Pierre

Briand, professor of theology at the University of Lyons. The good priest was foolhardy enough to sail in a ship ill-named *Jonas*. On a bright day in June 1613, the *Jonas* dropped anchor in a lovely Mount Desert cove. Father Briand and his Jesuit colleague, Father Massé, celebrated mass and named the spot Saint-Sauveur.

Mount Desert so charmed Father Briand that he decided to start his mission on the spot. The ship's company of twenty-five colonists and thirty-five sailors moved ashore, pitched tents, and left the *Jonas* at anchor while they set up camp and began searching for Indian souls to save. They spent a happy summer month encamped near Fernald's Point, meeting, befriending, and converting local Indians.

Then their luck turned bad.

Down the coast, off Blue Hill Bay, a small squadron of English ships were on the prowl, with the mission of chasing any French intruders off what England considered English soil. In command of the English was Captain Samuel Argall, a tough sea captain who had helped establish the English colony in Virginia six years earlier. As he cruised Blue Hill Bay, he met friendly Indians and invited them aboard. They told him other white men were nearby. Argall suspected they were Frenchmen. He got the Indians to act as his local pilots and together they sailed down the Western Way to Mount Desert. Argall soon saw smoke from the cooking fires of Father Briand's camp. He headed for it, aboard his 14-gun ship *Treasurer*, with all hands at battle stations. He found the *Jonas* at anchor and took her skeleton crew by surprise. In a brief fight, the *Jonas* got off one badly aimed shot and *Treasurer* quickly killed the man who had fired off the only shot. Argall captured the ship and sent his men ashore to round up Father Briand and all his soul-savers and sailors. The French surrendered with little resistance. Argall tore down their camp and erected a new protestant cross and a plaque inscribed with the name of the King of England, thereby establishing the claim to Mount Desert as the soil of England rather than France.

For the next seventy-five, years no new white settlement by either the English or the French was attempted on Mount Desert. It was a risky outpost, too close to the feuds between Indian, French, and English to tempt settlers.

But the area was nevertheless a bone of contention between the French and English crowns. In the hope that a military man would nail down the English claim to Mount Desert, King James I gave title to an admiral of the English navy, Sir Robert Mansell. The King hoped Mansell would go to Mount Desert to make certain that the flag of England flew unchallenged; but all Sir Robert did was change the name from Mount Desert to Mount Mansell. That bit of egotism failed to take hold. The French name of Mount Desert has stuck.

Sailors of all nations knew Mount Desert well, by sight. It was one of the biggest landmarks of the New World for ships from Europe. According to ships' logs, in clear weather a ship 60 miles out to sea could spot Cadillac Mountain. For example, when Governor Winthrop sailed by Mount Desert in June 1630 on his way to settle Massachusetts Bay, he drew the first known sketches of Mount Desert as it looks from 40 miles at sea. Sketches like the one drawn by Winthrop appeared in every edition of *The English Pilot* from 1706 on. The sea traffic past Mount Desert was frequent, but few set foot ashore.

One who did, and left his mark, was Antoine Laumet, son of a small-town French lawyer. Few have heard of him by that name, but his alias is a household word—Cadillac.

Laumet emigrated from France to Canada. In 1688, this adventurer obtained a land grant from the French Governor of Canada for 6 square miles in Maine, plus the Isle des Monts Deserts, almost abandoned since Captain Argall had captured Father Briand and the Jesuit colony in 1613. By the time Laumet got his land grant, he had changed his plebian name to the more aristocratic name of La Mothe, and added the fake title "Sieur de Cadillac," a little town near his birthplace in France. Laumet, now going by the grand name of Antoine La Mothe, Sieur de Cadillac, in 1688 took his bride to Mount Desert. The couple spent only one summer on the island, but Laumet now added the resounding extra title "Seigneur des Monts Deserts." In his own honor, he christened the highest mountain of his new domain Cadillac Mountain.

Laumet was a born hustler. After his one summer on Mount Desert, he upped stakes for Montreal. There he became a fur trader of importance and soon founded a trading station he called Detroit. Detroit returned the compliment hundreds of years later by naming its most prestigious car after him. To this day, the emblem of the Cadillac is Laumet's phony coat of arms, further emblazoned with the coronet of a count—an honor not even Laumet dared invent for himself. The adventurer Laumet kept on the upward move and ended his career as governor of French Louisiana.

Thus the highest mountain on the Atlantic coast and the most famous American automobile carry the name of the adventurer who came from a village in Gascony and spent one summer three hundred years ago on Mount Desert; but his imprint on the history of Maine was by no means over when the Seigneur des Monts Deserts sailed away from Cadillac Mountain.

Close to a hundred years after he left, Laumet's granddaughter arrived from France to the newly independent United States and filed claim to her grandfather's land on Mount Desert. Her name was Madame Barthelmy de Gregoire. She arrived in Boston from France in 1786, at the age of forty-one, with a husband and three children. She promptly filed suit with the General Court of Massachusetts (to which Maine belonged till 1820), claiming ownership of her grand-father's lands. She brought with her letters of introduction from Lafayette. Thomas Jefferson, who had close ties to France from his negotiations in Paris for French help during the Revolution, was in the White House. The young United States and France were enjoying a happy honeymoon period. So when this 41-year-old French woman presented her prestigious letters of introduction and her claim, the Court of Massachusetts listened in a kindly mood. They promptly gave her and her family American citizenship; and then gave the lady ownership of all the eastern half of Mount Desert, plus some of the adjoining mainland.

Madame de Gregoire and her family, ownership papers in her purse, sailed to Mount Desert and settled at Hull's Cove. She quickly opened the first Mount Desert real-estate office and began selling her land to squatters at the bargain rate of five dollars for 100 acres. That dribble of income was not enough. In 1792, she went after bigger money and sold most of the eastern half of Mount Desert for $6,000 to Henry Jackson of Boston. He, in turn, sold to Senator William Bingham of Philadelphia. When Madame de Gregoire died in 1811, Bingham bought the rest of her land.

The Binghams, already one of the wealthiest families in America, established the Bingham Trust, which soon had enormous holdings in Maine. To bankroll their land speculations, the Bingham Trust took into partnership the Baring family, bankers in London. Together, they embarked on still more land speculation. Their agent in these parts was Colonel John Black. He prospered hugely, as witness the Black Mansion at Ellsworth, a dazzling and extravagant display of classic Georgian architecture that Colonel Black built in 1802. In frontier Maine, the Colonel's house was a rich-man's palace. (Today it is open to the public.)

Madame de Gregoire's presence on Mount Desert triggered new French interest in the island. Soon after she came to Hull's Cove, wealthy and energetic Madame Bacler de Leval fled here from the French Revolution, bringing a large retinue of friends and servants. She bought land from Madame de Gregoire, with the idea of starting a center of French culture and trade. In the French-named town of LaMoine, she built a grand French-style home, "Fontaine Leval," complete even to a long driveway lined with French poplars grown from seeds she had brought from France. Her enterprise failed, but her retinue left behind descendants with French names who have become distinguished citizens of Mount Desert. One delightful French coincidence is that, on land owned in the 1790s by Madame de Gregoire and Madame de Leval, the Pierre Monteux School was established in 1964 by the widow of the famed French conductor Pierre Monteux. The music school is famous and flourishing today.

Another memorable French connection to Mount Desert is the famous Talleyrand, right-hand man to the Emperor Napoleon. Talleyrand came to Mount Desert with the purpose of buying land for French refugees from the Reign of Terror and the guillotine of the French Revolution. In the end, he bought no land here, but his presence gave rise to the story that Talleyrand had been born on Mount Desert—a story with no truth.

Samuel Eliot Morison, a man with deep ties to Mount Desert, gives a neat explanation for the origin of the story, which he tells in his excellent book *The Story of Mount Desert*. He says the myth of Talleyrand's birth on the island started because someone who saw Talleyrand strolling about said, "That fellow looks like the little French bastard who was running around Southwest Harbor thirty years ago."

The General Court of Massachusetts gave the eastern half of Mount Desert Island to Madame de Gregoire, granddaughter of the Sieur de Cadillac. What of the western part of the island? The Court of Massachusetts, still in a generous mood, gave title to that magnificent scenery to the Bernard family. The claims by the de Gregoires and the Bernards had a certain similarity.

In September 1762, while England still ruled the Massachusetts Bay Colony, Francis Bernard was the royal governor of the Province of Massachusetts. Bernard, who had a wife and ten children to support, cast envious eyes on the vast, empty land to the east. So the governor took a cruise Down East in the official sloop *Massachusetts*, to take a personal look at Mount Desert. While there, Governor Bernard gave official land deeds to the settlers already in place—the

Somes and Richard families, the Stanleys, Spurlings, Bunkers, and Hadlocks. Then and there he decided to provide well for his own future and issued deeds to himself for most of the western half of the island.

But there was not to be much future in America for him. The Boston Tea Party and the American Revolution put a sudden end to the dreams of Francis Bernard, the English governor and he beat a retreat to England. There King George III rewarded him by making him a baronet; but the American revolutionaries confiscated all his lands, and his hopes for a large slice of Mount Desert went down the drain.

However, his son, John Bernard, had not flown the coop to England. The son had stayed in Bath, where he was smart enough to join the winning Revolutionary side. After the War of Independence had been won, John Bernard went before the General Court of Massachusetts and petitioned to get back his father's confiscated lands. The kindly Court gave him title to all the western half of Mount Desert Island as a reward for sticking with the Revolutionaries when his father had fled home to the King. But once John Bernard had title, he turned tail. He mortgaged his land at Mount Desert to Thomas Russell of Boston, took the money, and caught a boat to England, where he made amends to the King and wound up with a civil-service job in the West Indies.

Thus, before the 1780s were out, one half of Mount Desert belonged to the son of an English baronet and the other half belonged to the granddaughter of that French adventurer who called himself Seigneur des Monts Deserts. From one or the other of these, all land titles on the island derived.

The first true white settler on Mount Desert has left his name on one of the loveliest villages here—Somesville, at the head of Somes Sound.

Abraham Somes sailed up Somes Sound in the summer of 1761. He came not as an explorer or as a colonist, but as a man from Gloucester looking to cut a boatload of barrel staves. He also had two ideas in his head that may have leaned him toward settling.

He had first sailed this way earlier in 1755 and on that trip had bought Greenings Island from an Indian for a gallon of rum. His shipmate, Ebenezer Sutton, had made an even better deal; he got a deed to the island, written on birch bark, for only two quarts.

His second idea had more substance to it. Somes had been promised plenty of free land by Governor Bernard if he and his new companion, James Richardson, would leave Gloucester and start a settlement on Mount Desert. They set sail. When Somes and Richardson reached the head of the Sound, both men liked the spot so well that they called it Somesville and brought their families up the following spring.

James Richardson was the son of an early version of *Lady Chatterley's Lover*. His father had been head gardener on the estate of a Scottish nobleman. He and the nobleman's daughter, Lady Jane Montgomery, enjoyed a love affair, got secretly married, and eloped to America. James Richardson, pioneer settler of Mount Desert, was their son.

Slowly, others followed the Somes and Richardsons. A chart drawn in 1772 by Samuel Holland shows six homes at Bar Harbor and Hull's Cove, four at Somesville, two at Southwest Harbor, four more on the Cranberry Isles, and one on Bartlett's Island. The population grew a little each year.

There were enough men to hold the first town meeting on March 30, 1776, at the home of Stephen Richardson. There it was agreed all settlers would join forces and build a road, and further agreed that no one would take any hay off the island to sell elsewhere, as all of it was now needed to feed local cattle.

Foreign visitors still came and reported favorably. In 1792, a Frenchman, Bancel de Confoulens, made a trip to Mount Desert to buy land for other French emigrants.

"I saw very well kept houses," he wrote, "and settlers honest, affable, and generous, living as well as people in Boston and Philadelphia. They cultivate enough land to provide themselves with potatoes, corn, barley, and vegetables, but spend most of their time cutting wood into shooks and barrel staves which they sell at a good profit. Each family has a small boat from which they catch cod and cure it and exchange it with the merchants for flour, sugar, soap, molasses, oil, and rum ... On the day of my arrival there were five ships in Frenchmans Bay, one of which sailed for London, one for Santo Domingo, and three for Boston."

Four years later, in 1796, Alexander Baring of London took a rather fancy cruise to Mount Desert on a vessel belonging to the Binghams. Women, children, and servants were aboard. Baring was here representing the London bank of his name, which had lent money to Senator William Bingham to buy land here and elsewhere. To cement the two families, in love as well as money, Alexander Baring married the senator's daughter and his younger brother married the senator's younger daughter. Baring, who had earlier visited

New York and Pennsylvania frontiers, reported that "the settlers in Eastern Maine are vastly superior in character to the pioneers in western New York and Pennsylvania."

By 1837, so many settlers were prospering here that Captain Joseph Smith, U.S.N., reported to the Secretary of the Treasury, stating that "there were six hundred ships in Mount Desert Harbor." By 1860, all the best farmland was under cultivation. By 1870, all the first-growth timber had been cut for ships and homes or sent away as barrel staves in cash trades.

A bridge to the mainland, built in 1836, speeded the influx. A group of enterprising islanders formed the Mount Desert Bridge Corporation, which built, owned, and operated the bridge from 1836 right up to 1917, when the county took it over.

The painter, Thomas Cole, can be credited or blamed for starting the transformation of Mount Desert into a famous summer resort. Cole came across the bridge on September 4, 1844, just eight years after it had been built, bringing his brushes, his paints, his canvases, and his romantic eye with him. Cole was the founder and centerpiece of those romantic landscape artists known as the Hudson River School. He led them all in his passion for the picturesque and the sentimental, and he exploited the fashionable urge of the wealthy to spend summers enjoying the "Good Simple Life of Nature." Having painted every view possible of the Hudson, Cole now began to paint Mount Desert.

With his declamatory oils and his purple prose, he sold the wealthy not only his paintings, but also his admiration for the joys of Mount Desert's simple life. He did for Mount Desert what artists and writers soon after him would do for the Isles of Shoals (as told in an earlier chapter), and what artists would do in the 1920s for Monhegan Island.

Cole popularized Mount Desert. His paintings persuaded Charles Tracy, a wealthy New York lawyer, to bring his large family here for a vacation. One of the Tracy girls grew up to become Mrs. J. Pierpont Morgan and soon the great banker was here with his great steam yacht *Corsair*.

"The Rustication Rush" was on in full flood. On an August day in 1855, Charles Tracy estimated he could see two hundred yachts under sail from Sargent Mountain. President Chester A. Arthur sailed in with the North Atlantic Squadron of the U.S. Navy; but the Russians had beaten him to it. In 1878 the auxiliary cruiser *Cimbria*, of the Imperial Russian Navy, spent six long and reproductive months at

Southwest Harbor. She had seven hundred sailors on board. Most nights a hundred of them had shore leave. It is said today there is considerable Russian blood on the island.

By 1887, there were seventeen hotels in Bar Harbor, four of them run by the four Higgins brothers, and seven of those hotels could each accommodate five hundred guests. There were five more hotels at Northeast Harbor, six at Southwest Harbor, three at Somesville, and two at Seal Harbor.

The Rockefellers, the Stotesburys, the Vanderbilts, the million-aires, the Episcopalian bishops, and the college presidents (notably Charles W. Eliot of Harvard) came to Mount Desert in droves. Some built cottages with bedrooms for forty servants. The Atwater Kents built a cottage with a garage for fifteen cars. During Prohibition, Mrs. Stotesbury had six hundred guests in for her dances, where they drank $6,000 worth of bootleg liquor of an evening.

Early in the 20th century, these millionaire "rusticators" so wanted to preserve the feeling of being simple country folk that they banned all automobiles from the island. Long after cars were common on the mainland, Mount Desert was still horse-drawn. In 1913, a patient died because a horsedrawn doctor could not reach him in time and the great automobile war was over. Cars by the thousands came to Mount Desert. So did the visitors. The influx was hugely accelerated by boats and overnight sleeper trains from Boston and New York to Hancock Point. Three times daily, Maine Central ferries carried train passengers from the Hancock Terminal to Mount Desert. Tourists who were less than millionaires now swarmed to Mount Desert.

The wealthy summer colony feared they would soon lose their rusticating haven. To protect "their" island from developers, they took up collections among themselves to buy thousands of acres. When they had 15,000 acres, they did not know quite what to do with it. The federal government finally agreed to accept all 15,000 acres in 1916 and Acadia National Park was born—the first national park east of the Mississippi.

Today, the park has expanded to 30,000 acres, with about half of that total on Isle au Haut and Schoodic Point. The beautiful land has been beautifully protected. Walks, bridle trails, mountain climbs, swimming holes, and camping areas have been handsomely installed, but now, with some three million visitors and campers a year, the park faces the danger of over-use. Engineers have built a splendid road, with many wonderful lookout points, to the very top of Cadillac

Mountain. The view across the Maine coast for 50 miles east and west and out across all the islands of Penobscot and Frenchman bays is spectacular beyond description.

The French adventurer Laumet, who named the mountain after the little French town near where he was born, would be astounded at the crowds atop the mountain that carries his name, but which he never climbed.

The Great Fire of October 1947 was the death blow to the great estates. So great was the glamor of Bar Harbor as America's haven for the very rich that the fire made headlines around the world. In Paris, the story took a new twist. The newspaper *Le Figaro* reported that the peasants of Mount Desert had staged an uprising and put the torch to the feudal castles of the rich.

The Great Fire

On the 30th anniversary of the fire, I went back to Bar Harbor to talk with people who had lived through it. Their words and their memories of that ghastly catastrophe tell the story more vividly than any re-hash. Therefore, let me extract from the newspaper piece I wrote for the *Maine Sunday Telegram* of October 23, 1977.

They ranged from George Abbott, who was the police chief, at the center of the action; to Charlotte Stuart, who handled the town switchboard; Albion Emery, who ran a pumper; Inez Henckler, who gave birth to a son; Cora Harris, a hystologist at the Jackson Laboratory, who still winced at the recalled smell of 90,000 suffocated mice; Fred Salisbury, who saw the great Satterlee estate, which he supervised, mostly burned to the ground; and Jimmy Cough, who, as a 14-year-old schoolboy, filled oil-tank trucks with water.

> They can smell the great fire still. They blink their eyes, and say they can still see, and will never forget, the fire blazing down the hills and leaping a thousand feet at a jump to come ever closer to their homes, their town and their bodies.
>
> The great fire peaked in its devastation and terror on October 23, 1947. It began October 17 and was declared officially out November 14. It burned 17,188 acres on Mount Desert Island; destroyed 237 homes. More than two thousand women and children were evacuated by truck convoys; and four hundred more were taken off by small boats, while gale force winds between 50 and 70 miles-per-hour fanned the furnace on shore.
>
> George C. Abbott was chief of police then, age forty-three. Thirty years later, he is still a vast, out-size man with crewcut hair and a presence that in full uniform could strike fear into any thief.
>
> Abbott and his wife live in a spacious and handsome, senior citizens housing project.

"Funny thing," he says, brown eyes laughing, "this apartment of ours is smack on the site where the Belmont and Malvern hotels burned to the ground that night. All five hundred rooms. Flame came down the mountain and both huge wooden hotels took fire, and blazed together back to back. Now, on their land stands this senior citizens' housing.

"I had a force of eight fulltime police and thirty reserves. For eleven days and nights they were on duty ... We got great help from 250 National Guard, wardens from Sea and Shore Fisheries, the Hancock County Sheriff's Department, and State Police.

"There was never any looting. Every hotel burned to the ground. Scores of houses of millionaires burned, with contents to match their purses. Almost 240 houses afire. And not one case of looting. It's a wonderful tribute to the people ... But one reason may be that I had the Governor ban the sale of all hard liquor, beer, and ale anywhere on the island."

Mrs. Abbott chimes in. "I was with the twenty-five hundred women and children being evacuated that terrible Thursday afternoon and night. We were packed first on the athletic field. Hauled there by Army trucks. Then the gale of wind shifted. They moved us all down to the Municipal Pier, because for a while it seemed the only escape would be by water."

The official Fire Department report states: "Soon after three o'-clock in the afternoon the wind began to veer from southwest to west and with increasing velocity swung into the northwest ... the Coast Guard clocked the wind between sixty-three and seventy miles an hour at 4 p.m. that afternoon."

No matter the velocity, it's a wind anyone on Mount Desert Island that day will never forget. It is remarkable that many people were not burned to death; for the fire, stirred to an inferno by the gales, descended on the outskirts of the town of Bar Harbor, jumping hundreds of yards at a time, sweeping all before it. One fireman reported he looked up, and it looked as though two gigantic doors had opened and towering columns of roaring flames shot down on his position.

Mrs. Abbott, huddled with her smallest son and the thousands waiting to be evacuated says, "From 5:30 until 7:30 that evening we saw a wall of flame coming at us. Cottages and hotels on Eden Street and West Street blazed and exploded. The gale fanned the furnace. Behind us on the pier the gale whipped up waves like mountains around the lobster boats trying to take people off."

Police Chief Abbott remembers that tense, packed crowd of women and children. "Their men were off fighting the fire. Some had been gone for days. Women and kids stood and some saw their houses burning ... I had Father Edward Fitzpatrick with me, the only clergyman left in town. He did wonders with the women and children, comforting and calming them. We got 'em loaded onto 150 trucks."

Bulldozers cleared burning rubble on the roads so convoys could escape through the fires. They took the evacuees to City Hall in Ellsworth, where families sought out each other, and the Red Cross volunteers provided food and shelter.

Amazingly, there were only three deaths. Helen Cormier, 15, was killed in a traffic accident in the evacuation. One man who had been fighting the fire hard took a breather on the wharf and died of a heart attack. An elderly man, about to be evacuated by truck, held his cat in his arms. The terrified cat jumped out and ran away; and the man ran after his pet into the danger area and was burned to death. About four hundred women and children went off by boats.

Cora Harris and Lester Bunker were working at the famous Jackson Laboratory. "Most of the men were out fighting the fire. The women workers were in the lab feeding the animals. We left about 3:30 p.m., Thursday, October 23, not knowing the fire was changing direction and would soon be headed this way. By the time we reached home, the fire whistles were blowing seven frantic blasts. That meant evacuation. Dr. Katharine Hummel and I were picked up by the National Guard, put in trucks and evacuated to Ellsworth. I couldn't get a pass to get back on the island till Monday. Nobody could move past all the road blocks without special passes. When I saw our labs, I wept ... And the smell; I can never forget that awful smell ... About ninety thousand of our mice died. Suffocation. It looked as if all the scientific work was lost. I wept. But Dr. Little, the director, swore "We'll begin again right now."

Inside of ten days Dr. Little had received responses from architects to his request for new plans. "And telegrams poured in from other labs around the world offering to help us get rebuilt." Jackson Lab. is famous for its genetic research.

Cora Harris, who specializes in making hystology slides, looks around the new lab buildings.

"I began work here in 1942. When the fire came in 1947, there were thirty of us. And ninety thousand mice. We saved four hundred mice. And all the people. Now we have 450 people working here and 700,000 genetic mice. So we rose."

Cora Harris and Luther Bunker smile at one benefit from the fire. "Our lab had been plagued by Harvard bedbugs, which came with mice sent from Cambridge. Since the fire—no bedbugs."

Charlotte Stuart works in a Bar Harbor gift shop, "But on that night of October 22–23, 1947, I was one of two telephone operators on duty. At three that afternoon my sister and her husband, Hugh Kelley, lost their dairy, the first in-town business to burn.

"I called home to reach my eight-year-old daughter. She'd guided some people to safety, and taken herself and them to my mother's camp. I didn't see or hear from my child till late the next day ... I got a call they needed me at the telephone exchange and went to work. It was a hot, humid day. I wore a silk dress and sandals, as though it were August instead of October. Then up came that awful gale—cold and strong and by night I was wearing winter boots."

The old telephone exchange was in the upper floors of a Main Street building. "We had a manual board. Lines kept burning out all over the island. But all night long we kept one circuit open to Southwest Harbor. And Southwest had one circuit to Ellsworth. We kept that one communication line to the mainland open all night.

"Lillian Ingalls worked all night with me. No electricity. We worked by candles. My home didn't burn, but I saw all the houses across the street burning. I remember one weird call from the milk man who worked for my brother-in-law's dairy.

"'Should I deliver the milk I've got?' he asked. I told him he might as well. He did, on Friday morning.

Inez Henckler gave birth to a son in the Bar Harbor Hospital while the great fire still burned.

"Most patients had been evacuated," she said. "It was pretty dark and only candles when we got there. We came in from Southwest Harbor. My time came suddenly. National Guardsmen and police stopped us all along the road, but helped when they knew our emergency. I remember the unbelievable, eerie sight of the sky and the burned buildings and rubble. I saw fires out my window. And the smell. I'll never forget that smell. But Dr. Weymouth and the nurses delivered Don okay."

Other fire-babies include a pair of twins—Paul and Peter Hodgkins of Lamoine, born October 22. Paul is the golf pro at Rockland Country Club. Peter works for the telephone company. And Carl 'Whitey' Griffin, another baby born in the fire, is a cook at Tripp's Restaurant across the street.

Fred Salisbury was superintendent at the big waterfront estate of Herbert Satterlee at Great Head.

"The fire burned our own home, and six others, on the estate to the ground. My wife had just put up four hundred quarts of preserves. She lost 'em all. And we'd fresh painted the house, and just hung $80 worth of new curtains. It all went. We lost six other estate houses and all furnishings. I evacuated my family to Lamoine. Saw flame a thousand feet up over our heads as we drove. The Army wouldn't let me back. The city manager of Ellsworth would not give me a pass to get back. Finally a county agent got me one. Took four days for me to get back to the estate. The fire was underground then. No flame to see. But before your eyes big trees would fall over— burned from underground. Kept burning until mid-November."

Fire Chief Sleeper's own report, written with Captain John Heath, makes stirring reading on this 30th anniversary of the terrible fire they fought.

"The catastrophic spread and intensity of the conflagration is indicated by the fire's sudden enormous expansion from approximately 1,900 acres at 4 p.m. to 16,000 acres by midnight on October 23 ... Right here it must be stated that the courage of the Bar Harbor people cannot be excelled anywhere in the world. When it became apparent that for twenty-five hundred of them the best means of escape would be by water, they were transferred to the Pier. With the bay whipped into mountainous waves by the gale wind, with their town being apparently obliterated at their back, with no certainty that any of them would get out alive, they calmly waited rescue without any sign of panic . . ." he wrote.

"The morning of October 24 dawned beautifully clear and quiet, as though nature was seeking to make up for the terrible things she had done to us the night before," wrote Sleeper. He ended his official report with these words: "Of the thousands of people who either fought the fire or escaped from it, all of them have interesting, and in most cases, thrilling stories. There is one thing they all cannot but be impressed with, and that is the utter helplessness mere man can possess when confronted by the full fury of nature on the loose. It is an experience they will never forget."

In Bar Harbor they are remembering still.

20

Heritage
Safeguarding the Islands

This book is a celebration of the Maine islands and Maine island people, and the island heritage beyond price that is given to us. Now we need to ask: What of their future? Will these staunch and beautiful islands be spoiled or safeguarded? What, if anything, should be done to protect them? And protect them from what?

The Maine coast is endowed with more than four thousand islands. They range in size from rocks only big enough for a basking seal to granite ledges with room for a lighthouse, and on to islands of thousands of acres and hundreds of inhabitants. But no matter their size, every one is important to some living human, bird, animal, or plant. These are the outposts of America from which our nation really began.

As such, they represent a national heritage of history, beauty, struggle, and courage in which the whole nation has a stake. The islands are also a very special preserve—a kind of wilderness in the sea—of the natural world of sea birds, sea life, plants, trees, and animals whose territorial rights to these islands deserves respect.

A new awareness of the special qualities of Maine islands has, thank heaven, become widespread and urgent in the past few decades. The State of Maine, which long ignored or despised these islands, is working toward safeguarding almost thirteen hundred of those that belong to it. The Maine Coast Heritage Trust, a private, nonprofit organization begun in 1970, is performing enormously valuable service to island landowners in helping them safeguard the future of the islands they love so well. In its first ten years, this organization helped protect under law the future of seventy-six entire

islands and portions of sixy-six other islands. The Maine chapter of
The Nature Conservancy, in its 45-year history, has played a leading
role in safeguarding the future of dozens of other islands. The good
work done by these organizations is possible only because of the ea-
gerness of island owners to ensure and safeguard the future of their
loved land.

Yet there is a tension, an inevitable conflict, that only goodwill
and common sense can resolve, between the desires to protect the
islands and the desires of ever more people to get to them and enjoy
them. There is something inherently wrong, even absurd, about a
battery of "No Trespassing," "Keep Out," and "Private Property"
signs along the shore of a Maine island. But they are going up on
more islands every year. Infuriating as such signs are to a boatsman
seeking to stretch his legs or swim from an island beach, there is, un-
happily, good reason for some hostility by island owners. Too many
islands are grossly abused. It is sickening for an island owner to see
rubbish left by picnickers, annoying to have his peace destroyed by a
noisy flotilla of invading boats, and it is downright terrifying to think
careless strangers may have begun a fire on a defenseless, tinderbox
island. Many island homes have been vandalized and robbed. Some
islands have been used as drop-points in million-dollar drug smug-
gling. Islands, which are the fragile habitats of seabirds, have been so
disturbed that the birds no longer nest upon them; rare lady slippers
and wild orchids that once filled an island meadow in glory have
been rooted out by thoughtless and uninvited visitors. Such are the
penalties to islands caused by easy access with modern boats.

Yet these islands cannot and should not become over-protected
private preserves, wrapped, so to speak, in cotton wool. Precious and
fragile as island ecology may be, the islands are also tough.

These islands were born as mountains a million years ago, created
in the tortured explosions of a boiling earth. They were transformed
from mountains to islands after the last Ice Age, some ten thousand
years ago, after the meltdown and movement of ice sheets, a mile
thick and weighing many million tons an acre, gouged out the land
and the sea poured in. These islands were once home to races of
people who vanished without a trace. But the islands survived.

These islands have survived Indians who summered on them
centuries before Christ; they endured English and European fishing
crews four hundred years ago and the first settlers in a New World
who clawed a toehold on their shores. They have survived wars and
revolutions, fires, and a million violent storms. Thousands of nesting

cormorants and herons and gulls have destroyed trees and vegetation on some islands. Lumbering operations have stripped others of trees and they have recovered. Sheep have gnawed the grasses to extinction on other islands. Granite by the millions of tons has been blasted out of island guts. But the islands have survived.

None of these perils, however, matched today's perils: popularity and easy access. Islands that were once hard to come to are now in easy reach of tens of thousands. For centuries, most mainland people despised or ignored the Maine islands. Now the islands are magical meccas. Islands that not long ago were the unwanted stepchildren of Maine are today's prize possessions. Islands that forty years ago were used only by lobstermen for storing traps are today sold for millions of dollars.

Let the record tell the story.

No sooner had Maine separated from Massachusetts, on March 15, 1820, than both states moved to rid themselves of the islands they owned but did not want. The Massachusetts government, by Resolves of January 30 and June 13, 1823, instructed George Coffin and the state treasurer to sell all islands inside Maine that still belonged to Massachusetts. They got rid of sixty-eight islands.

Then Maine acted. The newly independent legislature ordered James Irish, the first state land agent, "to sell all the islands and parts of islands belonging to the state in such manner as to him may seem fit." But he found few takers. After ten years, by 1830, only twenty-one islands had been conveyed from state ownership to private hands. In the next forty-six years, between 1830 and 1876, only twenty more state-owned islands could find buyers; and so the state made another try to be rid of the pesky islands. On February 11, 1876, the governor of Maine signed a new law by which "The Land Agent is hereby authorized and required to sell all islands on the coast belonging to the state at public auction."

Incredible bargains in islands were offered by land agent Edwin C. Burleigh at the public auctions held in Rockland in November and December 1876. He sold sixty-six islands, mostly in Penobscot Bay, at prices from 25 cents to $450. The record shows thirty-four islands sold for five dollars or less, ten islands sold for between five and fifty dollars, and only four islands fetched more than $50.

Bargains like that will never be seen again; yet they merit a place in this book on the islands. Here is a sample from the record of that memorable auction:

ISLANDS	Est. Acres	Where Situated	Amount
Barred islands	10.00	Northwest of Beach Island	9.50
Barred "	3.00	Southwest of Little Deer Isle	3.00
Barred "	4.00	West of Deer Isle	13.50
Bill's island	2.00	South of Deer Isle	4.00
Black "	9.00	West of Mt. Desert Island	10.00
B "	3.00	North of Mt. Desert Island	7.50
Burnt "	2.00	Southwest of Calf Island	2.50
Block "	2.00	Southwest of Calf Island	2.50
Burnt "	3.50	East of Stave Island	5.00
Compass "	10.00	Southwest of Little Spruce Head	13.50
Conary "	90.00	In Eggemoggin Reach	85.00
Crow Islands	7.00	East of Little Deer Isle	16.00
Crow Island	7.00	East of Swan's Island	16.00
Crow "	3.00	West of Grindstone Neck	1.90
John's "	2.00	In Deer Isle Thoroughfare	3.50
Lassell's "	148.00	In Penobscot Bay	440.00
Lazygut Islands	10.00	East of Deer Isle	21.00
Little Mark Island	1.00	In Deer Isle Thoroughfare	1.50
Lime "	1.00	North of Kimball's Island	1.05
Molise "	6.00	East of Lassell's Island	4.00
Mahoney "	5.00	South of Naskeag Point	14.00
Matinic Green "	10.00	South of Matinic Island	35.00
No Man's Land "	2.00	Northeast of McGlathery's Island	2.50
No Man's Land "	15.00	Northeast of Matinicus Island	31.00
Ned's "	5.00	South of Grindstone Neck	5.25
Outer Bar "	6.00	In Indian Harbor	3.75
Potato "	2.00	In Deer Isle Thoroughfare	7.50
Peggy's "	2.00	In Deer Isle Thoroughfare	1.00
Robinson's Rock	2.00	In Penobscot Bay	3.00
Ram Island	1.00	Northwest of Merchant's Island	1.00

The state sold sixty-six islands and realized the sum of $1,109.15 from the entire sale.

But the unhappy land agent still had unwanted islands on his hands. The next year, 1877, he was ordered to hold still another auction. He managed to sell seven islands off Washington County and realized a total of $251 for all seven.

Then suddenly the island market changed. Four years later, summer people were demanding to buy islands and pestering the land agent. His report for 1882 complains: "There are numerous applications now on file in the Land Office for islands on our coast, and as the land agent has no personal knowledge of their value and since their value does not appear to warrant the expense of a personal inspection, no action has been taken."

Seven years later, swamped with unanswered inquiries, the land agent registered yet another complaint. His report of 1889 contains this snide comment on island lovers: "The repeated calls for information about titles to islands is somewhat perplexing. Inquirers evidently think there is somewhere a schedule of all the islands on the coast and that they can easily learn whether the State has title or not." There was no such list. An attempt was made to compile one in 1892. "I have prepared a new list of all islands that have been conveyed by the state," wrote the land agent. "The general opinion is that islands not on this list are the property of the State, although there are many instances of pretended owners basing claims on the statement that their families have claimed them for many years." (Those words were prophetic; the same problem was to plague the state again in the 1970s.)

In 1913, the state legislature got another attack of "islanditis" and passed yet another island law. But this one was a total and complete reversal of all previous policy, which, for ninety years, had been to get rid of the pesky islands. The law of 1913 suddenly proclaimed that "Title to all islands not held in private ownership shall remain in the State of Maine and shall be reserved for public use."

The brave words produced a fine *Report on Island Land Titles*, by Melvin H. Simmons, the best bureaucratic and most readable document ever written on this topic. But the law did very little more; the state took no significant action to show it really gave a hoot about the islands it owned or the public enjoyment of them. Nor did most of the Maine population. A few close-in islands in Casco Bay were crowded with resort hotels and cottages; some, like Isle au Haut and Monhegan, had a small, intensely loyal summer colony. But on most islands, the resident population was decreasing. Each new generation moved in greater numbers to the mainland for jobs, the conveniences, the good life, and a better chance at marriage or wealth. All through the 1930s, '40s, and '50s, islands were for sale dirt cheap. A few dozen wise, lucky, and sometimes famous and wealthy families bought island paradises for the price of a car today. When the federal government, which had taken islands by eminent domain to make them into military posts, offered to return these islands as gifts to the state, town, or city, they had no takers—even though many of these islands now had paved roads, water and power supplies, and fine brick homes, all built at taxpayers' expense.

In the 1960s, change began and, by the 1970s, islands were in high demand, fetching premium prices, mostly from out-of-state buyers. A little island that sold for $3,500 in 1950 would fetch $35,000 by 1960 and upward of $200,000 by 1981.

Seeing prices rose like rockets, the state once again began to wonder which of the precious islands belonged to it. In 1972, the State Planning Office researched the titles of ownership to islands in Penobscot Bay, as a test sample. They found quite a lot of title claims had little or no basis in law, which was a surprise to the state and a shock to some presumed owners. As a result, a new state law of 1973 required owners of islands with fewer than four residential buildings on them to file claims of ownership with the local registrar of deeds by December 21, 1974.

The first result was chaos. So a year later the Coastal Island Registry was established within the Department of Conservation and the law was amended and clarified.

The result is that, today, really for the first time in history, Maine state government has an authenticated list of all the islands and who owns them and pays taxes on them. The Coastal Island Registry shows that most islands are privately owned.

No sudden bonanza of island real estate was dropped into the state's lap. The biggest of the unregistered, or state-owned, islands proved to be a 12-acre island, and the smallest a rock large enough for one man to stand upon without his dog. But the knowledge that the state owned more twelve hundred islands forced Maine to develop and publish an official written plan of how the state hopes to use and protect the islands and ledges that belong to it.

These islands are a mixed bag. The state owns bare ledge islands, which average only one-third of an acre. Certainly they are small and bare, but many of them are valuable seabird habitats. Several of Maine's largest cormorant rookeries are on bare ledge islands. The perky black guillemots, which are a favored prey of gulls, find safety on these bare ledges, build nests, and raise young in their rocky crevices. The ledges also offer safe sanctuary to the rare razor-billed auk.

The next-most-numerous state-owned islands are saltmarsh islands, mostly in estuaries and tidal river channels. They, too, are small, averaging two-thirds of an acre. But they are important producers of vegetation needed by wildlife and vegetation that reduces toxic chemical oxygen in estuary waters. Beaver, otter, muskrat, ducks, herons, and teal feed or nest on these saltmarsh islands.

Those spits and gravelly bars that often emerge only at low water are called "islands of unconsolidated marine sediment." The State of

Maine owns a few of these. No vegetation grows on them, though they sometimes make good spots for clamming. However, these gravel spits and bars are favorite nesting spots for common terns, arctic terns, and roseate terns.

Another category of state-owned islands includes the small islands, averaging just over an acre, called "shrub vegetation" islands. The state owns a couple hundred of these. Often in generations past, island farmers would graze sheep on them. The incessant gnawing by those sharp-toothed sheep, prisoners on a little islet, came close to killing all tree and grass growth. Now these islands are recovering and may soon again produce shrubs and trees. Goldenrod, raspberries, wild strawberries, primroses, wild asters, blueberries, and even gooseberries are already profuse on many of them. These islands are preferred nesting places for herring and black-back gulls and eider ducks. Where tall grasses grow, laughing gulls often nest, filling the islet with their strange cries. On the "shrub vegetation" islands that were not used to graze sheep, enough peaty soil is left so that Leach's storm petrels and Atlantic puffins burrow down to nest and raise their young below ground.

Finally, among the state-owned islands, are more than a hundred islands with trees and good soil, which average close to 2 acres, and these are the most attractive for human use. The biggest and best are Harbor Island, 11 acres, off Isle au Haut; Crow Island, 10 acres, in Eastern Penobscot Bay; and Hay Island, 9 acres, at Vinalhaven. These forested islands are favorites of the great blue herons, snowy egrets, and glossy ibises, all of whom are at the northern end of their breeding range.

Maine is now working for the future protection and management of the widely different types of state-owned islands. Whether it will work long-term depends on the ability of one state agency to persuade other agencies to take on responsibility for islands in their field of expertise. If those agencies are short of money or people, they may duck. If this happens, then the future of the state-owned islands could be grim. There is no existing office in Maine state government capable of safeguarding and managing more than a thousand islands. Because there is no "island lobby" with political clout in Augusta, the whole program could fall through the cracks and the state will again ignore its islands, as it has done for most of its 180 years.

What of the other islands and ledges that are privately owned? How may they fare in the future? Two forces on the side of the angels are at work. One is private money. The other is the growing ecology movement. Fortunately, the two often go hand-in-hand, at least on many privately owned Maine islands. From this happy combination, organizations such as the Maine Coast Heritage Trust, the Maine Chapter of The Nature Conservancy, the Maine Audubon Society, and the Island Institute draw most of their stature and effectiveness.

These organizations have become quiet but competent experts in such legal matters as "easements" and tax write-offs. Each has easy entree to rich island owners. For example, Thomas D. Cabot of Boston, and David Rockefeller of New York City, were largely instrumental in starting the Maine Coast Heritage Trust. Together, they own more island property in Maine than they care to admit publicly. They have safeguarded and protected the future of their islands by full use of easements and write-offs; they are, therefore, in good positions to influence other wealthy, concerned island owners to protect their loved land in similar fashion—and at the same time get a tax advantage. The Maine Chapter of The Nature Conservancy and the Maine Audubon Society have sponsors similar in clout and wealth to the Cabots and the Rockefellers.

In layman's language, the easements and restrictions recommended by these organizations are enough to prevent any future undesirable commercial development of island property, even generations hence. Land with such restrictions on it may often earn a lower tax assessment or a lower inheritance tax than land without restrictions. Frequently these organizations arrange for a third non-profit or governmental agency to take either title or responsibility for enforcing the restrictions.

In the years since it was founded in 1970, the Maine Coast Heritage Trust has helped landowners arrange hundreds of conservation easements for islands or parts of islands from Biddeford to Jonesport, and for headlands, beaches, and salt marshes on the mainland coast. Thousands of acres so far have been thus protected.

The Maine chapter of The Nature Conservancy, since it was founded by Rachel Carson and seven others in 1956, has been successful in safeguarding the future of dozens of Maine islands.

Encouraging as these accomplishments are, the fact remains that more than a thousand privately-owned islands have no formal safeguards for their future, except perhaps money. Good-size islands that might have a potential for truly commercial development now have values in the millions of dollars. Most families that own such islands are already very wealthy and have spent scores of summers on them, with their parents or their children and grandchildren. They are inclined to fight tooth and nail to prevent any gross change in their beloved island. They, of course, are the future "clients" that the Maine Coast Heritage Trust, the Nature Conservancy, and other similar organizations are seeking.

Important major islands, such as Monhegan, Isle au Haut, and Swan's Island, have safeguarded themselves through island ordinances. Others have fought hard and successfully when radical change threatened. One such instance, told in the earlier chapter on the Isles of Shoals, merits recapping here.

In 1973, Olympic Oil Refineries, largely owned by the late Aristotle Onassis, announced plans to build an offshore docking station between the Isles of Shoals and the mainland. Supertankers would unload crude oil near the Isles of Shoals into underwater pipelines to supply the 400,000-barrel-a-day appetite of a new refinery to be built on the mainland. A dozen organizations quickly formed to fight the proposal. It died a swift death at the Durham town meeting three months later, when local people voted 1,254 to 144 against the required rezoning.

When King Resources proposed a supertanker oil terminal at Long Island in Casco Bay, the organized protests from Casco Bay islanders roused all Mainers. The terminal was not built.

When the Pittston Company launched its proposal to bring supertankers into Eastport, coastal opposition was extremely vigorous; now, no tanker has come and no refinery has been built.

Yet, a new threat is imminent: exploration for underwater oil and gas off the New England coast. Dangers to the islands may come from the ocean bottom as well as from helicopters, hotels, hydrofoils, and ferries.

But the greatest danger to the islands is one that no laws, ordinances, or organizations can prevent.

This is the erosion of island families, year-round island residents, and the very special sense of values, caution, kindness, mutual support, courage, and confidence that island living breeds in them.

There is a rare and wonderful inner strength, inner kindness, and inner serenity found only among men and women who have lived close to the bone of man and nature on the islands of Maine.

On most islands out of commuter range, the year-rounders are dwindling down to a precious few. Maine, and the nation—indeed, the world—will lose an irreplaceable breed when they all are gone. The islands need to flower with something stronger and closer to the sea and the soil than even the best of summer people.

Perhaps some future swing in human values or economics will again make it feasible for a new wave of resilient men and women to live and love, to farm and fish, to raise children and bury their dead on some of the lovely but only half-used islands of Maine.

Further Reading

I have used and enjoyed many books in the preparation of this book on the islands of Maine. Below are some I suggest to anyone interested in further reading.

Chapter 1.   The Beginning: Ice Age to Indians

Antiquities of the Indians of the Kennebec Valley (Maine Historic Preservation Commission and Maine State Museum, 1980).

Discovering Maine's Archaeological Heritage by David Sanger (Maine Historic Preservation Commission).

Discovery of North America by Cummings, Skelton, and Gernu (American Heritage, 1971).

Chapter 2.   The Treasure Hunters and Explorers

Atlantic Crossings Before Columbus by Fred Y. Pohl (W.W. Norton).

David Ingram's Accounts (from *Magazine of American History*, March, 1883).

The European Discovery of America, The Northern Voyages A.D. 500–1600 by Samuel Eliot Morrison (Oxford University Press, 1971).

Hakluyt's *Principal Navigations, Voyages, and Discoveries*, c. 1587.

Leif Erickssen by E. Grey (Oxford University Press).

Ramusio's *Divers Voyages* (Hakluyt's Translation, 1582).

Sailor's Narratives of Voyages Along the New England Coast, 1524–1624 by George Parker Winship (Houghton Mifflin Co., 1905).

Verrazano's Letter to the King, 1582.

The Viking Explorers by Frederick J. Pohl (Thomas Y. Crowell, 1966).

The Voyages of Giovanni de Varrazzano by Lawrence C. Wroth (Yale University Press, 1970).

Voyages of the Northmen to America, editor Edmund F. Slafter (Prince Society, Boston, 1877).

Chapter 3.   Fish: The Silver Mines of Maine

Beginnings of Colonial Maine by Henry S. Burrage (Portland, 1914).

The Description of New England by Captain John Smith (London,

H. Lownes, 1616).

New England Canaan by Thomas Morton (London, 1632).

Tallman Lecture Series, Spencer Appollonio, Bowdoin College, 1976.

True Relation of Captain George Weymouth's Voyage by James Rosier (London, George Bishop, 1605).

Voyages of Samuel de Champlain, 1604–1618.

Chapter 4.   Men and Boats

Colonial Vessels by William A. Baker (Barre Publishing Co., 1962).

Elizabethan Ships by Gregory Robinson (London, 1631).

Frobisher's Second Voyage (London, 1577).

History of the State of Maine, vols. 1 & 2 by William D. Williamson (Glazier, Masters Co. of Hallowell, 1832, reprinted by Cumberland Press, Freeport).

The Maritime History of Maine by William Hutchinson Rowe (W.W. Norton, 1948).

The Maritime History of New England by Samuel Eliot Morison (Houghton Mifflin, 1921).

Thomas Prince's Chronological History of New England, 1736 (Massachusetts Historical Society).

Whimzies, or a New Cast of Characters by Richard Braithwaite (London, 1631).

Chapter 5.   Sir Ferdinando Gorges

A Brief Relation of the Discovery and Plantation of New England by Sir Ferdinando Gorges (London, 1622, reprinted by Prince Society, Boston, 1890).

Captain Smith's Description of New England

Gorges of Plymouth Fort by Richard A. Preston (University of Toronto, 1953).

The Real Founders of New England by Charles Knowles (F.W. Faxon Co., Boston, 1929).

Sir Ferdinando Gorges by Henry Morrill Fuller (Newcomen Society, 1952).

Chapter 6.   Popham, 1607

Beginnings of Colonial Maine by Henry S. Burrage (Marks Printing, 1914).

Historie of Travaille into Virginia Britannia by William Strachey (Hakluyt Society, London, 1849).

Memorial Volume of the Popham Celebration by Edward Ballard (Bailey and Noyes, 1863).

Popham Colony by Edward E. Bourne (B. Thurston, 1864).

Popham Colony by James Davies (University Press, 1880).

The Sagadahoc Colony by Henry O. Thayer (Research Reprints, 1980).

Chapter 7.   Isles of Shoals

Among the Isles of Shoals by Celia Thaxter (Houghton Mifflin, 1897).

Brief History of the Isles of Shoals by Rev. E. Victor Bigelow.

Isle of Shoals by Peter E. Randall (KJ Printing, Augusta, Maine, 1981).

Isles of Shoals in Lore and Legend by Lyman V. Rutledge (Star Island Corporation, 1971).

Murder at Smuttynose and Other Murders by Edmund Pearson (Doubleday, Page, 1926).

Ninety Years at the Isles of Shoals by Oscar Laighton (Star Island Corporation, 1971).

A Stern and Lovely Place by Susan Foxon (University of New Hampshire, 1977).

The Story of the Isles of Shoals by Louis C. Cornish (Beacon Press, 1936).

Chapters 8 & 9.   Casco Bay Islands

Buried Treasure of Casco Bay by Ben F. Kennedy (Vantage Press, 1913).

The Calendared Islands: A Romance of Casco Bay by Harrison Jewel Holt (1910).

Casco Bay Yarns by William Haynes (1916).

Chronicles of Casco Bay by Daniel C. Colesworthy (Sanborn and Carter, 1850).

The Isles of Casco Bay in Fact and Fiction by Herbert G. Jones (1946).

The Romance of Casco Bay by Edward Rowe Snow (Dodd, Mead, 1975).

Chapters 10, 11, & 12. Lighthouses and Keepers

Collection of thirty-four articles by Reverend O. Thayer, 1914–'15 (Maine State Library).

Lighthouses of Casco Bay by Peter Down Batchelder (Breakwater Press, 1935).

Lighthouses of the Maine Coast by Robert Thayer Sterling (Stephen Daye Press, 1935).

The Lighthouses of New England, 1716–1973 by Edward Rowe Snow (Dodd, Mead, 1973).

Chapter 13.   Monhegan

The Fortunate Island of Monhegan by Charles Francis Jenney (Vol. 31, *American Antiquarian Society,* 1921).

History of Monhegan by Herbert M. Sylvester (Stanhope Press, 1904).

Monhegan, The Cradle of New England by Ida Sedgewick Proper (Southworth Press, 1930).

Monhegan Island by W. W. Ellsworth (Hartford, 1912).

Chapter 14.   The Fox Islands—North Haven and Vinalhaven

Days of Uncle Dave's Fish House by Ivan E. Calderwood (Rockland, Maine

Courier-Gazette, 1969).

Fish Scales and Stone Chips by Sidney L. Winslow (Machigonne Press, 1952).

The Geology of the Fox Islands by George Otis Smith (1896).

History of Vinal Haven by Albra Josephine Vinal (Ellsworth, 1898).

Vinalhaven by the Centennial Committee (Press of the Star Job Print, 1900).

Chapter 15.   Granite

The Granites of Maine by Thomas N. Dale (Government Printing Office, 1907).

History of the Granite Industry by A.W. Brayley (National Granite Industry Association, 1913).

Tombstones and Paving Blocks by Roger L. Grindle (Rockland, Maine *Courier-Gazette,* 1977).

Chapter 16.   Isle au Haut

Here on the Island by Charles Pratt (Harper and Row, 1974).

Sailing Days on the Penobscot by George Wesson (Marine Research Society, 1932).

Chapter 17.   Lobstering

Fish and Men in the Maine Islands by W.H. Bishop (Reprinted from *Scribner's* magazine by L. Berliawsky, Camden, Maine).

Fisheries Industries of the U.S., edited by George B. Goode (Government Printing Office, 1887).

The Lobster at Home in Maine Waters by W.H. Bishop (*Scribner's* magazine, 1881).

Chapter 18.   Swan's Island

History of Swan's Island by H.W. Small (Ellsworth, 1897).

Swan's Island by Perry D. Westbrook (T. Yoseloff, 1958).

Chapter 19.   Mount Desert

The Jesuit Relations, edited by Charles H. Levermore (New England Society of Brooklyn, 1912).

Mount Desert, A History by George A. Street (Houghton Mifflin, 1926).

Pioneers of France in New England by Francis Parkman (Little, Brown, 1865).

The Story of Bar Harbor by Richard W. Hale, Jr. (Ives, Washburn, 1949).

The Story of Mount Desert Island by Samuel Eliot Morison (Little, Brown, 1960).

Chapter 20.   Heritage

Island Land Titles by M.H. Simmons, Maine Forest Commissioner,

Biennial Report 1914, Maine Legislature.
Newsletters and Annual Reports of the Maine Chapter of the Nature
    Conservancy.
Reports and Newsletters of Maine Coast Heritage Trust.
Unregistered Islands by Maine State Bureau of Land Resources, 1976.

General Reading and Reference
Along the Maine Coast by Dorothy Mitchell (McGraw-Hill, 1947).
The Coast of Maine by Louise Dickinson Rich (Crowell, 1962).
Islands of Maine by John B. Moore (Oxford University Press, 1933).
The Maine Coast by the Maine Development Commission, 1944.
Maine Islands by Dorothy Simpson (Lippincott, 1960).
Ranging the Maine Coast by Alfred Loomis (W.W. Norton & Co., 1939).
Seacoast Maine by Martin Dibner (Doubleday, 1973).

Index

If you enjoyed *Islands of Maine,* perhaps you'll also enjoy these other great books from Down East:

The Allagash
by Lew Dietz

In the heart of Maine's north country, the Allagash River is a woodsman's world of paddle and portage and the history of the region, as well as the river, is wonderfully told by Lew Dietz. Paperback, 282 pages.

The Old Somerset Railroad:
A Lifeline for Northern Mainers
by Walter M. Macdougall

Though it never did realize the goal of linking the Maine coast with Quebec, for fifty-six years the Somerset Railroad carried people and goods from the North Woods to southern Maine and New England. Walter Macdougall traces the history of the railroad, its development and construction, and the ways the lives of people living along the tracks became interwoven with the railroad. Paperback, 192 pages, 80 b&w photographs.

The Coast of Maine:
An Informal History and Guide
by Louise Dickinson Rich

No one has ever done it better than Ms. Rich. In her comfortable, witty, and vivid style, she takes readers on an armchair tour of Maine's coast. Her focus is on the unchanging character of Maine's land and people, so the book will always be timeless and fresh. Paperback, 400 pages, maps, and 25 b&w photographs.

The Great New England Sea Serpent
by J.P. O'Neill

This is the first book-length examination of sea serpents, and J.P. O'Neill has gathered fascinating accounts that document and support the existence of such sea creatures in New England and beyond. Paperback, 288 pages, b&w photographs and illustrations.

Available in bookstores, or by calling
Down East Books at 1-800-685-7962

Also available on-line at *www.downeastbooks.com*